BECOMING
A VESSEL OF HONOR

By Rebecca Brown, MD

Also by Rebecca Brown, M.D.:
He Came to Set the Captives Free
Prepare for War
Unbroken Curses
Cómo llegar a ser una vasija para Honra
El vino a dar libertad a los Cautivos
Maldiciones sin Quebrantar
Preparémonos para la Guerra

BECOMING A VESSEL OF HONOR

Rebecca (Brown) Yoder, M.D.
Harvest Warriors
P.O. Box 65
Clinton, AR 72031
e-mail: warriors@artel.com

ISBN: 0-88368-322-9
Printed in the United States of America
© 1990 by Rebecca Brown, M.D., 1992 by Solid Rock Family Enterprises, Inc.

Whitaker House
30 Hunt Valley Circle
New Kensington, PA 15068

Library of Congress Cataloging-in-Publication Data

Brown, Rebecca, M.D.
        Becoming a vessel of honor / by Rebecca Brown.
            p.   cm.
        Rev. ed. of: Becoming a vessel of honor in the master's service. 1990.
        ISBN 0-88368-322-9 (trade paper: alk. paper)
        1. Satanism—Controversial literature. 2. Occultism—Controversial literature.
        3. Christian life. I. Brown, Rebecca, M.D. Becoming a vessel of honor in the
        master's service. II. Title.
BF1548.B   1998
235'.4—dc21   98-22799

        7 8 9 10 11 12 13 14 15 16 / 09 08 07 06 05 04 03 02 01

Father, in the name of Jesus, I humbly come before your throne to make a petition. I am very well aware of my own helplessness apart from You. I know the words on the pages of this book are worthless unless YOU do the work. Therefore, I reverently ask You to send forth the Holy Spirit with each book to work IN POWER in the minds and hearts of every reader. May the blessed Holy Spirit do His work in spite of the frailties of this book. May He bring understanding to the readers and plant within their hearts a hunger and thirst for an ever deepening knowledge of Yourself and the riches that are in Christ Jesus.

May all power and glory and honor be unto YOU for ever and ever! In the precious name of Jesus I ask these things.

Amen,

Rebecca

"... And, Let every one that nameth the name of Christ depart from iniquity.

But in a great house there are not only vessels of gold and of silver, but also of wood and of earth; and some to honour, and some to dishonour.

If a man therefore purge himself from these, he shall be a vessel unto honour, sanctified, and meet for the master's use, and prepared unto every good work."

2 Timothy 2:19 - 21

TABLE OF CONTENTS

FOREWORD

I have known Rebecca Brown for quite a long time and have always found her very inspirational and challenging. It has been my privilege to work with her in several deliverances and see people set free from demonic bondage through the Power of the Precious Blood of the Lord Jesus. I believe that Rebecca is a servant of God! She has been used by God in the past, is still being used by God to reveal truths that need to be shared in this present age, and will continue to be used by God until He sees fit to call her home to her Heavenly Reward.

I have worked more than 25 years in the ministry of God's Word. I have checked what Rebecca teaches with Scripture and I am satisfied that she is very accurate and knowledge-able. It would do well for Christians to pay attention to the message that God has given to her to share. The problem with our modern generation of Christians is that we too often want to hide our heads and pretend that the things that are going on in society are not really there. We want to feel that things are just like they "used to be" and that the world is "getting better!" The fact is that Satan and his forces have stepped up their activities as they try to get ready for a world take-over that is predicted in Scripture. Things are not as they used to be. Demonic powers are at work in this generation with more force, fervor, and openness than ever before. The Christian who finds himself asleep to what is going on will someday regret his decision to hide from the facts and not prepare. Rebecca is one of God's servants who is sounding the alarm to the Church to awaken!

I thank God that Rebecca has had the courage to speak up in spite of opposition, persecution, and ignorance on the part of those who should be helping herald the message of the end times. It would do well if the Christian world would quit picking and bickering at each other and work together to reach a harvest of souls for Jesus.

Read what Rebecca has to say. Compare it to what is revealed in God's Word. Then, be ready to act in doing your part to reach a world that Christ died to save. It seems to me that prayer and obedience to God will go a lot farther in fulfilling Christ's Great Commission than will gossip and schism among God's people.

If the Church doesn't wake up soon and stop pretending that nothing is changing and that time will go on forever, we are going to be the victims and God will say, "I sent my servants to warn you, but you would not listen." God's people were asleep when Christ came the first time and they missed that wonderful event. The Church is asleep again -- it seems like we will never learn! Thank you, Rebecca for waking us!

Rev. William W. Woods
Church of the Nazarene
Stevenson, Washington

INTRODUCTION

I DID NOT WANT TO WRITE THIS BOOK! I DO NOT
WANT TO PUBLISH THIS BOOK! In fact, just recently,
I have strenuously petitioned the Lord to release me from
doing speaking engagements.

You see, I had what I thought were very good reasons. That
is, until the Lord straightened me out.

In the past few years, the antagonism against me within the
Christian community has escalated. I am hated by so many.
Newsletters are being printed all over the place supposedly "exposing me." Lies and false accusations are flying --
especially through the Christian bookstores, by letters and
word-of-mouth amongst Christians. Not once has anyone
printing a newsletter contacted me to find out if there might
be another side to the story! Rarely does any Christian stop
to contact me to see if what is being said is true. Few stop
to think that Satan usually destroys people by framing them
and setting up all sorts of accusations against them, which
is what happened to me. In fact, I have discovered that many
Christians love gossip above everything. They justify it to
themselves by calling their lies "exposing the truth."

But, what really brought everything to a head is some contacts my husband and I have had recently from some people
in very high positions within Satan's kingdom. They said,
"We really do not have to spend much time or effort in trying
to destroy the Christians anymore. They are so busy stabbing each other in the back and destroying each other that
we no longer have to worry about them. We hear what you
are saying, but we cannot see any advantage in choosing to
serve your God. The servants of your God are no different

than us. In fact, most of them are worse than us. At least we do have some code of honor. They have none, as far as we can see. Your God is a weak God. He must be to tolerate what is going on in His own kingdom."

I was heart broken! I have had such an incredible burden for the salvation of these people for so long. My tears flowed, but my horror grew as I tried to share my grief with another Christian in a public ministry. "You can't let that bother you." he said. "You can't listen to them. After all, they are just Satanists. They lie."

I spent days in tears and prayer. What was the use? So many Christians do not even care if their lives are driving others away from Christ, and don't seem to want to listen or to know what is happening in the real world. Truly this scripture is fulfilled in my own life:

> "And ye shall be betrayed both by parents, and brethren, and kinfolk, and friends; and some of you shall they cause to be put to death." Luke 21:16

"Oh Lord," I begged. "Please release me and let me shake the dust of the organized Christian churches off of my feet and go out into the highways and byways to the heathen who have never even heard of You. That is where my heart longs to be."

Silence.

Finally, one day about a month ago, as I was watching the sun come up with the Lord, He spoke to me so very clearly. "Child, I am God."

"Yes, Father, I know you are God." I replied. The simple statement came again. "Child, I am God." I sat thoughtfully a minute. "Well Lord, I must be missing something. What am I missing about the fact that you are God?"

The thoughts poured in from the Holy Spirit, both convicting me and giving me a blessed hope at the same time. They went something like this.

"You have been petitioning me to release you from speaking to my people to warn them that they must put sin out of their lives so that they will be prepared to stand in the coming persecution. I will not release you from this command for I am a just and holy God. I have said in my word:

> 'For the time is come that judgment must begin at the house of God: and if it first begin at us, what shall the end be of them that obey not the gospel of God?'"
> 1 Peter 4:17

"The end of the age is near. This country will fall. But, because judgment begins in MY house, my people will be persecuted before the unbelievers will suffer. Therefore, you and others must go forth and warn my people first."

As I was sitting soberly thinking about that, the Lord spoke to me again.

"Do not despise my people. You are falling into that trap. Tell me, if I had moved in judgment upon you for your gossip and back stabbing fifteen years ago, where would you be today?"

"I would be in a terrible position." was my immediate answer.

"Do not forget, I am not only a God of holiness and justice, I am also a God of mercy. It is in mercy that I tarry, waiting for my people to repent of the evil they are doing. Satan has no mercy at all. In fact, Satan has always interpreted mercy as being weakness. His people follow a certain code of honor because there is no mercy in Satan's kingdom. If they disobey that code they are dead. It is that simple. Therefore, Satan's servants think that mercy is a sign of weakness. But I tell you that I displayed the greatest power I have ever displayed when I allowed my only son, Jesus, to be tortured and killed upon a cruel cross! My mercy paid the price for your sins.

"Always remember. I love my people! Even though they are prideful, sinful and even destroy my servants, I still love them and wait in mercy for them to repent for their wrong doing. They WILL answer to me for what they are doing one day. The blood of many will be required of them at the judgment seat of Christ but, do NOT despise my people because I love them. (see 1 Corinthians 3:13-15, Romans 14:10)"

I repented for the anger I felt towards others at the terrible testimony they were giving to the world. But my heart was still heavy. "What can I say to those who have been stumbled by the sins of Christians, Lord? How can I effectively bring them to Jesus?" I asked.

Once more, that simple yet sublime statement was flooded into my mind and heart. "Child, I am God. It is YOUR responsibility to share the good news with these people, to tell them about Jesus Christ. It is MY responsibility to prove Myself to them. You cannot prove Me to anyone. Only I can do that. You tell the good news, then you pray, and you challenge them to pray and ask me to make Myself real to them. The rest is up to Me."

Praise the Lord! How true it is. We human beings cannot prove God to anyone. God Himself must, and will, do that. We are responsible to preach the gospel to all men. God will do the rest. Hallelujah! What a wonderful God we serve.

I have no need to defend myself. The Lord is my defender. Why should I run around trying to defend myself when I have done nothing wrong? Those who will listen will listen, and those who will gossip will gossip. It is my prayer that all Christians everywhere will heed the warning the Lord has given to me and to others in His service. A persecution is fast sweeping down upon us in this land. I pray that YOU, His child, will be prepared to stand strong, bringing glory to this wonderful God of ours. Stand strong in the power of Jesus Christ, God almighty, bringing glory to God the Father for ever and ever. Amen.

Chapter 1

TESTING THE COVENANT

The shadows lengthened in the cold dusk as the sun began to slip quickly below the horizon of mountains of barren rock. Winter twilight lasts only a few minutes up in the high desert where Elaine and Rebecca lived. This particular evening of December 21 , 1988, the wind was stilled and everything seemed to be hushed, waiting for the events of that night. Evil stalks, always, under the cover of darkness. This night was of particular significance because December 21st is the night of the winter solstice, a high day for the satanists.

This particular day was also to be the day of the death of Elaine and Rebecca. Once again the age-old battle lines were being drawn -- the forces of Satan against the forces of our Lord and Savior, Jesus Christ.

God's most recent covenant with Rebecca was about to be tested (See *Prepare For War*: chapter 2, "Covenanting with God" and chapter 7, "Hearing God"). The first of December, 1988, God had covenanted with Rebecca, giving her His promise that the valley in which they lived would be a haven for people coming out of Satanism. The Lord directly promised her the lives of everyone coming under her care or working with her in the ministry. He told Rebecca she would have many battles and some "close calls" but in the end, their lives would be saved. Shortly, they were to see the mighty arm of God warring against Satan on their behalf.

As darkness fell, Rebecca went around and re-anointed and sealed their home. The warm lights from the windows shone out in stark contrast against the dark, cold evil outside. All was still as dark figures began to gather on the edge of the property. Rebecca and Elaine's home was in a country-type area with a yard of **a** little more than an acre. Sheba, their dog, began to pace the floor from one room to another with a continuous low growl in her throat. This was her warning signal of danger on the property. But everyone in the house already sensed the growing evil outside.

How would they attack? Elaine and Rebecca were the targets. One of Satan's top assassins, and her associates planned to have the two for their winter solstice sacrifices this night.

Esther (not her real name,) Elaine, Rebecca and Betty (not her real name) gathered together in the family room for a short time of prayer. There wasn't much to say, except to thank the Lord for His covenant and promise to keep them alive and ask Him to work in this situation in whatever way He saw fit to bring the most honor and glory to Himself. As darkness fell fully, Sheba increased her pacing and growling. The girls peeked out of the front windows and saw some shadowy figures around the edge of the property. There was a dark van out in the street in front and another on the side of their property. Several of the men were armed with what looked like shotguns, but it was difficult to tell clearly in the darkness.

Esther began to cry. "I'm so scared. Those people look dangerous. Is God really strong enough to stand against them?" Her slender body was shaking with fear. Rebecca went over to her and took her hand. "Listen, Esther, you KNOW Jesus is stronger. You have seen His power demonstrated over and over again. Now you must stand with us in faith and rebuke fear in the name of Jesus. Father promised us a haven here and He NEVER goes back on His word."

Chapter 1
Testing The Covenant

"But are you sure you heard Him right?" was the tearful response.

"Yes, I am sure. He also confirmed the promise to Elaine and Betty. There is no doubt in our minds. Come, Esther, let us sing praises to our Lord and stand and watch to see how He will fight this battle for us.

Betty put on some soft praise music and they all started to sing together. Time passed and the tension grew. Everything outside was deathly still, but the demonic pressure built steadily. They peeked out the windows again. There seemed to be even more shadowy figures out on the lawn, some were coming towards the house.

Betty spoke up. "Listen, it is silly for us to stand here and be nervous and afraid. Let's do something constructive, like make chocolate chip cookies."

The others laughed. "Cookies!" Elaine exclaimed. "Well why not? I just hope the Lord doesn't let those guys come in for some!"

So, they all gathered together in the kitchen. No sooner had they started the cookies than suddenly they heard a loud THUMP which shook the house. Then another and another and another and another. Five in all. Esther cowered against the counter in the kitchen.

"I'll bet they plan to start a fire on our roof. That's typical for how these folks work," Elaine said thoughtfully. "What do we do now?"

"We stand. We just stand!" was Rebecca's reply. "If Father lets them come into the house then we will know that we must share the gospel with them, but I don't think He will let them come in, or start the fire." No sooner were the

Chapter 1
Testing The Covenant

words out of her mouth than they heard the sounds of a tremendous scuffle taking place on the roof. Their house was typical of most desert homes -- single story with a flat stone roof. The noise of the commotion and fight went back and forth from one end of the roof to the other.

The cookie making was suspended as the girls stood praying and looking up at the ceiling as the noise increased. Suddenly, after about five minutes, there was a yell and loud cursing and a thud just in front of the house. There were more yells and thuds as the girls ran to peek out the front window. There, before their astonished eyes, they saw five men, cursing wildly, picking themselves up off the ground. One had landed in the large cactus growing up against the front of the house. He cursed the loudest of all! The girls shouted with laughter and rejoiced and praised the Lord while the men went back to the van to regroup. Still laughing, they went back into the kitchen to continue with the cookies.

"Wow! Would I like to see what those men saw," exclaimed Betty.

"I wonder if the Lord let them see the angels that they were fighting with?" Rebecca commented thoughtfully. "I hope so, that will really shake them up. If they don't see the angels, I'm afraid they will just think they are fighting against more powerful demons."

"Oh, I have no doubt He did," said Elaine. "I vividly remember the time I went against God's angels! It was a humbling experience, to say the least. We couldn't get through no matter what we did. It sure did start me thinking. Satan wouldn't tell me what they were, but inside I KNEW they were God's angels. It sure made me realize Satan wasn't as all-powerful as he said he was."

Chapter 1
Testing The Covenant

About a half an hour later, they heard the men climbing back up on the roof. Sounds of an intense struggle again came from the roof. Shortly, the men were thrown off the roof again. But this time the men did not get to their feet. Instead, each one was grasped under his arms by an unseen force and dragged off the edge of the property. The girls did not see the angels, but there was no doubt in their minds that they were there. The men were unceremoniously dumped out into the street. The fight was over. The satanists lingered around the property for another couple of hours, but they were unable to set foot back on the property. Finally they gave up and left.

The girls ate cookies and praised the Lord for His wonderful deliverance from their enemies. As always, the Lord had kept His covenant.

Once the victory had been won in this area, they were quickly faced with a new attack and a new battle with new lessons to be learned.

(Author's note: I am writing some of our adventures for a purpose. I want you, the reader to know that our God still lives and works today just as He did down through the pages of Scripture. We still have a miracle-working God! We are alive today ONLY because of His direct protection and working in our lives. We also have a God who speaks to His people today just as He did in the days of the scriptures. We MUST rely on His guidance daily. Satan has a vast kingdom, but OUR GOD sits above the earth and heaven. Our God is the Creator of all. He sees all and knows all. Satan makes endless schemes and plans, but our Captain, Jesus Christ, reaches down His hand and plucks up a person here and a person there, frustrating Satan's best laid plans.)

Chapter 1
Testing The Covenant

Chapter 2

PUSH-PINS

"Rebecca, this call is for you," the receptionist said holding out the phone. Rebecca was at the veterinarian to get medicine for their cats. They had been under such a heavy attack by witchcraft that every animal in the house was sick. Rebecca's heart was heavy as she stepped up to the counter to answer the phone.

"Rebecca," a weak voice on the other end said, "come quickly, I think Elaine is dead and I don't think I can last much longer. They are here to get us. They are outside. I ... " her voice faded out and the phone clattered as it fell to the floor.

"Annie!"(not her real name) Rebecca called, "Annie, answer me, what's going on?" Silence, except some strange background noise. Annie did not pick up the phone again. Rebecca handed the phone back to the receptionist. "I'm sorry. I'll have to get the medicine later. I've got some sort of trouble at home. I have to run." So saying, she dashed out the door to her car. She was about a ten-minute drive away from home.

The sun was rapidly setting and the shadows lengthening as Rebecca raced for home. "Oh Father," she prayed, "I come before your throne and stand on your covenant with me. Satan cannot have the lives of anyone in my household. I counter petition Satan, Father, in the name of Jesus. You promised me the lives of everyone coming under my care, now I am standing on that promise." Rebecca drove as quickly as she could. The short drive seemed endless. Her mind was whirling. What was happening? What could have

happened in the short time she had been gone? She had
only been away from the house about 30 minutes.

The intensity of the spiritual warfare had been rapidly
building in the past few weeks ever since Annie and her son
Timmy (not his real name) had come to live with them.
Annie had spent all of the almost thirty years of her life in
Satanism. She was what is known as a "breeder." She was
given to the high priestess of the coven when she was an infant to be raised for this purpose. She had known nothing
but the most terrible abuse from her earliest memories. She
was used extensively in child pornography, then as a
breeder. She had her first baby at the age of eleven. She had
ten children, nine of whom were sacrificed. The tenth child,
Timmy, had not been sacrificed and was now six years old.
Annie had gotten into contact with Rebecca, desperate to
get out of the craft. She had then come to the Lord and
eventually Rebecca had brought her into her home. The
satanists were not pleased!

As Rebecca turned the last corner before her street the sun
slipped below the mountains. Darkness would fall completely in just a few minutes. This hour of sunset seemed to
be the time when the satanists always launched their
heaviest attack. As Rebecca reached her street, she saw a
helicopter circling low over her home. So low, that the trees
were whipping in the wind from its blades and many of the
smaller branches were breaking off and blowing all over the
lawn. As she approached her driveway, she noticed a dark
van parked on the edge of the property and three men
standing spaced across her driveway.

The urgency within Rebecca was so great that she just acted
without taking much time to think. She pulled up and
jumped out of her car shouting to make herself heard above
the deafening noise of the helicopter. "I rebuke you in the
name of Jesus Christ my Lord! You have 20 seconds to get

Chapter 2
Push-Pins

out of my way or I will run you down! In the name of Jesus Christ I command every one of you demons to be bound and break every incantation you have done! Now, get out of my way!"

So saying she jumped back into her car and backed down the street a short way. Then she stepped on the gas and headed for the driveway. The men were obviously surprised. They jumped to the side with only inches to spare as Rebecca rushed by. She hit the garage door opener and roared into the garage, shutting the door as she entered. Screeching to a halt she jumped out of the car. Heart pounding, she ran to the door of the house and rushed in.

"OOF!" Rebecca was knocked flat onto the floor as soon as she got through the door. She lay there gasping for breath for a few seconds. She had not been expecting such an attack. It was extremely rare that the demons could ever get her down physically. Shaking her head to try to clear her mind, she spoke aloud, "You demons, I command you to get off of me in the name of Jesus!" With that, she picked herself up off the floor and headed into the living room.

The demonic oppression in the house was so heavy it was difficult to breathe. Evil was everywhere. The noise of the helicopter above made it difficult to hear anything. Fear was a palpable thing.

As Rebecca entered the living room she quickly sized up the situation. Elaine was blue from lack of oxygen, lying on the floor having a grand mal seizure. Annie was lying unconscious in the kitchen. Her son was sitting next to her screaming and crying. Rebecca knew she could not resuscitate them all at the same time. Her heart cried out to the Lord for guidance.

Chapter 2
Push-Pins

She quickly turned Elaine on her side, pulling her head back to open her airway so she could breathe. In the name of Jesus she commanded the demons causing Elaine to have a seizure to leave. Immediately the convulsive movements began to slow down. Then the Holy Spirit spoke to her, "Seal the house, child, seal the house!"

Rebecca jumped to her feet. She grabbed a bottle of oil and set a new record for anointing the house. She ran as fast as she could from door to window to window to door, praying as she went, asking the Lord to cleanse and seal her home. As she reached the last door she shouted, "In the name of Jesus I command every demon and human spirit in this house to leave at once! This house belongs to my God, you have no right to be in here." "Father," she prayed, "in the name of Jesus, I ask you to totally cleanse this home and make it holy for You. AND, Father, would you PLEASE make us invisible or something to get rid of that helicopter? I can't hear myself think above the noise of that thing!"

Then Rebecca ran back to the girls lying on the floor. She rejoiced as she saw that Elaine was breathing freely again. Her color was starting to improve and Annie was moaning as she began to regain consciousness. Rebecca took Timmy into her lap, holding him in her arms, trying to comfort him.

Suddenly the helicopter left, leaving them in a deathly silence. Rebecca quietly moved between the three, anointing and praying over each one. They were all in a lot of pain, but they were alive! The Lord had again kept His promise. They were safe and alive.

The next couple of hours were busy ones as Rebecca helped each one into bed. She called Betty who came over in about half an hour to help. By then it was fully dark and the van had withdrawn a ways down the street, but still lurked menacingly outside.

Chapter 2
Push-Pins

Finally, everyone was somewhat recovered and in bed. Betty and Rebecca sat up in the family room talking. Rebecca quickly filled Betty in on the events that had taken place. "We seem to be entering into a different phase of warfare," Rebecca said thoughtfully. "It's been a very long time since a demon was able to knock me down, and it was a really close call for the others, especially Elaine. I don't like it, I don't like it a bit!"

"The thing that bothers me is how did they manage to get in? The house was sealed, wasn't it?" Betty asked.

"Yes, it was. In fact, I just re-anointed it last evening because I felt so much oppression." Rebecca sat pondering the events of the evening. "That helicopter bothers me too. Annie said the high priestess of her coven has used helicopters before. What is even more troublesome is the fact that this house was obviously an open thoroughfare for every demon they wanted to send in. Something had to break the seal but what?"

Betty chuckled, "Yeah, what? That's the $10,000 question."

"Yes, I know," Rebecca replied, "I don't want to go through another evening like this one. That was much too close for comfort!" Little did Rebecca know just how many more times she would have to go through this type of attack.

The next day, she went to the veterinarian's office again for medicine. This time going while it was still broad daylight. All the animals were sick, and Rebecca had no doubt that it was because of curses being sent towards them. Later that evening as she was fixing dinner, they all felt the oppression building again. Rebecca had called Betty to come over and stay the night to help.

Chapter 2
Push-Pins

"It sure feels like the witching hour again," Rebecca muttered to Betty as they worked in the kitchen. "This is getting real old real fast."

"Yeah, I know," Betty said, "I wonder what they'll try this evening?" No sooner were the words out of her mouth than...CRASH! The sound came from the living room. Betty and Rebecca dropped what they were doing and rushed to see what was going on. Elaine was on the floor with a lamp on top of her. She had grabbed at it as she fell, trying to regain her balance. She was groaning and rolling on the floor.

"Elaine, what's happening?" Rebecca asked as she knelt down beside her.

"They're ripping my guts out," Elaine moaned, doubling up. Betty ran for the oil. Evil was sweeping into the house. Again the air seemed to be thick with it so that it was difficult to move or breathe.

"Oh no, not again! Help, Lord! How can I stop this?" Rebecca cried out desperately.

"The seal on your house is broken again," was the immediate reply from the Holy Spirit.

"Rebecca, where are you?" Betty called. "Annie is down too."

Rebecca headed for the kitchen. "I've got to anoint the house, hang onto them as best you can" she called to Betty. Once again, Rebecca raced around the house, anointing and sealing and cleansing it. Once she had finished they were able to gain control of the situation and put a stop to the demonic attacks. The girls were becoming very weak and sick from the damage done to them by the demons.

Chapter 2
Push-Pins

Rebecca and Betty worked steadily together until they got all three, Elaine, Annie and Timmy settled in bed. There would be little sleep for any of them that night. Rebecca and Betty spent most of the night in prayer. Clearly, they were missing a key somewhere. What was breaking the seal on their home? Why could the satanists send in demons to wreck havoc in the house? Earnestly they sought the Lord for answers.

Early the next evening, as soon as the sun started to set, Rebecca went around and anointed and sealed the house again. "No one is to go outside," she told the others, "I want to see if we can prevent such an attack from happening."

They prepared and ate their supper in an uneasy silence. Finally, Rebecca spoke up. "We are certainly missing a key here somewhere. Those demons have legal ground to come in here, or the seal on our house couldn't be broken. Do any of you have any idea what it is?" (Legal ground is a "doorway" of sin that grants Satan legal access into your life. See *Prepare For War*, chapters 9 & 10 for additional explanation.)

Both girls shook their heads. "No, I don't know," said Elaine.

"Me either," added Annie.

"Well, we never had such an attack before you came here, Annie. There MUST be legal ground in your life somewhere! I want you to really get on your face before the Lord and seek Him for the answer." Annie agreed that she would seek the Lord for an answer.

No one slept much that night. About the middle of the night, Sheba started growling. Rebecca got up and peeked out the front windows. Men were again on the edge of the property, but seemed unable to actually walk onto the property.

Chapter 2
Push-Pins

Rebecca sighed, how glad she was she had obeyed the Holy Spirit and had walked all around the edge of their property that evening, claiming it holy for the Lord's use and asking Him to seal it with His angels.

Suddenly, the Lord gave Rebecca a glimpse into the spirit world. All around the edge of their property stood a shining line of huge angels. They stood shoulder to shoulder facing outwards. They were dressed in pure white with gold belts, swords ready in their hands. They were silent as they stood motionless, waiting. Light radiated from them. All of the property seemed to be covered with a soft blue light. There were many more angels up by the house as well. Rebecca offered up a prayer of intense thanks to the Lord for His wonderful provision. "And Father, please thank the angels for me as well," she prayed. "They certainly have been busy around here recently. I do appreciate what they do. Thank you Father so much for your faithfulness in caring for all of us. I thank you in Jesus' name."

Much comforted, she returned to bed.

The battle raged for three more weeks. Over and over again the girls were hit with demons and knocked to the floor. Everyone was very ill the whole time. Night after night Rebecca fell onto her knees, crying out to her God for answers and grace to continue the fight. They were all becoming more and more weary. There seemed to be no end to the fight, and no answers either.

Finally, the Lord spoke to Rebecca and told her that she must take Esther, Annie, Betty, and Elaine and leave town for a week to rest.

Rebecca discussed it with Elaine and Betty "Father says we are to get away for a brief rest. Goodness knows we all need

Chapter 2
Push-Pins

it, but HOW are we going to get any kind of rest with the satanists following us everywhere?"

"Well, for one thing, we won't tell the others ahead of time where we are going," Elaine suggested. "I don't think they would deliberately let the satanists know, but they certainly seem to have some sort of pipeline to them."

"Where can we go?" Betty asked.

"Oh, I believe Father is indicating to me that we should go to Hawaii. I have a special hideout there. So far Father has completely protected Elaine and I at this place. Fortunately it's not so expensive flying there from California. I'll make the arrangements and keep them as secret as possible. Let's also pray and ask Father to close all the ears of demons and satanists so they won't know where we are going. We're all exhausted, that's for sure."

"I sure hope you're successful." Betty said.

Carefully, their plans were made. At last the day came when all of them boarded a plane for Hawaii. They rejoiced as they did not see anyone who seemed to be following them. In fact, the first two days on the island were completely peaceful. BUT, their peace was to be short lived. The third evening, at dinner, Rebecca and Elaine thought they saw two men whom they had seen following them back in California. When they asked Annie, she denied knowing the men, but refused to look Rebecca in the eye. Clearly, her behavior was different. That evening, they weren't back in their room very long before they were attacked by demons. Once the situation had been dealt with, Rebecca sat Annie down.

"Now listen here," she said, "I've had all I can take! I have no doubt you DO know those men. And, I am just as sure

Chapter 2
Push-Pins

you KNOW how those satanists knew where we are! It only took them two days to find us. Now, you MUST have some kind of demonic transmitter or homing device on you. You'd better start talking and fast, or I'm going to put you out there and let them get you. We've played this game long enough! On the walk back to our room from dinner this evening father told me you know very well how they found you."

Annie hung her head.

"I'm waiting, Annie" Rebecca said in an exasperated tone.

Finally, Annie spoke up. "Well, yes, those two men are satanists. I was afraid to tell you."

"So HOW did they know where to find us?"

Annie looked down and shuffled her feet uneasily. Finally she spoke again, "Well, it might be my push-pins."

"What on earth are push-pins?" Rebecca and Betty asked in unison. Elaine smacked her forehead. "Of course, why didn't I think of it?"

Rebecca turned to Elaine. "Do YOU know what these push-pins are?"

"Yes."

"Well why didn't you tell me before?"

"Well, because you didn't ask me, and I didn't think about them."

Rebecca fell back onto the couch. "Well really! Here we are fighting tooth and nail for over a month and you guys just

Chapter 2
Push-Pins

don't happen to remember a little detail like push-pins!'"
She was so exasperated she couldn't talk.

Betty spoke up, "What, exactly, ARE push-pins?"

"They are tiny metal pins which are inserted under the skin in a special ritual. Demons are attached to the pins for various functions," Annie said. "They enter the person when the pin is inserted."

"Let me guess, they function as a sort of radar homing device, I suppose?" Betty asked dryly.

"Yes, and also for purposes of destruction. The demons associated with the pins are supposed to destroy the person if he or she ever leaves the craft." Annie was squirming and looked very uncomfortable.

"May I ask just WHY you never saw fit to tell us about these things?" Rebecca asked.

"I didn't know what to do. They told me the demons with the pushpins would kill me before I could get them out. They're like time bombs, there's no way to escape them."

"Annie, Annie," Rebecca sighed. "How can you believe such a lie when you have been privileged to see the Lord work in such power and in so many marvelous ways?"

Annie looked down at her hands. "Well, I was afraid," she muttered.

Once again Rebecca was faced with the stubbornness and fear that marks everyone coming out of Satanism. "No wonder we couldn't keep the house sealed," she thought, "every time Annie went out and then back into the house she broke the seal by taking demons into the house with

Chapter 2
Push-Pins

her." Everything was beginning to make sense. That was why the girls could be affected in such a devastating way by the demonic attacks.

Another thought came to Rebecca. She turned to Elaine. "Did you have one of these push-pins?"

Elaine nodded. "Yes, I did, but I was afraid to tell you about it. So I asked the Lord to help me get it out. He did so. He literally pushed it out through the skin. It hurt a lot, but I did get rid of it. It's been so many years that I had forgotten all about it. They are sometimes also called 'inserts', or 'curse-pins' in some areas of the craft.(See chapter 6 for a more in-depth discussion of inserts.) In other countries, they use different things instead of metal. Sometimes small flat pieces of rock, a small piece of wood, a tooth, or a piece of human bone. The purpose is the same, though, it is for control. A tooth or piece of human bone is also frequently used here in the U.S. Once a person has a push-pin, the people in the craft always know where they are. AND, when they leave, the demons attached to the pin rise up to try to kill the person physically."

"Well, now that we finally know what the problem is, what can we do about it?" Betty asked.

"For two cents I'd like to take a knife and just carve them out!" was Rebecca's exasperated response.

"No you don't! Not on me!" Annie exclaimed.

Betty laughed. "You'd have to catch her first, Rebecca."

Rebecca didn't answer because she was sitting praying, asking what to do in the situation. They all fell silent for a few minutes, listening to the steady pounding of the waves

Chapter 2
Push-Pins

on the beach and the soft rustling of the palm branches. Finally Rebecca stirred.

"The Lord has been so faithful to us thus far, I believe He will be again. This problem must be dealt with and dealt with immediately. All of our lives are in danger until those push-pins are gone."

"But how are you going to get rid of them?" Annie asked.

"I'm not going to, the Lord is," was Rebecca's response. "We can't very well go to a doctor and give a story such as this! No, I'm going to ask Father to burn them out, vaporize them, or whatever is necessary to get rid of them. I believe He will. Now where are they and how many do you have?"

Annie did not like pain, and she especially did not like the idea of anything being "burned or vaporized" out of her skin. "Will it hurt?" she asked.

"I don't know, that's up to Father. You little wretch, after all the difficulties we have been through because you have refused to tell us about these things, I should just get a knife and cut them out! However, you are fortunate that we serve a very merciful God. Now where are those pins?"

Annie pointed, "There is one in my leg and one in my hand."

Rebecca got the oil and sat down next to Annie. "O.K. let's see what the Lord will do." She took the oil and covered the area over the pin in Annie's leg. Then she prayed, "Father, we come before you in the name of Jesus. You know our problem. I am asking you to flow your power into Annie's leg and vaporize or burn out this metal pin, or whatever is necessary. I also am asking you to completely remove any and all demons associated with the pin."

Chapter 2
Push-Pins

"STOP! OUCH!" Annie interrupted. "Rebecca, my leg feels like it is on fire. Ask the Lord to stop! It's hurting too much!"

"I will do no such thing! If you had told me earlier, we could have gotten it removed by a doctor with a local anesthetic. Now, you'll just have to put up with the pain."

Annie continued to wiggle and squirm, but Rebecca held firm. She thanked the Lord for answering her prayer. The burning pain continued for about ten minutes, then stopped. Prior to asking the Lord to remove it, Rebecca had been able to easily feel the push-pin under Annie's skin. Now it was completely gone. Her skin was red, but no pin could be felt. They rejoiced and praised the Lord for His wonderful provision. One-by-one, all the other push-pins were destroyed as well.

Once again, the Lord had remained faithful. Everyone went to bed for the first peaceful night's sleep in a very long time.

Chapter 2
Push-Pins

Chapter 3

MEMORIES

Rebecca put another log on the fire which was crackling merrily on the hearth. Flames of blue and green and orange licked over the fresh log as she carefully pulled the screen across the fireplace.

"There, that should do it for awhile," she said as she settled down on the couch next to Joyce. (not her real name) The house was quiet as everyone else had gone to bed. The cold winter wind whipped around the house outside, and the shadows from the flames danced warmly in the room. Everything was cozy and peaceful as Joyce and Rebecca settled down with mugs of coffee for a quiet talk. They had much to share. But, they had no idea just how soon their peace would be shattered by the rapidly approaching events of the night.

Joyce is a young woman in her mid-thirties who had been involved in witchcraft for 12 years. She rose through the ranks of WICCA, becoming a high priestess, and, eventually, a "courier" between WICCA and a major network of covens. She had accepted Jesus Christ as her Lord and Savior about six months before meeting Rebecca, who helped her kick out all of her demons. Now, about a month after her deliverance, Joyce had come to visit Rebecca and Elaine. (Joyce has, at the time of this writing, been out of the craft for a little more than two years.)

"Rebecca, you will never know what an impact the cover of your first book had on me," Joyce commented. "I received Christ, and was then nearly killed by the demons beating me up. I didn't think I would survive. A man at the church introduced me to Chick Publications, so I called them up and asked them if they had anything on Satanism. They said yes they did, and I thought, "I bet!" I figured it would be surface material. But, when I first saw the cover of that book I freaked out! I knew without a doubt that someone KNEW the truth about Satanism. Then when I started reading about Sister Courage I could hardly believe my eyes! I had been told that she was dead. I could hardly believe that she was still alive."

"You mean you knew Elaine while she was still in the craft?" Rebecca asked in surprise.

"Oh Yes. And, I knew Sedona, Elaine's associate. Sedona (her craft name), was totally hateful. She seemed to especially hate me. Boy was I glad when Sedona lost her position not too long before I came to Christ!"

Rebecca smiled. "I've had a few encounters with Sedona myself. That was years ago when Elaine first came out of the craft. In fact, Elaine took me to her house once. Boy, talk about an evil place! I have heard recently, from someone coming out of the craft, that Sedona is still very angry with me."

"What do you mean?" Joyce asked.

"Well, you see, one day Sedona astral-projected into my home to try to kill me. Instead, I ended up forcing her to bow down to Jesus with her nose right on the floor. I described the incident in my first book, *He Came To Set The Captives Free*, only I just gave her the name Sally in that book instead of using her craft name."

Joyce laughed. "I remember, you mean THAT was Sedona? No wonder she hates you so much! Bowing to Jesus would

Chapter 3
Memories

be an insult she would never forget! I was surprised when I read about that incident. Astral-projecting into another person is very rare."

"Yes, I know that now -- I didn't know that at the time. People who develop that degree of skill in astral-projection pay a high price in their physical body. Sedona has aged very quickly as a result."

Joyce nodded. "Yes. I spent a lot of time learning to astral-project. My hair started to turn gray while I was in my twenties because of it." Joyce chuckled again, "So you made Sedona bow before Jesus. No wonder she hates you so much!"

"Well, I figured she may as well start getting used to it, she is most certainly going to bow to Him AND confess that Jesus IS Lord, in the end!" Rebecca chuckled. Then she sobered. "You know, I have no doubt at all that Sedona had a hand in the satanist's set-up and frame job they did on me when they destroyed my medical practice and everything I had. I know that a rather prominent craft member has recently been trying to set up another frame by accusing me of selling drugs or some such. He has gained some prominence on the national scene in law enforcement by going around lecturing on occult related crimes. He does what he does to protect his network of covens from exposure and to keep people thinking that satanists don't really have any power.

"There is another one working on the same frame-up who poses as a "Christian" pastor. He is also involved in the CIA. I also know that Sedona is out here in California currently. If she continues to come against us she is certainly going to further her education in experiencing the power of our God."

Chapter 3
Memories

Joyce nodded thoughtfully, "Unfortunately, what these satanists don't understand is that they can't touch us unless the Lord allows it."

"Yes, and sometimes He DOES allow it. I am a good example. I am sure they thought they had a tremendous victory when I lost my medical practice and they got all those lies published about me. But what they don't understand is that my God was in control of it all. What Satan meant for evil, He has turned to good. I was in a very hidden and somewhat limited ministry then, and although I did reach many in Satanism while I was in practice, I am now in literally a worldwide ministry and reaching thousands more than I could ever have reached if I had stayed in a busy medical practice." She sighed. "That WAS one of the toughest tests I've ever had to walk through, but it is wonderful to be able to rest in the fact that Father IS all powerful and all wise. Everything that happens to us is for a purpose."

"The thing that irritates me is that the Christian community is so eager to pass around those false accusations against you without even wondering why none of the documents submitted in your defense are included with the package of accusations. People just don't stop to think!" Joyce said.

"I know, but God is my defender. I am trying to reach those in Satanism to win them to Christ. Those involved in Satanism already KNOW about that frame-up and that the accusations against me were false. They KNOW that I am a servant of Jesus Christ. I am satisfied with that, because the satanists are the people God has called me to minister to," Rebecca commented slowly.

Both girls fell silent. After a thoughtful pause Rebecca spoke again.

Chapter 3
Memories

"You know, Satan appeals to people with such glamorous promises of power and riches. So many people swallow the bait hook, line, and sinker. Some do indeed gain incredible power and riches through their service to Satan." Rebecca said. "But in reality, the price people have to pay to gain the cooperation of the demons is tremendous! The suffering, degradation and corruption the demons bring into their lives is terrible."

"You are so right," Joyce commented with a shudder. "Talk about bondage, witchcraft is a terrible bondage! I was always having to worry about whether I performed each incantation exactly right. One tiny slip up and the demons would beat me horribly. I was in total bondage to all sorts of rituals, festivals and high days. On top of all of that, I was always having to look over my shoulder. There was always someone else who wanted my position and was willing to kill me to get it. They also pulled me deeper and deeper into sin. Just before I came to Christ they forced me into blood sacrifices. I couldn't stand it, but there seemed to be no escape. Every day, there were rituals I had to do. How different it is now that I serve Jesus!"

"Yes, you really can appreciate that scripture in Matthew 11, can't you?" Rebecca commented. Quietly she quoted the beautiful passage:

> "Come unto me, all ye that labor and are heavy laden, and I will give you rest. Take my yoke upon you, and learn of me; for I am meek and lowly in heart: and ye shall find rest unto your souls. For my yoke is easy, and my burden is light."
> Matthew 11:28-30

Joyce nodded in agreement. "Anyone coming out of the occult has a real appreciation for that promise. I can't tell you what a release it was to realize that I didn't have to do any

Chapter 3
Memories

more rituals, keep track of any more special days, always be aware of whether it was the full moon or new moon or a thousand other things. That's the basic difference between white witches or pagans, and satanists. The satanists do blood sacrifices to appease the demons to get them to cooperate with them and give them power. The so-called white witches and pagans have to perform endless rituals to gain the same thing. AND they dress the demons up with fancy names and call them spirit entities or gods or energies or vibrations instead of demons.

"Basically, satanists don't have the patience and discipline to spend so much time and effort performing meticulous rituals. It is much quicker and easier for them to do sacrifices. They gain the cooperation of more powerful demons that way. The others deal with the less powerful demons, but they are demons just the same no matter what you choose to call them. You learn very quickly in witchcraft that there are NO such things as impersonal energies. They are all VERY personal. You are either dealing with demons or the power of God, and humans cannot control the power of God. So anyone that is controlling an "energy" or "power" of any kind is dealing with demons. It is just that simple. It is so very different to serve a Master who will forgive you instead of taking great delight in punishing you for any little thing. Jesus gives life. The demons always bring death."

Rebecca stared thoughtfully into the gently flickering fire. "What a difference there is between serving Jesus and serving Satan," she said. "If ever there were any man on this earth who had the power to do everything Satan and his demons can and much more, it is Jesus. He created everything. But when HE came to earth, He never showed off. When He did miracles they were frequently done in such an unobtrusive way that people sometimes questioned whether a miracle had even been performed or not. What an example Jesus set for us to follow."

**Chapter 3
Memories**

There was a pause, then Rebecca continued slowly. "ALL satanists like to show off and be in the lime-light. But then, what human being doesn't? Naturally all of us would, and all of us would enjoy having power. Any one of us would use it to show off and make ourselves look big. I have no doubt of that. The desire to show off and look big is the very root of our sin nature. Satan had that problem too, and got himself kicked out of heaven for it. The demons cooperate with people to make them look powerful in front of others just to trap them into eternal destruction. But our God knows us through and through. That's why Jesus set such an example of humility for us. If we are going to serve Him, we MUST follow it. What terrible sins we would fall into if we were given the kind of power demons give to their servants!

"When we become servants of Jesus, we quickly recognize the fact that we are NOTHING but sinners saved by grace! We have NO power of our own, neither do we control the power of our Master."

Joyce spoke soberly, "It is a VERY big change for someone coming out of the craft. I was used to having the power to do what I wanted to do when I wanted to do it. Now, I am utterly dependent upon the Lord without any power at all of my own. Oh, I realize the demons were just cooperating with me, but I considered their power to be under MY control. As long as I obeyed them, that is. Now that Jesus is my Master instead of Satan, I am finding out what it is like to wait on somebody else's will rather than doing what I want."

"Yes," Rebecca said, "but unfortunately, sinful human nature being what it is, far too many Christians try to develop ways to force God to perform when THEY want Him to. Just look at the number of so-called Christian leaders who gather together thousands of people to put on a show. If the Lord is really healing through them, why don't they quietly

Chapter 3
Memories

go from person to person instead of calling together so many people to watch the spectacle? I am very uncomfortable with these long, so-called prayer lines for healing and such. Going forward as individuals to kneel before the altar to do business with the Lord is one thing, but lining up a bunch of people before a crowd and then praying over them and having them fall over is something else. It seems like too much of a show to me. Pretty heady stuff for the person doing the praying and healing. Everyone looks up to them as being a 'powerful man of God, or woman of God.'

"Jesus, on the other hand, went quietly through the crowds healing. So many times, the person didn't even know just WHO had healed them. Over and over again in the gospels, Jesus avoided the public eye, and he certainly NEVER put on a show. Our God simply will NOT perform when WE want Him to! When people think they can control God's power, or at least use it when THEY want, they end up with demons performing the supposed miracles for them and pulling them deeper and deeper into deception."

After a moment Rebecca spoke again, "You know, in the ten years I've been in this terrible battle, not once have I ever been 'in control' so to speak. I am ONLY a servant, that's all. I have NO power, and NO control. I simply do what my Master tells me to do. Sometimes I get impatient and wish I could have control of a particular situation, but in the long run I'm glad the Lord works as He does. The awesome power of God is so much greater than anything Satan or the demons or any of us human beings could ever think of having! You know Joyce, I'm PROUD of my Master! He is so utterly wonderful and wise and powerful and glorious I just don't have the words to describe Him! My heart nearly bursts when I stop to think about Him. He is so incredibly strong, yet He can be so very gentle and tender. What a combination! I'm just so proud of Him! In Isaiah 42:8 God says that He will NOT give His glory to

Chapter 3
Memories

anyone else, and I'm glad! I'm so glad! God is so utterly glorious, I'm thankful to the depths of my being that He will never change or give away His glory to someone else!"

Tears streamed down Rebecca's face. "I can't begin to tell you how privileged I feel that this great God will actually allow me to be HIS servant! How thankful I am that He created me to give me the glorious privilege of experiencing Him! It doesn't matter that I am nothing. It doesn't matter that I have no powers. My master has it all! I can completely rest in the total security of knowing that He is profoundly wise and ALWAYS works in my life in the right way, the best way. HE is in total control of every situation. You know, Satan has so many complex schemes and conspiracies. We can't begin to fathom them all. But to MY Master, they are all very simple. Oh, how I long for that day when I can finally go home and actually see Him face-to-face!"

"Amen to that!" Joyce said with deep feeling. They were silent for a few minutes. Then Joyce spoke, saying, "Unfortunately not only do too few Christians really appreciate the wonderful privilege God gives us to be in His service, they also refuse to acknowledge the reality of the spirit world. No matter what the Bible says!"

"Yes, it really grieves my heart, the number of Christians who want to bury their heads in the sand and refuse to believe that any of this is real." Rebecca commented. "The Bible has so much to say about the spirit world and Satan and his kingdom. It is amazing how many people choose to ignore it rather than learning how to defeat it through the power and authority of Jesus Christ."

"I know," Joyce said, "since I have come out of the craft I have been amazed at the resistance of so many Christians to simple things, like the truth about satanic infiltration of

Chapter 3
Memories

the churches. The Bible has a lot to say about it, but they don't want to hear it. Did you know that Wiccan's are also trained to infiltrate and destroy Christian churches?"

"Yes, I knew that. In fact, I know someone who has accessed one of WICCA's main computers. They found a rather complete 'hit list' of Christians they want to discredit and destroy."

"Mary, (not her real name) was one of the people who trained me in how to infiltrate churches. That was her specialty. I also went to one of several special training camps for witches on how to destroy churches. It was taught by one of the well known "Christians" on T.V."

"Really. I'm not surprised," Rebecca said. "Paul wrote that Satan's servants would reach positions of leadership within the churches. He told the Ephesian elders that from among THEM, the church leaders, would come ravening wolves to destroy the sheep. (Acts 20:30) But tell me, what did Mary teach you?"

Joyce laughed. "I'll never forget the first time Mary commanded me to come to a certain city in Kansas where a big evangelistic crusade was being held. It so happened that a crusade was being held by a particular denomination. Mary instructed me that I was to wear long sleeves, a long skirt and had to have long hair. I had to get a hair piece because my own hair was fairly short at the time. I had never worn such sedate clothes in my life. I thought I looked terrible! Of course, my ideas about clothing have changed a lot since I started to serve Jesus."

"Anyway, I was to meet Mary at her hotel room. She knew some of the top people involved in the crusade and was there to make sure they followed their orders. When I arrived at her room, I thought I had done very well with my

Chapter 3
Memories

clothing. I had never been in a church of their denomination before. When Mary opened her door, she took one look at me and grabbed my arm. 'You come in here girl,' she snapped. 'You can't go looking like that! Remember, you must dress and act as they do or they won't accept you.' She dragged me into her bathroom and took a washcloth and proceeded to wash every scrap of make-up off my face. I was horrified. But Mary, I protested, I look terrible without makeup, I never go anywhere without at least a little."

"Mary was very impatient. 'How many times do I have to tell you that you MUST dress and act according to their expectations? If you look like them and act like them no one will question you to see if you really are a Christian or not.'"

"And you know, she was right. We could move freely throughout the many people at the crusade and everyone accepted us as being Christians without questioning us at all. It was during that weekend that Mary taught me more about slaying in the spirit. Oh, I could already knock people unconscious just by touching them, but Mary told me that wasn't enough. She told me that because they were violating their own scriptures (James 5:14) by allowing anyone to lay hands on them and pray for them without even checking to see if they were a true servant of Jesus or not, that we were free to do whatever we wanted. Their God wouldn't protect them because they were in direct disobedience to His word."

"Mary understood that when people knelt before us, or even bowed their heads before us, that they were actively submitting themselves to us and accepting whatever we wanted to give to them. Of course they thought we were praying for them, but their submission to us gave us the legal right to put demons into them. They also directly opened the door for it by allowing their minds to go blank without testing the spirit knocking them out. Mary showed me the proper in-

Chapter 3
Memories

cantations to do and how to have the people hold their hands up like this." (Figure 3-1)

"Then she would tap them first on one hand then on the other, then on their forehead, making the sign of an upside down cross." (Figure 3-1)

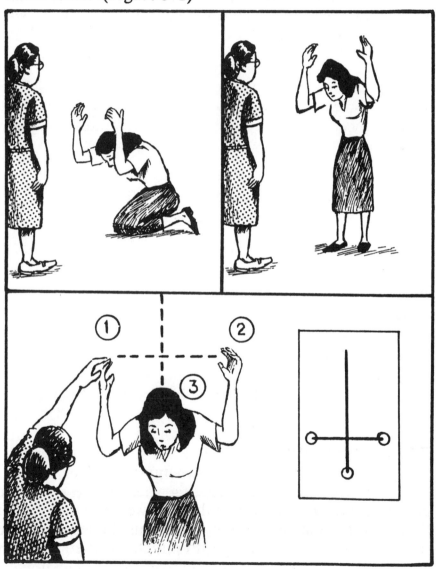

Figure 3-1

Chapter 3
Memories

"Out they would go, every time. She then did it to me and I fell over unconscious. I guess I was out for five minutes or so. When I awoke, I found that I had acquired a new demon. Mary told me this special demon would put demons into the people I prayed for. And so he did. I'm sure that isn't the only way people put demons into people by having them hold their hands like that, but that is how we did it."

"You know, I have always wondered about the widespread acceptance of this 'slaying in the spirit' by Christians. Have you ever stopped to think that they all fall backwards? In the Bible, in every instance, when God's people fell before His presence, they fell FORWARDS, prostrate onto their faces in an attitude of worship. For example, John 18:6 says:

> "As soon then as he had said unto them, I am he, they
> went backward, and fell to the ground." The NIV says,
> "...they drew back and fell to the ground."

The Greek word for "ground," in that verse is "chamai" (Strong's number 5476) meaning prostrate. One definition for prostrate in Webster's New World Dictionary is:

> "Lying with the face downward in demonstration of
> great humility or abject submission."

It seems like that verse may be saying that the men actually stepped backward, then, fell forward on their faces. I have never seen anyone 'slain in the spirit' fall forwards," Rebecca commented thoughtfully. "I don't have the answers to this question, but I can tell you I am really seeking and searching. I am very uneasy about the practice. I am not surprised that Satan's servants take advantage of the practice."

"Yes, you are right," Joyce said. "I am horrified now as I look back at the number of Christians I put demons into through that practice! They were so eager and willing to go uncon-

Chapter 3
Memories

scious that they accepted anything I chose to put into them. I frequently put demons of false tongues into them. Then they would wake up speaking in tongues and think they had been baptized by the Holy Spirit."

Rebecca nodded. "Yes, it is sad. All the gifts of the Holy Spirit ARE REAL and operative today. The gift of tongues is real. BUT, so very many Christians try to put God into a box and demand that He work when and how they think He should, that they accept all sorts of demonic deception as being the working of the Holy Spirit. Of course Satan is going to try to duplicate the gifts of the Holy Spirit. Satan knows the power in them. What a victory he wins when he can get Christians to accept demonic counterfeits of the real gifts!"

"How true that is!" Joyce replied. "Also, those to whom I gave demons of divination, would receive all sorts of what they considered to be 'words of knowledge' from the Holy Spirit. Those so-called words of knowledge were nothing more than information from a demon of divination. They were accurate, of course, but then the demons have so much information about everyone."

"Yes, I know," Rebecca said. "I am sometimes amazed how many Christians accept false words of knowledge as being from God just because the information is accurate. They completely overlook that scripture in Deuteronomy."

"If there arise among you a prophet, or a dreamer of dreams, and giveth thee a sign or a wonder, and the sign or the wonder come to pass, whereof he spake unto thee, saying, Let us go after other gods, which thou hast not known, and let us serve them; Thou shalt not hearken unto the words of that prophet, or that dreamer of dreams: for the LORD your God proveth you, to know whether ye love the LORD your God with all your heart and with all your soul. Ye shall walk after the LORD your God, and fear him, and keep his com-

Chapter 3
Memories

mandments, and obey his voice, and ye shall serve him, and cleave unto him. And that prophet, or that dreamer of dreams, shall be put to death; because he hath spoken to turn you away from the LORD your God, which brought you out of the land of Egypt, and redeemed you out of the house of bondage, to thrust thee out of the way which the LORD thy God commanded thee to walk in. So shalt thou put the evil away from the midst of thee." Deuteronomy 13:1-5

"This scripture clearly shows that servants of Satan can do all sorts of signs and wonders and prophesy prophecies that come true. These do NOT validate them as being from God. How it must sadden God the Father's heart to see His children running after signs and miracles and accepting all sorts of demonic signs and miracles as being from Him!" Rebecca said.

"Yes, and that scripture shows that God allowed people such as myself and Mary to function within His church to test the people to see where their hearts were. They literally DEMANDED signs and miracles from the Lord. We were only too happy to give them to them. They NEVER tested any of us. If we could perform, then they decided we must be from God. It just showed that they desired a miracle so much that they were willing to accept a demonic miracle rather than testing to find the true source. We DO serve a God of miracles, but He never performs them when we demand them. That's the total difference between serving Satan and the one true God. Satan and the demons usually gave us the miracles we wanted when we wanted them, to encourage our selfishness and pride and self-centeredness. God always works to discipline our flesh (sin-nature) and helps us to conform to Jesus Christ."

Rebecca nodded soberly, "I know, and the tragedy is that most Christians are willing to serve Jesus only so long as it

Chapter 3
Memories

benefits them. They are completely unwilling to suffer in any way, especially not physically or financially."

"You know," Joyce said, "that's where Mary was so very useful to Satan. She was willing to study the Bible to find out the places where Christians were going against God's Word. She was smart enough to know that the instant Christians were disobedient to God we could very effectively come against them. Satan taught us that we had legal right or legal ground, as he called it, to put demons into them or afflict them with demons when they were walking in disobedience to their God. That's one time I know he was telling the truth. I saw it happen over and over again. It is a very sobering thing to think about now that I am a Christian myself. How I wish more people would listen to the testimonies of those of us coming out of Satan's service."

Rebecca shook her head. "Yes, I will never understand why so many Christians think they are automatically protected from Satan and his demons EVEN if they actively sin against God! They completely overlook the scripture in Galatians 6:7-8 which says we WILL reap what we sow. There is another practice in the churches that is so common yet is against scripture. I consider it to be very dangerous. It is the practice whereby anyone from the congregation can come up and lay hands on, and pray with, those at the altar. It doesn't matter if you are a first time visitor in some churches, they will still let you do whatever you want. It provides a free-for-all for the infiltrating satanists."

"Did you know that's how I got the very powerful demon of divination I had?" Joyce asked.

"No, tell me about it."

"Well, I was in just such a church that allowed that practice. They completely overlooked the scripture in James 5 that

Chapter 3
Memories

says you should have the ELDERS anoint and pray for you. There was a woman in that congregation who was a Christian. She had inherited a very powerful demon of divination. I recognized it immediately, of course. So, one day she went up to the altar for prayer. I went forward and told her and the pastor that 'god' had told me to come pray for this lady, and that she was having a problem with a demon of divination. The lady knew she was having problems, so they readily agreed with me. I laid hands on her and commanded the demon to leave her. What they did not know is that I had, with my spirit, called the demon to come into me because I wanted it. The demon promptly left her and came into me. They thought I was a really powerful Christian because the woman felt great relief as the demon left. They never knew that I was actually a witch who wanted her demon of divination! I'm sure we have no idea just how many times such things go on every day within the Christian churches."

Both girls fell silent for a few minutes, each busy with her own thoughts. The fire was dying down, leaving only the light from a small lamp in the room. Suddenly the clock began to strike . . . bong, bong, bong . . . "Oh my goodness, it's midnight already and I forgot to call home to let my husband know I got here safely," Joyce exclaimed, jumping to her feet. "I must at least leave a message on our answering machine. Can I use your phone?"

"Of course," Rebecca replied, "use the one in the bedroom." As Joyce left the room Sheba suddenly got up and began to growl a warning.

"Hmmm, I wonder what's going on?" Rebecca thought. Just then Joyce came out of the bedroom.

"Rebecca, doesn't your phone normally have a dial tone?" she asked.

Chapter 3
Memories

"Of course, try the one in the kitchen."

Sheba's hair stood up along her back. She began to pace from the door to window to window growling steadily. An evil presence began to sweep into the room. Rebecca jumped to her feet.

"This phone is dead too!" Joyce exclaimed.

Then Rebecca reached for the lamp, clicking off the light, plunging the house into complete darkness. "Now what," Rebecca muttered, heading for the windows on the front of the house. "Rats!" she exclaimed quietly as she looked outside. There on the front lawn were five dark figures. Two of them carried what looked like shotguns. A sixth figure came creeping around the end of the house. "He must be the one who cut our phone line," Rebecca thought. "That means they plan to come in for a visit and the purpose of their visit isn't very friendly, I bet."

Elaine roused from her sleeping place on the couch in the living room. "What's going on?" she whispered.

"Don't turn on a light," Rebecca warned, "they have guns."

Elaine joined her at the window. "What?" her question trailed off.

"They cut the phone line," Rebecca said quietly.

"Oh great! Now what?"

Rebecca was praying quickly and silently. "Oh Lord, what is your will. Is it your will for us to lay down our lives at this time?" "NO!" came the immediate answer. "Stand your ground." Rebecca heaved a big sigh of relief.

Chapter 3
Memories

"Listen, Elaine, I know you're sick. You go back to bed and I'll keep watch. Father says He will protect us." Elaine nodded her assent and stumbled back to the couch.

By that time, the figures outside had five black candles burning on the front lawn in the shape of a pentagram. As their soft incantations rolled, demons swept into the house. Rebecca felt their evil presence. Suddenly she thought about Joyce and the other two girls. "I'd better check on them."

She felt her way through the darkness into the kitchen. "Joyce," she whispered, "where are you?" She heard a soft moan and stumbled over Joyce who was pinned down onto the kitchen floor by a demon. Rebecca knelt down beside her and put her hands on Joyce's shoulders. "You demons, I rebuke you in the name of Jesus Christ my Lord," she said firmly, "You have NO right to Joyce. Get off of her NOW, I command you in the name of Jesus."

Joyce began to move and struggled to her feet. "Those people are sending in some big guns!" she whispered.

"I know," Rebecca replied, but Father has promised to protect us. "Come to the family room and wait there, I must find out what is happening to the other girls."

Rebecca found Sue (not her real name) pinned to the floor in the hallway, and Rita (not her real name) pinned on the floor in the other bedroom. Both were extremely frightened. She helped them rebuke the demons pinning them down and brought them into the family room. They all joined together in prayer, asking Father to protect them. Silence fell. The presence of evil continued to increase. Rita and Sue were shaking with fear.

Chapter 3
Memories

"Listen this is nonsense," Rebecca exclaimed. "There's no reason for us to sit here in fear. Father has promised to protect us, therefore WE have much more power available to us than they do. Let's use it!"

"Sounds good, but how?" asked Sue. She and Rita had been living with Rebecca and Elaine for two months.

"God's word, that's our strength," Rebecca replied. "Let's see how many scripture verses we can quote between us. We dare not turn on any lights to read, so we will have to do it from memory."

Joyce was quick to catch on. "Good idea, we have rebuked the demons and commanded them to leave, but they aren't budging. If they're going to hang around, then they'll have to listen to the Word of God."

"Just one thing, Joyce, don't you dare quote any verses about 'going down into the pit.' If you do I'll wring your neck," Rebecca said laughing.

So they started out quoting scripture verse after scripture verse. Rita and Sue had not memorized any, but Joyce had been started on an intensive scripture memory program by Rebecca and had memorized a lot. As the two girls sat and quoted the beautiful words of scripture out loud, they all could feel the thick presence of evil begin to recede. Back, back it went towards the front windows, and finally, completely out of the house.

Suddenly the Holy Spirit spoke to Rebecca, "Go to the windows now, I want you to see my power." She told the others and they all jumped up and went to peak out the front windows. The six figures were standing by their candles. Suddenly, all five candles went out all at once! The figures tried to relight them, but to no avail. NOTHING worked. They

Chapter 3
Memories

could not relight the candles. They began to look around and suddenly all of them started to run off of the property. They ran down the street and disappeared around the corner. The girls shouted for joy, praising and thanking the Lord for His wonderful work.

Then they all went to bed and slept in peace the rest of the night.

Rita and Sue had learned a rather severe lesson. They had refused to memorize scripture. When they needed it the most, they did not have it available to them. They could not turn on lights to read a Bible.

The Word of God is a sword. It is very powerful. The ONLY way to have it constantly available to you is to MEMORIZE it.

Would YOU the reader have had God's Word in your memory had you been there?

Chapter 3
Memories

Chapter 4

CAGES & CURSES

Ring . . . Ring . . . Ring . . . Rebecca fumbled in the dark motel room for the phone. Ring . . . "I'm coming, I'm coming," she muttered. Finally she found the phone. Betty's voice was on the other end.

"I'm sorry to bother you, but I think you should know what's going on."

"What time is it?" Rebecca asked, reaching for the light.

"Well, it's ten o'clock here," was Betty's response.

Rebecca clicked on the light and looked at her watch. "Yeah, well it's one a.m. here. What's going on?"

Rebecca and Elaine were in the eastern part of the U.S. on a speaking engagement. They had been asleep only one hour. Just long enough to make it very hard to wake up. They were both exhausted as they were nearing the end of a grueling week of seminars.

"Esther and I were over at your house this evening. I am very concerned about the couple Sara (not her real name) has staying there."

Rebecca was still a bit fuzzy with sleep. "What do you mean? Sara knows that when she is house sitting for us she isn't supposed to let anyone into the house without our personal permission."

"I know, but I think she is very deceived and controlled. She thinks this couple are servants of Jesus Christ. The man calls himself a 'Prophet of God' but I really question just which god he is serving," Betty explained.

Rebecca sat up alert. That got her full attention. "Where did this guy come from and how long has he been there?"

"Well, I don't know just where he came from, but he has been there a couple of days. He and his wife travel in an R.V. Apparently Sara met them two or three years ago. This 'prophet' says he was sent to your place by 'god.'"

"So what has he done to make you think he isn't a true servant of Jesus Christ?" Rebecca asked.

"Several things. First of all, his wife sits on the couch rolling her eyes up and back into her head humming what sounds like quiet chants, rocking herself back and forth while her husband is expounding on something. I tried to speak to her a couple of times, but she didn't respond. She seemed to be in a trance of some sort. The thing that really caught my attention was when he started telling us about how he had a dog which he loved very much. He told us that 'god' told him that he loved the dog too much. So, he had to sacrifice it like Abraham had to sacrifice Isaac. He said he took the dog out and killed it and sacrificed it! Also, he told us that he sees into the spirit world ALL the time. He talked a lot about seeing werewolves. He says he sees demons continuously and that he sees the werewolves in the spirit realm. Christians DON'T see into the spirit realm all the time like that. I never could get any kind of statement out of him as to who he serves. He always sidestepped my questions and kept saying that he is 'a prophet of god.'"

"Oh no!" Rebecca groaned. "Didn't Sara think that sounded a bit strange? Especially the part about sacrificing his dog!"

Chapter 4
Cages & Curses

"No, that's the problem," was Betty's sober reply. "I wouldn't be surprised if she didn't even hear it. She seems to be totally controlled by that guy. She thinks everything he says is wonderful. Every other sentence out of all of them is 'Praise the Lord!' and 'Hallelujah!' But I can tell you there is a terrible demonic oppression in your house."

"What's going on?" asked Elaine who was, by then, awake as well. Quickly Rebecca filled her in on what Betty had been telling her.

"Well, we know Sara IS a true servant of Jesus Christ," Elaine commented. "This so-called 'prophet' must have caged her."

"Whoa, wait a minute, what's this business about 'caging?'" Rebecca asked. "You never told me anything about that before."

"I know, I know, but I haven't had any reason to think about it before," Elaine said.

Rebecca turned back to the phone as Betty was speaking again. "Jack met him today down at work as well and had no peace with him at all. He couldn't get him to give any kind of testimony as to who he serves either. He told Jack also that he is a 'prophet of god.' Jack thinks that he could be a servant of Satan."

"That brings confirmation. I'm glad Jack met this man," Rebecca said thoughtfully.

"He also kept saying that 'god' told him NOT to work. That sure goes against II Thessalonians 3:10!" Betty said.

"Do you have Esther with you?" Rebecca asked.

Chapter 4
Cages & Curses

"Oh yes, I couldn't leave her there as uneasy as I am about this guy."

"Good," Rebecca said in relief. "Keep her with you at your place until we get home. I'll get hold of Sara and tell her that couple must leave immediately. No telling what will be in our house by the time we get back." Rebecca had no idea just how much they would have to face when they got home!

After Rebecca hung up she turned to Elaine. "Now, tell me more about this 'caging incantation' you mentioned."

"It's a very powerful incantation that is commonly used by servants of Satan. The person is literally put in a cage, spiritually, so that they cannot see the wrong actions of someone, or so that they will believe lies about someone. It's kind of like putting mental blinders on someone. You know, like the blinders they used to put on horses so they could see in only one direction. Satanists use it VERY commonly against Christians so that the Christians cannot discern that they are not true servants of Jesus. Once a person is caged, then it is easy for the satanist to place all kinds of wrong thoughts into their minds and they will not realize that the thoughts are inconsistent with God's word. That's one way so much demonic doctrine gets accepted in the Christian churches."

"That sounds like a very dangerous incantation -- for the Christian, that is," Rebecca said soberly. "How can we protect ourselves from being caged?"

"I'm not sure," Elaine said. "I just learned how to use them, not how to prevent them. When I was in the craft, I was always alert to other people trying to influence me or control me. I would always send a caging incantation their way first to keep them from caging me."

Chapter 4
Cages & Curses

"Wow, what a mess!" Rebecca exclaimed.

"Indeed it was. My whole life was ruled by fear. I always had to be on the lookout because so many people wanted to knock me out of my position. There is NO peace when you serve Satan !"

The two sat in silence for a few minutes thinking and praying. Finally Rebecca spoke, "Well, any incantation can be broken in the name of Jesus, but I'm afraid the person who is caged is going to have to be the one to break it. That's no small project to get someone already caged to recognize that they need to break such an incantation. They won't believe they are under any kind of demonic influence because they are caged."

"Exactly," Elaine said. "But you know, when I was in the craft, I found that I couldn't cage Christians who refused to accept anything or anyone at face value but tested everything against God's word. They were the ones who didn't fall for someone just because of his or her charisma. I guess you could say they were like the Bereans Paul commended so highly for searching out the scriptures to see if what Paul was preaching was true. I could easily cage those people who really didn't think for themselves and who were susceptible to following people with a lot of charisma."

Rebecca nodded. "Yes, that is precisely one of the greatest problems within the Christian church today. Too many people obtain positions of leadership simply because they have very charismatic personalities which naturally attract people. I have often wondered just how much so called 'charisma' was really demonic power. I'm sure some of it is natural, but I'll bet a lot of it may be demonic."

Chapter 4
Cages & Curses

"I'm sure you are right. A satanist who knows how to use his demons well will have people flocking to him thinking that he is the kindest, most caring person they know. Kind of like bees to honey."

"Well, scripture is clear. Satan has always worked by deception and always will. So do his servants. I am very concerned, though. I am going to pray regularly against any caging incantations sent against me," Rebecca said as she lay down again. Two more days and they would be home. What would they have to face when they got there, she wondered.

"The prophet" and his wife were gone by the time Elaine and Rebecca arrived home. Sara left almost immediately as well. Betty and Esther came over for supper that night. The demonic oppression within the house was very intense. Rebecca and Elaine were exhausted.

"Wow!" exclaimed Betty as she walked in the door. "This house is loaded with demons!"

"Yes, I know," Rebecca said wearily. The trouble is I'm so tired I just don't have the strength to go through the house thoroughly tonight."

"I planned to stay with you tonight," Betty said. "I think you can use the reinforcements. I'll start going through and anointing the house while you finish dinner." She got a bottle of oil and started anointing the house.

"I doubt that just anointing will be enough," Esther said. "While I was here, that 'prophet' went around and anointed and 'blessed' every room in the house. He also said he was going to walk the property and 'bless' it as well."

Chapter 4
Cages & Curses

"Oh No! That's all we need!" Rebecca groaned. "That means we'll have to wash down all the places he might have put oil to fully remove the curses."

It was getting late in the evening by the time they finished supper. As the sun set, the demonic oppression began to build up within the house. Every one felt weak and ill and exhausted. They decided to try to survive the night and start a major house cleaning on Saturday, which was the next day. Joyce was arriving the next morning to stay the weekend. She would help also.

Everyone decided to sleep on the floor in the living room so they could all be in the same room for the night as they were expecting a fight. They had just started to doze off when Esther jerked upright. "Look," she pointed.

Rebecca sat up. A patch of blue light came floating through the patio door. "I rebuke you in the name of Jesus Christ. In the name of Jesus I command you to flee! You must leave my house at once!" The blue light extinguished. "I can tell this is going to be a bad night." Rebecca muttered, lying down again.

They managed to sleep a couple of hours. Then the blue light came into the room again waking first Rebecca, then the others. It extinguished as soon as Rebecca rebuked it. The rest of the night passed, but no one slept well.

Joyce arrived the following morning. They all sat down to discuss what they should do.

Betty started out. "First of all, I want to know more about these caging incantations."

Chapter 4
Cages & Curses

"Oh, they are very common within the craft,"Joyce said. "They are easy to do but hard to break. That is, it is hard to recognize when you are being afflicted by one."

Elaine got a pad of paper. "Here," she said," let me show you some of the symbols you can be on the lookout for. You may find a piece of paper with symbols on it like this."
(Figure 4-1)

"That's right,"Joyce agreed. "Many times, though, the incantation will be placed on the person's property. I'll bet we could find some on yours if we looked carefully enough. It can simply be done with four sticks or branches or reeds. They are placed on the ground like this. They look like sticks that have just fallen naturally onto the ground."
(Figure 4-2)

"That's right,"Elaine spoke up. "In the center of the square or rectangle is placed some object such as a hair, a button, or it could even be something as small as a piece of lint off your clothing. They can also write your name or initials on the ground rather than placing an object there."

Joyce agreed.

"Does the piece of paper have to be placed in the person's home or on their person in order for the incantation to work?" Rebecca asked.

"No,"Elaine and Joyce said together. "Those are just things you can be on the lookout for. If you see them around then you know for sure such an incantation has been done."
"We should also look for ley-lines," Joyce said.

"What's that?" Rebecca asked.

Chapter 4
Cages & Curses

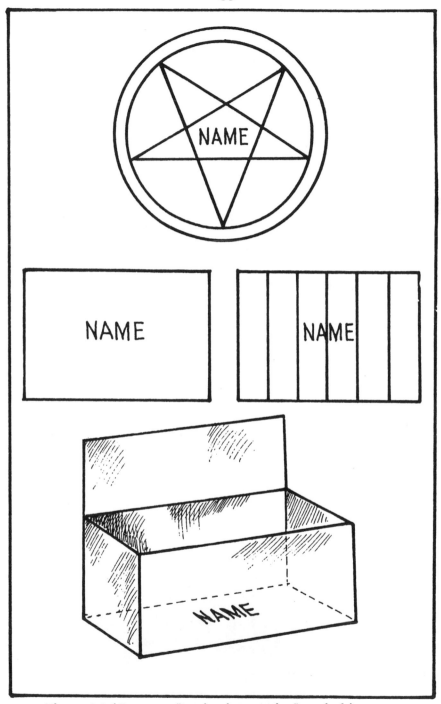

Figure 4-1 (Common "caging incantation" symbols)

Chapter 4
Cages & Curses

"To do ley-lines you do an incantation over a stick which is then used like a wand. They can drag it along the ground beside them. It looks like they are just playing idly with the stick. But everywhere the stick touches the ground a ley-line is placed. If you look very carefully you can sometimes see a very thin line in the dirt where the stick was dragged along." (Figure 4-3)

 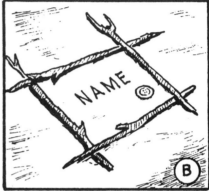

Figure 4-2 (Sticks used in a caging incantation)

Figure 4-3 ("ley-lines")

Chapter 4
Cages & Curses

Joyce continued. "When you walk around a property and put ley-lines all around it, it is like a giant cage around the whole property. It is used for the following reasons:

1. To claim the property for themselves and Satan.

2. To place demons all around the edge of the property to guard it.

3. To place special 'doorway demons' or 'openers,' as they are sometimes called, so that the satanist can easily astral-project onto the property. You see, it isn't so easy to find your way around when you are astral-projecting. So if you leave specific demons in the places where you will want to go, you can just astral-project to them.

4. Place specific sentinels. These are demons who are watchers. They communicate to the satanist about anyone that comes onto the property or anything that happens on it.

5. And lastly, the demons placed there are to bind and blind everybody coming onto the property. To cage them, in other words."

"I see," Rebecca commented. "We walk the ground to declare it holy for the Lord asking Him to place His angels around it. The satanists do essentially the same thing, only they place demons and claim it for themselves and Satan."

"Yes, that's it exactly." Joyce said.

"O.K." Rebecca said. "The first thing we will do is carefully search the whole property outside to remove any and all curses. I want to be sure to command off any of those 'opener' demons so those folks can't astral-project onto our property so easily. I'll bet that's why we have had so much

Chapter 4
Cages & Curses

trouble with astral-projecting human spirits these past several months. I didn't know to get rid of those opener demons. After we cleanse the property we'll start on the house."

They all agreed and went outside. It took about an hour to carefully walk over all of the property. They found several places where there was melted black candle wax, and sure enough, there were slender branches arranged as illustrated above in each of the four corners of the property. The sticks were removed and the incantations broken and the demons commanded to leave.

Next, the girls turned their attention to the inside of the house. This was not an easy project as there were a multitude of places occultic objects could be hidden. As the day progressed, the demonic oppression became more and more severe in the house. A terrible rotten sulfurous odor began to permeate every room. Demons stink! That is why you will always smell incense being burned in occult book stores. It is burned to hide the stench of the demons.

As the girls searched, they found a crystal door knob in Elaine's bedroom. "I haven't seen one of those since I was a little girl," Rebecca commented. "I know for sure that we have never had anything like that in our possession. What a strange thing to leave."

"Not really," Joyce said. "Anything crystal can be used for communicating with demons. Who would suspect that a door knob could be used for that? That's why crystals are so popular with the New Age Movement. We used to just call them 'hag stones' before the New Age Movement popularized them. This type of door knob is frequently placed in the homes of higher level satanists. It's sort of a status symbol."

Chapter 4
Cages & Curses

The door knob was destroyed. By the evening, everyone was feeling sick, Esther most of all. They gathered together in the family room for prayer. Elaine got up to get the oil to anoint her. Betty, Joyce and Rebecca stood up to gather around Esther. As Elaine walked back from the kitchen, she was suddenly struck from behind by an unseen force and pitched headlong over the back of the couch, yelling all the way. There she stuck, head down in the pillows, feet kicking wildly in the air! Every one burst out laughing. Elaine is so short, she fit perfectly in the corner of the couch.

"Hey, quit laughing and help me up!" she shouted.

Joyce and Betty helped her back onto her feet. "Well, these demons certainly are unhappy about our little prayer meeting," Rebecca said, still laughing.

The laughter helped lighten their mood and they began to feel a bit encouraged. After they had prayed, the girls had supper and went to bed. They were all exhausted. Again, the blue light kept floating throughout the house waking them up. Sometimes it started flashing like a strobe light. It extinguished when rebuked, but quickly came back again.

About the middle of the night, Esther got up to go into the bathroom.

CRASH! "Hey, stop that!" she yelled. CRASH! "I command you to stop in the name of Jesus!"

Betty and Rebecca dashed for the door, only to find that they couldn't open it. "Esther, open this door," Betty called.

The door knob rattled. "I can't!" Esther said. "It's not locked, but I can't open it. Those wretched demons knocked me into the bath tub."

Chapter 4
Cages & Curses

Rebecca got the oil. Only after they had anointed the door knob and commanded the demons off of it could they open the door. Esther was bruised, but otherwise unhurt.

In the very early morning, Joyce got up to go to the bathroom and stumbled on something soft in the living room on the way. "YUCK!" she exclaimed when she turned on the light. The house had been completely closed and locked up all night, but there, in the middle of the living room floor was a dead bird. Its wings were spread out, and feathers carefully placed below it in a pentagram. That was the end of their sleep for that night.

The stench in the house grew worse. The girls washed down walls, scrubbed carpets, looked under furniture, tore apart beds, but still could not find the final doorways the demons were using to have such free access to the house.

Taking showers became a real challenge as the demons would turn the shower head around and around, spraying the water on the walls and ceiling. The water would run hot and cold, hot and cold. They learned to shower with one hand on the shower head.

Several days later, they were almost in despair. They had prayed intensely, asking the Holy Spirit to show them the things they were missing. Finally, Betty found the last problem.

"Hey, look what I found!" she called from Esther's bedroom. They all went in to see. The ceiling of all the rooms in the house were of textured white plaster. There in the plaster were tiny nails, driven into the ceiling in the shape of a pentagram. They looked in the other bedrooms, and sure enough, there was a pentagram made in nails in the ceiling of each room. That was the final key. Once the nails were

Chapter 4
Cages & Curses

pulled out and disposed of and the curses associated with them broken, the house was clean at last.

In all, it took almost two weeks of hunting before Rebecca's home was finally cleansed. They found symbols in oil on the pictures that were framed with glass over them. These were very hard to see unless you looked at an angle so that the light would catch the clear oil.

Curses had been placed on the mirrors so that these could be used as doorways for demons to enter the house. That seemed to be the main doorway for the demon that manifested as a blue light to come and go. Once they cleansed all the mirrors the blue light no longer appeared. Mirrors are a rather common doorway as beginning witches frequently use mirrors to establish communication with the spirit world.

Rebecca's house was cleansed and peace again restored. But the damage done by the caging incantations of this couple to their relationships with several other people will probably never be repaired this side of eternity.

All Christians must be alert to this source of trouble, especially pastors and Christian leaders. NEVER overlook the possibility of being afflicted by a caging incantation. These incantations can either blind you to the wrong actions of someone, or turn you against someone who has done nothing wrong at all, leading you to believe as truth all sorts of lies about them.

If you think someone may be sending such an incantation your direction, simply command any and all caging incantations to be broken in the name of Jesus Christ. Command all the demons associated with such incantations to leave you at once in the name of Jesus. Terrible damage is being done within Christian churches and in relationships be-

Chapter 4
Cages & Curses

tween people because of these incantations. We must always be alert and sensitive to the guidance of the Holy Spirit.

NO ONE IS IMMUNE TO THIS TYPE OF ATTACK!

Chapter 4
Cages & Curses

Chapter 5

THE ARMOR OF GOD

As the last dryer clicked off, silence dropped like a blanket over the laundromat. Joyce jerked out of her thoughts, startled by the silence. She was folding her last load of laundry. She looked up and glanced around, to find that she was the only person left in the building. She was growing uneasy. Quickly she grabbed up the last of her clothes and plopped them into the basket without folding them. As she did so she heard the back door open.

She glanced up and froze.

There, just inside the door stood two very large young men. They stood side by side looking at her in silence. They radiated evil!

"Oh Lord, HELP!" Joyce prayed. She grabbed up her basket of clothes and her car keys and headed for the front door. The two men by the back door did not move.

As she hurried towards the front door, a white limousine pulled up in front of the laundromat. Two more large men walked up to the front door and took up positions one on each side of the door outside.

"Lord help me get through!" Joyce cried out in her mind. Fear rolled over her in waves.

As she reached the front door and stepped outside onto the sidewalk, the back door of the limousine opened and a woman stepped out. At first glance there was nothing remarkable about her. She was rather sloppily dressed in tight black pants that revealed she was somewhat pudgy. Her shoulder-length hair was mostly gray. BUT, she radiated powerful and evil demons.

Joyce stopped in her tracks, swaying as the demonic force of the demon lord Dantallion hit her. The woman was Sedona -- Joyce's mortal enemy when she was still in the craft.

Waves of fear rushed into Joyce. Flashbacks poured through her mind in rapid succession. Horrifying scenes of torture and torment. She struggled to think, struggled to breathe. It was as if she was sinking into a sea of mental torment.

Summoning all of her strength and will against the onslaught she forced her feet a couple of steps forward, hanging onto the laundry basket and her keys for dear life. Sedona stepped forward, blocking her path.

"Just WHERE do you think you are going?" she snapped.

Joyce shook her head, trying to clear it. "I'm going home," she stammered.

"Oh NO you're not! You're mine!"

With the last bit of strength she had left Joyce spoke as firmly as she could. "Oh no I'm not! I rebuke you in the name of the Lord Jesus Christ. I belong to Jesus!"

Sedona hesitated a moment, but only for a moment. She reached out and grabbed Joyce's arm at the elbow in a cruel grasp. Joyce jerked back and tried to pull away, but was unable to break free. Pain shot up her arm and enveloped her in waves. Burning pain. Instantly, the mental torment in-

Chapter 5
The Armor of God

creased a hundred fold. Pictures were whirling through her mind. Terrible pictures of demons and torture of other human beings. She jerked back again, but was unable to utter a word.

Sedona dropped her arm. "I've got you now! The full moon is in four days -- you are now MY prize, MY sacrifice to Lord Satan."

Again Joyce shook her head, but did not have the strength to speak. Sedona continued, her words coming like rapid fire shots.

"I know your every move." Then she proceeded to list with 100% accuracy everything Joyce had done the preceding week. "I can get you anytime I want," she boasted.

Something moved Joyce's feet. She started to walk, she didn't know how. She was detached, unable to control herself. Inside, she cried out to the Lord for help. She just couldn't think! Those horrible scenes continued to fill her mind.

Sedona was furious, but seemed strangely unable to do anything further. "You're mine!" she hissed. "I'll get you anytime I want to! I'll make you pay for humiliating me! I'll get you . . . soon!"

As she spat out those last words she climbed back into the limo.

Suddenly Joyce was running. Across the parking lot she ran. Her car was parked on the far side of the lot. It seemed like miles, but at last she reached her car. As she opened the door with trembling hands, the limo roared out of the parking lot. Joyce climbed into the car and pushed the key into

Chapter 5
The Armor of God

the ignition. Then she passed out and remembered no more.

How much time passed? Joyce didn't know. Suddenly she opened her eyes. She blinked in surprise as she realized she was driving into her driveway! She had no memory of the drive home at all. She pulled the car into the garage and somehow got out of the car and into her apartment. There she collapsed in tears onto the floor.

"Thank you Lord Jesus!" she wept. "Thank you for getting me home." That was as far as she got. Dantallion attacked with redoubled fury. Pain exploded in her head and down into her arm and stomach. She doubled up in pain. The horrible horrifying pictures rolled in her mind -- scenes too terrible to describe.

"I rebuke you and bind you demons in the name of Jesus," Joyce muttered weakly. The attack lessened a tiny bit. She crawled toward the phone. The demons attacked again. She started beating her head on the floor. "NO! in the name of Jesus NO!" she cried. She grasped her head in both of her hands and forced it to stop. "I command you to stop in the name of Jesus," she said again, this time with a little more strength. Once again she crawled for the phone. "I must call Rebecca and Elaine for help," she thought.

At last, she reached the phone, but she was too weak to stand. She fumbled, trying to reach the phone on the kitchen counter. Ah, at last, her hand found it. She knocked the phone down on top of her on the floor. A bottle of oil that was sitting on the counter next to the phone fell with it. "Thank you Jesus," she breathed as her hand closed around the bottle of oil, only to have it fall from her hand as the demons struck again, knocking the breath out of her. She felt as if a huge hand with claws was ripping her guts apart.

Chapter 5
The Armor of God

"The oil, get the oil. Bind the demons put in your arm by Sedona." The thought from the Holy Spirit cut through the chaos of tortuous scenes exploding in Joyce's brain. "Yes Lord," she sobbed. "Please help me Jesus!"

She scrabbled forward and grasped the oil bottle again. "Stop in the name of Jesus!" she commanded again. This time she got the top off the oil bottle and poured it over her arm where Sedona had grasped it." "Owwww" she cried out. Burning pain shot up her arm. "In the name of Jesus I command every demon put into me by Sedona to be bound! Leave in the name of Jesus!"

The pain eased up and her mind began to clear a little. She picked up the telephone and dialed. Elaine answered. Rebecca wasn't at home, but Elaine joined with Joyce in prayer. The demons were forced to back off some, but they didn't leave.

"I'll call Rebecca," Elaine said. "She's down at work but I'll get her to call you."

Joyce hung up and waited, praying for strength. Praying with Elaine had helped. She was at least able to think now. She was gaining strength. She got up off the floor and sat on the couch. "'Well at least I'm making progress," she thought with a wry smile.

Ring . . . it was Rebecca. Briefly, Joyce described what had happened.

"Tell me Joyce, did Sedona put an insert, or curse-pin in your arm?" Rebecca asked.

Joyce hadn't thought of that. Carefully she felt her arm. There it was! "Yes," she said slowly. "I can feel it, now I see where it went in. It feels like it is working its way in deeper."

Chapter 5
The Armor of God

"Yes, I expect it is. The demons like to do that. It has to come out of there and fast. Do you have any oil there?" Rebecca said.

"Yes, I've already anointed it," Joyce responded.

"Good, but you must do so again. We must ask the Lord to stop that thing from going into you any deeper. I'm also going to ask Him to push it back to the surface. You anoint your arm and I'll stand with you in prayer."

"O.K." Joyce smeared the oil on her arm again over the area where the curse-pin was. Rebecca started to pray.

"Father, in the name of Jesus we come before your throne. I counter-petition Satan for my sister Joyce. She belongs to You, Lord. Satan has no right to her. In the name of Jesus I ask You to stop this curse-pin and bring it out to the surface. In the name of Jesus I command every demon associated with this pin to be bound!"

Joyce moaned. Her arm was starting to burn again, and the demons were ripping at her stomach. Then the pain began to ease. "I feel better now," she told Rebecca. "I can see a dark spot, I think it's the end of the pin."

"Good, you hang in there, I'll be home as quick as I can -- it will be about an hour."

"That's O.K." Joyce said. "I'm really feeling better now."

By the time Rebecca arrived home Joyce had improved enough to drive over to her house. She was there waiting for her. She was still being tormented with flashbacks, but not as severely. The curse-pin was easily visible just under the surface of her skin and easily removed. It was a tiny

Chapter 5
The Armor of God

metal pin, about one-half inch long, the size of a largish splinter -- but VERY deadly. As soon as the pin was removed Joyce commanded Dantallion and all the demons associated with the curse-pin to leave at once in the name of Jesus. They did so and she was clear at last." (Figure 5-1)

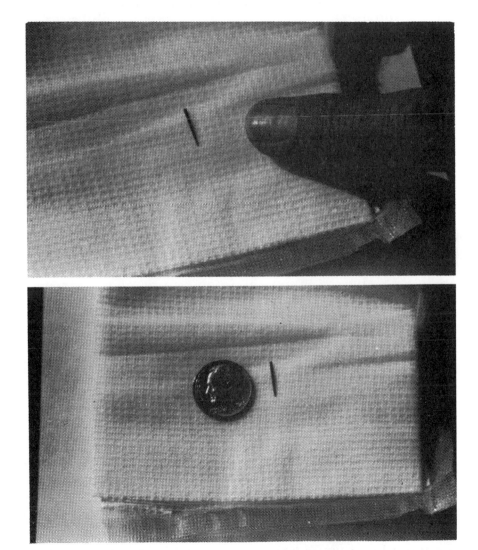

Figure 5-1 (Photos of curse-pins)

Chapter 5
The Armor of God

"I'm not sure that's the end of all this," Rebecca spoke thoughtfully.

"Well, if this is the kind of incantation I think it is, it probably isn't," Joyce agreed. "Sedona knew to use Dantallion because he is a particular demon lord who really hated me. I recognized him immediately. He has a peculiar ability to afflict the mind. This pin looks like an effigy pin used in voodoo. I think I know the incantation Sedona has done."

"I am afraid because I have been through several previous rituals which set me up for this incantation. I had wires placed in that arm that could be used. I never expected that anyone would use them, but Sedona knew about them."

"Why would you do such a thing knowing the possible consequences?"

"For power."

Rebecca sighed. "Of course! Satan's servants will do anything to gain more power. Well, I have no doubt Sedona could have done this death incantation," Rebecca commented. "Let's see, after tonight there are three more days until the first night of the full moon. This incantation was to be completed then, I suppose. That would go along with her threat to have you as a sacrifice this full moon."

"Yes, that's right. This type of incantation takes place over three or four days. You obtain a large black candle in the shape of a male or female. Then the incantation is done which includes a blood sacrifice of some sort. Part of the incantation involves lighting the candle and sticking six to nine effigy pins into the candle at specific positions depending upon what you want done. All but one pin is inserted into the candle. The last pin must be inserted into the person you are placing the incantation against. Then, in this

Chapter 5
The Armor of God

particular death incantation, as the candle burns continuously over the three or four days, the pin in the person is manipulated by the demons. It literally seeds other pieces of metal which correspond to the total number of pins. The pieces of wire previously placed in my arm are demonically controlled after the insertion of the curse pin. As the candle melts down, the pieces of metal grow together in the person in the shape of an upside down cross. On the first night of the full moon the incantation is completed and the upside down cross in the person is completed. As the candle burns out, the person dies. It is a very old and powerful voodoo curse."

"Well, we have the main pin out of you, but I am still concerned about those other wires and the seeds." Rebecca said. "Do you suppose the demons had time to place them in you?"

"I don't know, but I wouldn't be surprised," Joyce said slowly. "What can we do about it?"

"What we always do," Rebecca said, "we ask Father to take care of it" We'll anoint your whole arm and ask Him to bring to the surface any other pins or metal before the final night." So, they anointed Joyce's whole arm and prayed accordingly. (In fact, three days later, on the first night of the full moon, a red, raised, blistered upside down cross began to form on Joyce's arm. Three more pieces of wire were removed from her arm along the lines of the upside down cross. As the wires were removed and Rebecca again anointed her arm the red lines disappeared and the curse was completely broken! Joyce is alive and well. ONLY the power of Jesus Christ can break such a powerful curse!)

After praying and anointing Joyce's arm, they sat quietly for a few minutes. Then Rebecca spoke again. "Listen Joyce,"

Chapter 5
The Armor of God

she said soberly, "there is a lesson to be learned here. That was too close for comfort."

"Yes I know" Joyce said with feeling. "It was ONLY the hand of the Lord that saved me! Father has honored His covenant with you again." He saved my life. Only God kept Sedona from abducting me right there. She seemed strangely unable to do anything but make threats."

"Yes I know," Rebecca nodded. "But Joyce, she should never have been able to touch you!"

"How could I have prevented it?" Joyce asked. "I was hemmed in on every side by those men."

"You should have started fighting immediately. Remember how I have been telling you the armor of God is real? It is real in the spirit world but it affects the physical realm also."

"Yes, but I just don't understand how I could have used it. I did rebuke her in the name of Jesus."

"That wasn't enough. You took a purely defensive posture. You just stood there. Because you didn't fight, you submitted to Sedona. That's why she could do what she did. You allowed fear to take over. You should have taken aggressive offensive action from the beginning. If you had, she could never have gotten her hand on you at all. She should never have been able to put that curse pin into your arm."

Joyce rubbed her forehead tiredly. "I'm sorry, but I just don't understand."

Rebecca stood up and put her arm around her, giving her a hug. "That's O.K. You are too tired to go into it tonight. It is late and you have to go to work in the morning. Go to bed and we will talk about it tomorrow when you have had some

Chapter 5
The Armor of God

rest. In the meantime let's pray and ask Father to help you understand. Stay here tonight where you are safe."

Exhausted, Joyce agreed and stumbled off to bed.

The next day, Joyce returned to Rebecca's house from work about mid morning. She was excited. "Rebecca listen to this. Last night the Lord gave me a dream showing me the armor and how to use it. I understood, finally. Then today He gave me a chance to try it."

"Great! Tell me about it."

"I got to work this morning to find that they were over staffed. So, I volunteered to take the day off. As I went down the hall towards the nurses locker room to change, I saw a man dressed in the uniform of the maintenance people coming towards me. No one else was in the hallway. When he saw me he quickened his pace. I immediately recognized him as being one of the men that had been with Sedona yesterday. He had something in his hand that looked like a knife. I wasn't about to go through what I did yesterday!"

"So what did you do?" Rebecca asked.

"As he came close to me I said 'NO, STOP in the name of Jesus! You are not going to touch me!' Father had showed me how the shield goes on my arm. (Figure 5-2) I held up my forearm in front of me and stepped directly toward him, He looked so shocked. I didn't see the shield, but I have no doubt that he did. I literally pushed him right up against the wall without ever touching him physically. He stood flattened against the wall with his mouth hanging open. I commanded all of his demons to be bound in the name of Jesus and told him again that he could not touch me. He just stayed there, up against the wall. Then I turned and darted

Chapter 5
The Armor of God

into the locker room. When I came out he was gone. I did not see him again."

"Wonderful!" Rebecca exclaimed. "That's exactly what I was trying to talk to you about last night. Even though we do not see the armor of God, it IS real armor in the spirit world. We can use it in the physical world if the Holy Spirit so directs."

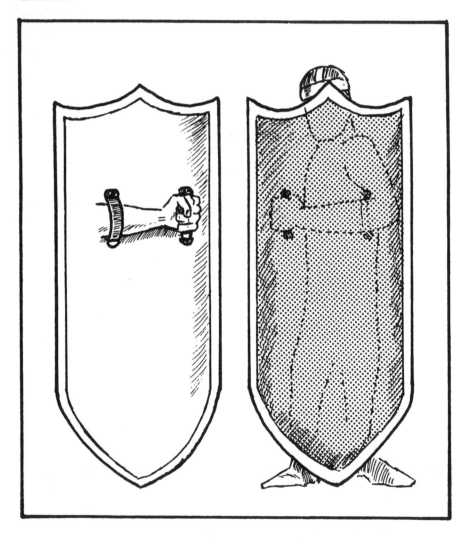

Figure 5-2 (shield of faith)

Chapter 5
The Armor of God

"Yes, that is exactly what Father showed me in that dream. He showed me how the helmet of salvation comes down over our head to protect it. He told me that when those demons of fear first hit me I should have instantly rebuked them in the name of Jesus, commanding them to flee, refusing to accept them because I was protected by the helmet. They got to me because I accepted the attack instead of repulsing it. Then He showed me the breast plate of righteousness and how it protects our chest. The belt of truth is like a girdle and is the only piece of armor that goes around our back. You know, like the armor the Roman soldiers wore. The shield is big, almost as tall as we are. And, the sword is exactly as you had it drawn on the front of your two books. It is pure white light with a golden handle."

Rebecca nodded. "Yes, how do you think I knew how to have the artist draw the sword?"

"You never told me you had seen it." Joyce said. "But, come to think of it, I suspect there is quite a lot you haven't told me."

Rebecca laughed. "Yes, I suppose there is. I remember very well a few occasions when I had to use the armor of God in the physical world. I first learned about its reality when the Lord allowed some demons to physically manifest and try to kill me. Then, the Holy Spirit showed me that we have that armor by faith and can use it when He directs us to do so."

"So when did you use it?" Joyce asked.

"Well, one time was several years ago when I was still in medical practice. I had gone back into the hospital to see a patient in the middle of the night. The parking lot for the doctors was a short walk from the hospital, and the hospital wasn't in a very good section of town. I had to walk alone

Chapter 5
The Armor of God

to my car that night. It was about 3 a.m. I was uneasy. Everything was too quiet, and it was just a couple of nights before the full moon. The satanists were really getting angry with me because I was bringing so many to Christ."

"This particular night, I reached my car and stopped to look around because I sensed that someone was in the parking lot, but I couldn't see anybody. I tried to put my key in the lock, but it wouldn't go in. Something was blocking it! I commanded any demons to leave at once who were interfering with my lock, but nothing worked. I heard a sound and whirled around to see four big tough looking guys coming my direction. Their demons radiated. I had no doubt at all that they planned to serve me up as the main dish for their sacrifice to Satan that full moon. It's a wonder that I didn't have a heart attack on the spot I was so frightened! I am sure they were throwing every demon of fear at me they could."

"What did you do?" Joyce asked impatiently.

"I commanded them to stop and commanded their demons to be bound in the name of Jesus, but that didn't seem to faze them. They just kept right on coming. I continued rebuking them, and they started to laugh at me."

"You are sadly mistaken if you think your Jesus can protect you from us," the leader said jeeringly. They were about ten feet away from me by then.

"Suddenly the Holy Spirit spoke to me. 'Don't forget the armor,' He said. So, in faith, I just asked the Lord to put His sword in my hand and make those guys see it. Then I held my hand across the front of me as if there was a sword in it. Immediately the men stopped in their tracks in surprise. They shielded their eyes as if against a bright light. I was delighted."

Chapter 5
The Armor of God

"O.K. boys," I said. "If you want a fight, come on! I'll fight you with this."

"They stood still for a minute and then the leader spoke up and said, 'Yeah? I'll bet you don't know how to use that thing.'"

"Want to bet?" I said. "Then come on and I'll show you. I do not fight with my own power, but with the power of my master Jesus Christ. You and your demons are no match for Him!"

"They looked uncertain at that point. I pressed my advantage and took a few steps toward them, rebuking them again in the name of Jesus. They stepped back a step, so I continued walking toward them, still holding my hand in front of me. It's a good thing they didn't know how my knees were trembling! I learned early on that I could NEVER show fear or pain."

"They shuffled their feet uneasily. Then, suddenly, they broke and ran. I hurried back to the car and this time the key worked in the lock just fine. Boy did I get out of there as quick as I could!"

"Did you see the sword?" Joyce asked.

"No, I didn't. I had to stand in faith that it was there because the Holy Spirit had told me to use the armor. But they obviously saw it. Satanists can see in the spirit world most of the time anyway, but the demons screen what they see. That is why I asked Father to make them see the sword. Otherwise I was afraid the demons might have kept them from seeing it. I wish I could have seen it but I didn't. I suppose if I had seen it then faith wouldn't have been necessary. We always have to walk this walk in faith."

Chapter 5
The Armor of God

"Yes, and sometimes that's very difficult," Joyce commented. "Tell me about some of the other times."

"Well, rather than talking about myself, let me tell you about an experience someone else had recently who also came out of the craft. Do you remember Annie (not her real name)? I think you met her once while she was here didn't you?"

"Yes, I remember her."

"She stayed with us about five months. She was horribly abused in the craft. Her mother tried to take her and run when she was about seven years old. They were caught and taken back. Annie was then forced to watch her mother be sacrificed as punishment. She was used as a breeder and in all sorts of pornography, both as a child and as an adult. She tried to get out once, about three years before I met her. Two big thugs from the craft caught her and took her back and horribly abused her sexually as punishment. She accepted Jesus as her Lord and Savior this time though. That makes all the difference in the world!"

"You're telling me!" Joyce said with feeling. "It is impossible to get out of the craft and live, any other way. ONLY the power of Jesus can keep you free!"

"About a month after Annie was fully delivered, a day came when she needed to go out to the shopping mall and I couldn't go with her. I can't protect everyone all the time. It's times like those that really test my faith. But I know these folks have to learn to stand on their own feet with the Lord. I let Annie go, but I was very concerned. Esther went with her."

"Later that evening, the Holy Spirit spoke to me telling me to pray, that Annie was in trouble. I had company here at

Chapter 5
The Armor of God

the house, so I asked them to join with me and we all stopped to pray for Annie's safety."

"About an hour later, Annie and Esther came home. Annie could hardly walk in from the car. Here is what happened as she and Esther told it to me."

"Just that morning on the day Annie went out for the first time on her own, I had been talking to her about the armor of God as given to us in Ephesians 6. I told her about the reality of it. I remember telling her that sometimes if you get in a tight spot it is helpful to pass your hand up and down in front of you and say something like 'I KNOW I have a shield right here in front of me, a shield of my faith in Jesus Christ.' It is not necessary to do this, of course, but it helps you stand in faith in a difficult situation. Little did I know that Annie would have to use that shield later that same day."

"As Annie and Esther were walking along in the mall, suddenly Annie stopped short as she was confronted with three huge men. Annie is a tiny thing, she is short and only weighs about 90 pounds. All three men were well over six feet tall. Two of them were the same two satanists who had caught her three years previously when she had tried to run. They were the same ones who had abused her in such a cruel way sexually as punishment for trying to run from the coven."

"The mall was busy, as usual, and hundreds of people streamed past without ever taking notice of the incredible scene unfolding there. Esther took a couple of steps back in fear, not knowing exactly what to do. Annie just stood there in silence looking up at those three men."

"The leader spoke menacingly, 'YOU are coming with us!'"

Chapter 5
The Armor of God

"Annie was trembling with fear, but she managed to speak. 'No I am not! Things are different this time. I now serve Jesus. I no longer serve Satan.'"

"'So what?' the man jeered. 'You are coming with us. You won't get off so easy this time!'"

"Annie was so afraid she didn't know what to do. Suddenly the Holy Spirit flashed into her mind what I had said about the shield of faith earlier that day. She took a deep breath and passed her hand up and down in front of her saying, 'NO! You cannot take me. You see, I have a shield in front of me. The shield of the power of Jesus Christ my Lord.'"

"The three men laughed. 'What shield? I don't see any shield,' the leader said. 'But I'll tell you what, if you want a fight I'll take you on. My power against your power!'"

"Even when Annie was in the craft she was no match for this man. She had never had demons as powerful as his. She was shaking so hard that she could hardly speak, but she said, 'O.K., but I don't have any powers any more, so it will have to be my God against your god!'"

"The men laughed and jeered again. Annie just stood there. As the men started sending demons against her she was overwhelmed with terrible flashbacks. She said the only scripture she could remember was Luke 10:19 which she kept repeating quietly over and over again.

> "Behold, I give unto you power to tread on serpents and scorpions, and over all the power of the enemy: and nothing shall by any means hurt you." Luke 10:19

"The battle raged in the spirit world as Annie just kept standing. The demons afflicted her horribly. They tor-

Chapter 5
The Armor of God

mented her in her mind and body. She swayed under the onslaught, but continued to stand."

"The men began to look puzzled, then they began to look uncertain. After a couple of minutes they took a step backwards, then another. Annie continued to stand. Suddenly, all three of them turned and literally ran out of the shopping mall!"

"Praise the Lord!" Joyce exclaimed.

"Amen! What a victory that was!" Rebecca agreed. "Annie was battered, but she stood! The shield of her faith in Jesus Christ protected her. Our Lord was faithful as always. She had demon bite marks on her neck and was very weak and sore, but she was alive, and they did NOT get her! We anointed her wounds with oil and commanded all the demons afflicting her to leave in the name of Jesus. The marks all disappeared over the next hour and she recovered.

"I know of another incident that happened just recently with T.G. "Rebecca said. (T.G. is a young man that recently came out of a high position within the craft.) "After his deliverance I was talking with him about the reality of God's armor. I told him that I wouldn't be surprised if the demons attacked him in physical manifestations as well as from the spiritual realm. A few days later he shared this incident with me."

"T.G. was sleeping in the back of a van. In the middle of the night he was awakened with a jerk when the back doors of the van blew open with tremendous force and he was sucked out of the van and landed on the ground about fifteen feet away. As he struggled to his feet, he was confronted with one of the demons who had been one of his spirit guides. The demon was in a physical manifestation and told T.G. that he was going to kill him. T.G. said that somehow

Chapter 5
The Armor of God

he had hung onto his pillow when he was blown out of the van. He was so frightened that he could hardly think what to say. He rebuked the demon in the name of Jesus, but it just kept on coming at him. He said that then he remembered about the armor of God."

"T.G. told me that he didn't have the faith to just stand there without anything in front of him, so he held up the pillow saying, 'See this, this is the shield of the Lord. You cannot touch me because I am protected by Jesus.'"

"The demon just laughed and said, 'You think that little pillow is going to protect you from me? I'll show you!'"

"Then the demon proceeded to reach out and claw at the pillow viciously. The pillow was torn to shreds, but the demon could not reach beyond it! Although T.G. could not see it, clearly there was a shield in front of him! Try as the demon might, he could not get through that invisible shield! After a few moments, he gave up and disappeared. T.G. came over and showed me the shredded pillow the next morning. He told me that in all his years in the craft he would never have attempted to ward off a demon with just a pillow! But praise the Lord, behind that pillow was a very real shield! The precious shield of his faith in his new master, Jesus Christ! If only Christians would realize the reality of the spirit world and of God's armor, there would be many more victories against Satan's kingdom."

Joyce nodded soberly. "Yes, and we are fast entering a time when we will be seeing more and more direct confrontations between satanists and God's people."

(Author's note: It is my prayer that Christians everywhere will begin to wake up and realize what wonderful provisions have been made for us by our Lord. We do not need to fear Satan and his servants. However, we must never under es-

Chapter 5
The Armor of God

timate them because they are powerful and their power IS REAL. But, praise God, they don't have any power at all compared to the awesome power of our Lord Jesus Christ!)

Chapter 5
The Armor of God

Chapter 6

DEMONIC WOUNDS

The more I work in this ministry of helping people out of Satanism, the more I learn about demonic wounds. By this, I mean injuries directly caused by demons. The Lord has graciously made provision for the healing of these wounds, but we must be able to recognize them and know how to treat them.

Those of us who have never been involved in Satanism must understand that those brothers and sisters in Christ who were once in Satan's service are peculiarly vulnerable to demonic wounds. I don't know why, unless it is a part of the reaping process they must go through.

The first characteristic of any demonic wound is the inability of the wounded person to recognize the demonic cause of the wound. The first thing the demons do is try to blind the person to the fact that they are dealing with demons. As long as the wounded person doesn't recognize that demons are the primary cause of the wound, they will not rebuke the demons or drive them away. This leaves the demons free to continue doing damage.

> "And Jesus answering said, A certain man went down from Jerusalem to Jericho, and fell among thieves, which stripped him of his raiment, and wounded him, and departed, leaving him half dead . . . But a certain Samaritan, as he journeyed, came where he was: and when he saw him, he had compassion on him, and went to him, and bound up his wounds, pouring in oil and wine, and set him on his own beast, and brought him to an inn, and took care of him." Luke 10:30-34

> "Is any sick among you? Let him call for the elders of
> the church; and let them pray over him, anointing him
> with oil in the name of the Lord: And the prayer of faith
> shall save the sick, and the Lord shall raise him up; and
> if he have committed sins, they shall be forgiven him."
> James 5:14-15

The keys to dealing with demonically created wounds are found in these two scriptures. The Lord has clearly indicated in these scriptures that the pouring in of the oil and prayer of faith in the name of Jesus is necessary. However, what too many people overlook is this: **IF** the person, who has been wounded or is ill, has unconfessed or active sin in his/her life the sin must be taken care of at the same time or they won't be healed.

It has been my experience many, many times that **if someone who has come out of the craft is getting wounded frequently, there is legal ground in their life for the demons to afflict them.** They may not always know what it is, but if they will ask the Lord to reveal it to them, He is always faithful to do so. Sometimes people are wounded simply because they forget to ask the Lord to place His full armor on them each day. I cannot emphasize strongly enough the importance of the armor of God.

There are four basic types of demonic wounds:

> direct physical damage
> poisoning
> inserts
> illness

Chapter 6
Demonic Wounds

DIRECT PHYSICAL DAMAGE

The most common wound in this category occurs in what seems to be an accident, but is actually caused by a demon. Let me give you an example. A couple of years ago I was rushing to get ready to go to a wedding. I finished ironing my dress and leaned over to pull the plug of the iron out of the wall. Suddenly my arm was caught and held against the iron. My natural reflex was not enough to pull my arm away from the hot iron. I had to use my other hand to do so. Naturally, I received a deep burn on the side of my left arm as a result.

Because my natural reflex was not sufficient to pull my arm away from the hot iron, I should have immediately realized that the wound was demonic in addition to the physical burn. It was more than just an accident. However, I was in a terrible hurry, and the demons did their best to block my mind from recognizing that they were involved in the wound. I hastily placed a dressing over the burn and rushed off to the wedding. I had a speaking engagement that evening and again the next day. My arm was extremely painful, but I did not stop to think about it long enough to recognize the demonic component of the injury.

Finally, two days later when I had a chance to slow down, I started thinking about the burn. I had applied aloe vera which normally always relieves the pain of a burn. In my case, it increased the pain! So did every other ointment I tried. Also, I noticed that the area of the burn was getting bigger and was, by then, so painful I could hardly stand it. This is not normal for a second degree burn. The pain should have started to lessen by the third day in the case of normal healing. But, this wasn't a normal burn. As I looked at the burn and began to pray about it, the Holy Spirit brought back to my mind the circumstances of the "accident." Especially the fact that my natural reflex had not been enough to pull my arm away from the iron. Immediately I realized that this was a demonic injury.

I got out my bottle of oil and literally poured it over the entire burn saying, "In the name of Jesus Christ, I command every demon associated with this burn to leave me immediately. I command you to stop afflicting and extending this burn, and in the name of Jesus I command pain to leave NOW! Father, in the name of Jesus I ask you to bring healing and pain relief to this burn. I thank you for it in the name of Jesus." Immediately the pain lessened, and the burn then started the normal healing process. However, because I had let it go so long, it had extended to twice the area of the original burn and took almost three weeks to heal, leaving a scar. I have no doubt at all that if I had stopped and anointed the burn immediately, I would not have had such a severe wound.

I have found that pure olive oil is not harmful in open cuts or burns. I have used it repeatedly in such cases. In the parable of the good Samaritan, the alcohol in the wine was used to cleanse the wound and the oil was used for healing. I will always anoint with oil first, then cleanse the wound with some sort of antiseptic, add whatever healing ointment I have available and bandage the wound.

Here is another example. Sam (not his real name) was a martial arts expert before accepting Christ. After he came to Christ, he was working on the lawn of his pastor's home one afternoon. The demon that used to be his spirit guide appeared to him and threatened to kill him if he did not renounce Christ and go back to serving Satan.

Sam, being a very young Christian, instead of simply rebuking the demon and commanding him to leave in the name of Jesus, said something like, "No way, bug off!" The demon

Chapter 6
Demonic Wounds

lashed out and clawed Sam on the head leaving three gashes to the bone extending the full length of his scalp. Sam was knocked unconscious on the ground. The Holy Spirit alerted the pastor that Sam was in trouble. He went out and found him unconscious in a pool of blood on the ground.

The pastor picked Sam up and took him to a nearby hospital where the three lacerations in his scalp were stitched closed. However, the pain did not lessen. Instead, it continued to increase over the next two days. That's when Sam came to see me. The pastor had anointed Sam with oil, but both he and the pastor had been afraid to put oil on the lacerations because of the stitches. Sam's pain was extremely severe by the time I saw him. There was no evidence of inflammation around the stitches, although the wound did not show the normal healing it should have for three days. I took olive oil and poured it over the three lacerations covering them completely. At the same time I rebuked the demons and prayed as I did in the above example with my burn. Within a few seconds the pain was gone out of Sam's head. We simply used clean gauze to daub the oil off the stitches and left the lacerations open to the air as they had done at the hospital. The wounds proceeded to heal normally.

There is another common type of direct physical injury caused by what the craft calls BRUSH ACID. Those skilled in astral-projection use this preparation extensively. It is simply a mixture of hydrochloric acid (occasionally some other kind of acid is used) mixed with agar. Hydrochloric acid burns the skin the just the same as a flame. It is easily obtainable from any laboratory supply house. Agar is a thickening agent ,which is used as a basic ingredient for mediums used to grow bacteria in any laboratory. It is cheap and easily available. Agar thickens any solution similar to gelatin. The agaracid mixture is about the consistency of runny jello. It is clear and easy to apply to any surface.

Chapter 6
Demonic Wounds

Anyone brushing against the acid, or getting their hands into it can receive a severe acid burn.

Satanists astral-project and put this brush acid on such things as car door handles, door knobs of homes, counter tops, etc. Those extremely skilled in astral-projection can carry the brush acid and directly place it, or brush it, onto a person in the physical realm.

The physical person cannot see the spirit carrying the acid, and the acid cannot burn a spirit. (I know this sounds really farfetched to those who have never been in the craft, but those who have served Satan know that what I am writing is true.)

People use it in the physical realm also, of course. We have most frequently found it on the handles of our car doors. It is simple to remove by flushing with water, but you CAN-NOT touch it with your bare skin. We usually flush the area with plenty of water and then wash it with soap and water and then anoint it with oil. If you receive a burn from such a source, you should immediately flush the affected part with copious amounts of water and then anoint it with oil as I have described. Then treat the resulting burn the same as you would any other burn.

Once I received a terrible burn in my mouth from tooth-paste. We were traveling on a speaking engagement. Apparently somebody got into our motel room and injected acid into my tube of toothpaste. Since that time I have never left medicines or toothpaste in a hotel room in my absence.

Also be careful of any unusual insect bites. Demons can use spiders and such, but do not do so commonly. If you suspect demonic involvement in an insect bite, simply cover the bite with oil and command the demons to leave. Demonic insect

Chapter 6
Demonic Wounds

bites will always produce a much more severe reaction and inflammation than a normal insect bite.

Demon bites are also a reality. They show up on the skin as a physical bite mark, or sometimes a pattern of tiny spots of red, called petechiae, in a circular pattern. These, too, are simply treated by anointing with oil.

Another type of demonic wound that is very common is a physical injury for which you have no memory of its origin. It is not uncommon for one of us to become very weak or ill. When this occurs, usually we start looking for some sort of injury. Frequently it is a significant cut somewhere and we will have no memory of when the cut occurred. Normally an injury of this type would cause enough pain that we would clearly remember when we got it. These, too, must be anointed with oil.

POISONING

Almost from the beginning of time, poisoning has been a very popular method of doing harm to an enemy. This is certainly true of those in the craft as well. However, their poisons are ALL mixed with demons and demonic powers. Therefore, there are two things to be dealt with: the physical poison and the demons. Some common substances which are available in most any occultic bookstore are not, in themselves, very toxic. But, when combined with special incantations, they can be deadly. Others are very deadly and must be ordered "under-the-counter" in occult bookstores or through occultic supply houses.

Some of the common substances used in poison potions are:

Ova ursi oil	Tannis root
Valerain root	Wormroot
Vervain oil	Cyanide
Muckroot	Hemlock
Mandrake	Curare
Bloodroot	Ginseng root
Quick silver (mercury)	Double-cross powder (cyanide)

Unfortunately, as modern scientific technology progresses, witchcraft takes advantage of all the advances. One of the most significant is the use of DMSO. DMSO stands for Dimethylsulfoxide. This is a chemical that was developed originally for use in horses. It is an excellent anti-inflammatory agent. It is rubbed on strained ligaments, inflamed joints, etc. In 1988 it was finally approved by the FDA for use in humans. DMSO has one property that makes it particularly valuable to the occultist and to drug users. It is absorbed through the skin into the blood stream within twenty seconds. Thus, most anything mixed with DMSO is ALSO absorbed through the skin into the blood stream in twenty seconds. The occultists love to mix their various poisons with DMSO. The unfortunate person who then gets the solution on his/her skin gets into trouble very quickly. DMSO is readily available at most any veterinary supply store. Frequently the poisons and DMSO are mixed with gum arabic to make it more sticky and harder to get off the skin.

Be careful! If you suspect a poison has been placed anywhere within your reach, use rubber gloves to handle the article and to wash off the substance. If you have put your hands into something that contains DMSO, wash the area GENTLY with copious amounts of water and then with

Chapter 6
Demonic Wounds

soap and water. If you rub your skin hard with DMSO, blisters will be raised on your skin and the rate of adsorption will be increased. You can be alerted to the fact that you have gotten into DMSO by the fact that, as it is absorbed through your skin into your bloodstream, you will experience a peculiar smell similar to that of oysters or fish as the DMSO travels in your blood through your nose. Many times you will also experience a taste of fish as well.

Some poisons also come in powdered form and can be placed on paper or on gummed stickers or labels. The poisons can be absorbed through your skin from the paper, or taken into your body by licking the stickers, etc. There have been cases of children poisoned with LSD through gummed stickers or stars which they licked to stick on their papers, or through stamps.

Those of us in such a ministry as this must ALWAYS be alert to guidance by the Holy Spirit. Only HE can alert us to these dangers. One characteristic common to most all occult poisonings is that the symptoms of the illness frequently come on every day at the same time as the poisoning occurred. Such things as intense headaches, muscle aches, fever, weakness, etc. Also, it will frequently get worse at sunset as the demons become much more active at dusk and throughout the night.

Some of the most powerful poisoning incantations come out of writings called the "Grimories." These are very old books that were written by the alchemists of the middle ages in Europe. They were the "scientists" who tried to turn common substances into gold, and bring life out of inanimate substances. They were, in reality, very powerful sorcerers. These volumes are still available today, for a price, but are strictly under-the-counter type materials.

Chapter 6
Demonic Wounds

I have been told that three of the common demons used in the various poisoning incantations from the Grimories are:

> VALEFOR, king of all occult medicine and death. Valefor cannot be called up without a human sacrifice.
> ALLOCES, king of torment.
> ANDRES, lord of swift destruction -- especially mentally.

Occultic poisonings that are mostly all demonic have limited time intervals in which they can work. These are governed by the astrological signs AND astronomy. Most poison incantations are done at the rise of a particular planet, such as Saturn, and run out when the planet sets. This is usually a period of one to three months. If it is a bad time of the year for the stars, they will use a more deadly physical poison. The demonic portion of a poisoning can be rebuked and driven away by prayer and a simple anointing with oil. But the effects of the physical poisons can be lasting. I know. I have personally been very close to death four times in the last year because of physical poisons. However, I believe that I am alive today because I NEVER put so much as a sip of water into my mouth without first praying and asking the Lord to purify and sanctify it according to I Timothy 4:5. Mark 16:17-18 has been fulfilled in my own life a number of times.

In purely demonic poisonings, many times the person can actually feel a burning or tingling sensation traveling up his/her arm immediately after getting their fingers in a poison, or getting something such as a splinter in their hand. You MUST anoint immediately with oil to stop the spread of demonic power into the rest of their body. I learned this lesson the hard way. You must apply the oil like a tourniquet above the level of the spread of demonic power, and

Chapter 6
Demonic Wounds

then drive the demons down and out of the extremity. (Figure 6-1)

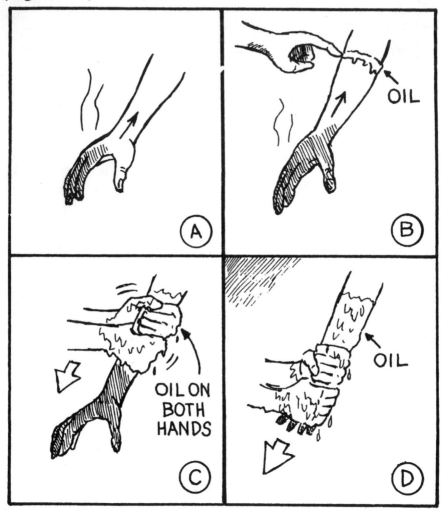

Figure 6-1

If the person is alone and does not have someone to help them, they should apply the "oil tourniquet" first, then wash the area thoroughly to remove any physical poison, or remove the splinter or insert, and then drive the demons

Chapter 6
Demonic Wounds

down and out of the extremity by using the oil as in the illustration.

Also, be careful. If you are involved in a ministry similar to our own, the craft will place their people as employees in all the restaurants in your area. We have been severely poisoned more than once through fast-foods restaurants. NEVER develop a routine! The safest restaurants to eat in are smorgasbords or buffets. It is impossible for craft employees to poison all the food on a buffet or salad bar. We rarely eat out except when we travel. I tend to cook everything at home. It's much safer that way.

INSERTS

Inserts are just about anything that gets inserted under the skin or into the body that has a demon, and sometimes physical poisons (the most common is cyanide or mercury) attached to it.

Not only is it impossible to completely clear a person of demons while these inserts are still in place, but the demons associated with the inserts frequently cause amnesia. The person will sometimes be unable to remember all of the inserts they have, and/or important rituals in which they have participated.

As you look at other cultures around the world, you will find the use of inserts everywhere. For example, Hindu women in India frequently wear a particular gem or stone imbedded in the skin in the center of their forehead. This is the position of the "third eye" (see chapter 10). This links them with their god and supposedly gives them special vision into the spirit world. Various African tribes are well-known for pieces of bone inserted into their noses, ears or lips.

Chapter 6
Demonic Wounds

I think it is no accident the gay movement has popularized ear rings for men. What effect does the placement of such ear rings have in a non-homosexual young man? I would be very concerned about this if I were a young man. I am not saying that all jewelry is demonic. However, some of it is. We as Christians need to be much in prayer about everything we do.

There are at least seven categories of inserts:
> Push-pins (see Chapter 2)
> Curse-pins (see Chapter 5)
> Nail-pins
> Satan's Web
> Crystals
> Demonic I.U.D.'s
> Dental inserts
> Splinters

Nail-pins are basically the same as push-pins. They are inserted into the bed of the finger nails or toe nails. Most commonly, the finger nails. They have the same functions as the push-pins.

Satan's web is a piece of fine silky material about two by three inches in size. It is swallowed in a ritual. The web is placed as sort of a time bomb which goes off if the person ever turns against Satan. It produces an intense acid in the stomach and will eventually destroy the stomach completely. It produces all sorts of severe stomach pain and even bleeding, but little is found on physical examination because the process is purely demonic. The Satan's web must be specifically renounced and the person must ask the Lord to completely remove it. Once this is done, the symptoms quickly disappear.

Chapter 6
Demonic Wounds

Crystals are extremely small and are actually demonic parasites. Although they are crystalline in nature, they are a living parasite. I have seen these under a microscope. They are usually inserted behind the ear drum, into the blood stream, or simply under the skin. They are about the size of one to three grains of salt. Some are red, some are white. In the craft, the red crystals are frequently called the "red devil's crystals." If a woman has a baby that is delivered on a satanic altar, or in the presence of other satanists, these crystals are often inserted into the artery and veins of the umbilical cord of the baby as the cord is cut. Both the baby and the mother are affected demonically by the crystals. It is not possible to completely clear someone of demons until these crystals are specifically renounced and the Lord is asked to remove them. If possible, they should be physically removed. They are capable of creating devastating illness, even death within four to six months of placement.

Demonic I.U.D.s are often placed through various procedures. These may be made of metal, but they always have a demonic component. Both the metal and the demons must be removed. In fact, I have been told by more than one high ranking satanist who has turned to Jesus, that the whole concept of the intrauterine devices were devised by craft doctors in the first place. (One of these was a man who was a physician who participated in extensive research in the various Satanic medical procedures. He also told me that much research is currently going on that makes what was done in Hitler's concentration camps look like nothing.) An I.U.D. does not prevent conception. It prevents implantation of the early fetus in the uterus. In essence, it causes an abortion. The craft doctors considered these I.U.D.-caused abortions to be sacrifices to Satan. The I.U.D. went over big at first, but quickly many women started having major problems with them. Heavy bleeding, cancer, etc. Finally, the government withdrew approval for them because of these problems. Why so many problems? Was it only be-

Chapter 6
Demonic Wounds

cause of the physical presence of the I.U.D.? I doubt it. I think it may well have been because of the demonic component as well. How many innocent women had an I.U.D. placed simply for birth control, never realizing the original purpose for which it was developed. Please note, I am NOT saying that the companies that manufactured the I.U.D.s were working for Satan. They very well may have had no idea at all of the original purpose for their design. Remember, Satan ALWAYS works through deception.

Any Christian woman who has an I.U.D. should have it physically removed and then close the doorway. Remember, all abortions are human sacrifices to Satan. If you have had an I.U.D., you should ask the Lord for forgiveness and cleansing and then command all demons that came into you through the I.U.D. and I.U.D.-caused abortions to leave you at once in the name of Jesus.

Dental inserts are common amongst the higher satanists. These are usually computer chips that can literally be traced by satellite. Thus, until these are removed, the person can be traced anywhere in the world. Their location is known at all times. A variation of these computer chips are currently being introduced into the general population of the U.S. and other countries. They have been used in animals for several years. In the winter of 1989 and 1990, the craft began pushing the implantation of computer micro-chips into children, either under the skin of their right hand or in their forehead. The stated purpose is to prevent the many kidnapings here in the U.S. The micro-chip contains information as to the child's identity and medical history. The child's location can then be traced by satellite quickly in the event they are abducted. The various "Child Finding" organizations are beginning to push this in some states already.

Also, I have heard from some higher craft members who have just recently come to Jesus, that these computer chips

Chapter 6
Demonic Wounds

will be placed in driver's licenses and credit cards in the near future. Thus, the person carrying the license or credit card can be located at all times. I have been told that the only thing that can shield these chips from detection by the various scanners is lead. Lead is also effective in shielding from the infrared scanners which can locate any living creature by the heat emitted from its body. Is that why there is such a move recently to recall all lead and to out-law the use of lead in our country?

Are these computer micro-chips the "mark of the beast?" I think they very well could be. A person with such a computer chip in place cannot hide anywhere in the world because of the satellite access. Scientific technology is so advanced that the world can be photographed and mapped by satellite with a resolution of inches or less. With the rapid shift towards a totally cashless society, what would seem more logical than the implantation of such a record keeping and identity mark? Afterall, credit cards can easily be lost or stolen. New Zealand, as of 1990, is very rapidly moving to a cashless society. Everyone will use a bank card or credit card. No one will use cash any more. Secular newspapers in both Australia and New Zealand are currently running articles and cartoons showing the switch from the credit card to a mark of some sort on the person's hand or forehead. Scripture IS being fulfilled in our day:

> "And I saw a beast rising out of the sea...And the beast was given a mouth uttering haughty and blasphemous words, and it was allowed to exercise authority for forty-two months...Also it was allowed to make war on the saints and to conquer them. And authority was given it over every tribe and people and tongue and nation. And all that dwell upon the earth shall worship him whose names are not written in the book of life of the Lamb slain from the foundation of the world...And he causeth all, both small and great, rich and poor, free and bond, to receive a mark in their right hand, or in

Chapter 6
Demonic Wounds

their foreheads: And that no man might buy or sell, save he that had the mark, or the name of the beast, or the number of his name...." Rev. 13:1-17

Please note, scripture says the mark shall be received IN the hand or forehead, not ON. Could this be because the Lord knew an insert would be used rather than a simple surface mark? I suppose you could say that the "mark of the beast" is the ultimate satanic insert.

Many different demonic things are implanted in people through "ritual sex." During ritual sex, usually a female is placed on an altar and/or is used as the altar. This person is then sexually used by humans, demons or animals. I have found that complete deliverance is not possible until episodes of ritual sex are renounced and every demon kicked out that was placed into the person during the rituals. Many times push-pins are placed in various areas of the reproductive tract during these rituals. Commonly, children abused in Satanic rituals describe "hot needles" being placed in various areas of their genital and reproductive tracts. They are describing inserts.

The simplest way to deal with these is by asking the Lord to burn out or remove these pins or implants, and by commanding every demon associated with the implants to leave in the name of Jesus Christ. I know that the memories of such rituals are extremely painful to the person who participated in them. I usually explain to the person that they must bear the pain of remembering long enough for us to deal with the problem. Then, as each episode of ritual sex is confessed and the demons are kicked out, I always pray and simply ask the Lord to completely wipe out the memory of the ritual from the person's mind forever. Our Lord is so very gracious, He has been faithful in answering my prayers in this area.

Chapter 6
Demonic Wounds

Children who are ritualistically abused are always put through some form of ritual sex. Inserts are commonly placed in these children. Push-pins are frequently placed in the reproductive and urinary tracts. These are hard to X-ray because of the demonic component. Demons can and do hide things on X-ray. This is a very commonly missed source of trouble in children who have been abused. Once again, I have found that the Lord is very gracious and will remove the pins directly. Our Lord has such a special love for children. He deals with these little ones very gently and tenderly.

Splinters of wood or metal are most commonly used. Demons are experts at handling these. Again, most often the wound seems to be "just an accident." However, the consequences can be very grave.

In the case of inserts, the demons CANNOT be removed from the person until the physical substance placed under the skin is removed.

DEMONIC ILLNESSES

These are physical illnesses caused by demons. Sometimes the demons simply set a physical problem in motion which then continues on its own. Sometimes, they remain and continue the problem themselves. in the first case, rebuking and driving away the demon will NOT stop the physical illness. A very common method of demonic discipline within the craft is by kidney stones. Demons can very easily create kidney stones. These are extremely painful to pass. However, once the physical kidney stone has been created, removing the demon will not have any effect on the course of the problem. The stone will still pass unless the Lord chooses to directly intervene and supernaturally dissolve the stone.

Chapter 6
Demonic Wounds

seen upside down crosses blistered into the skin
who has come out of the craft as a result of an
n. The result of such a wound is usually some
p.   with the organ located underneath the cross, such
as the kidney or stomach. Such things must always be COM-
PLETELY covered with oil and the demons commanded
away in the name of Jesus. I also always command all incantations to be broken in the name of Jesus.

REMEMBER, demons can, and do, cause illness. But NOT
ALL illness is demonic. We must remember that physical
as well as spiritual death was the result of Adam's fall. The
alteration in our physical bodies caused by sin makes us vulnerable to an array of physical illnesses. We must always
look for a purely physical cause of any illness, AND seek
the discernment of the Holy Spirit to alert us when there is
a demonic component also.

Through the years I have found that one of the first things
demons affect is the rapidly reproducing cells. These are
found in such places as the bone marrow and the lining of
the intestinal tract. VERY commonly, people who are
severely afflicted with demonic illness are completely unable to break down or adsorb complex proteins or fats. This
is because demons can so readily affect and damage the cells
lining the stomach and intestinal tract. It is rather a joke
amongst my friends (some of them physicians also) that
anyone involved in spiritual warfare is usually on Tagamet
or Zantac, medicines that help reduce the hyperacidity and
ulcers which are common because of the demons' peculiar
ability to hit in this area.

ALL demonic illnesses create a tremendous protein drain.
The body's natural defenses are quickly affected by protein
deficiencies. The white blood cells, which fight infection,
quickly become unable to function as they normally would
when a protein deficiency is present.

Chapter 6
Demonic Wounds

I have found two items that are very effective in handling this type of problem. They require a prescription from a physician, but I hope some Christian physicians will take heed to my experience. There are two products called Vivonex HN and MCT oil. Vivonex is a preparation of pure amino acids, the building blocks of protein. It is directly absorbed through the gastric and deuodenal mucosa without requiring any digestive process. It comes in an oral preparation. BUT, it tastes terrible! The way to make it palatable is to mix it with jello and add unsweetened Kool-Aid as flavoring. The MCT oil is most frequently used for premature babies. It is a medium chained triglyceride which is an essential fat. It, too, is directly absorbed without needing digestion. When I was in medical practice I saved many patients lives by using these two simple remedies.

I have also found that demons love to create very painful paresthesias. Paresthesias are severe burning pains on various areas of the skin, sometimes accompanied by intense itching. Usually there is nothing abnormal about the appearance of the skin, but it will be very tender to the touch and extremely painful. In these cases, if anointing with oil does not stop the pain, I have found that often injectable Vit. B12 in large doses over seven to ten days is helpful. (One of the very few uses I ever found for B12.) Usually in amounts of 1000 mcg. per injection per day. When anointing with oil, it is important that the entire area that is painful be covered with the oil.

Shingles is also common with demonic affliction. Anytime anyone has repeated bouts of shingles, they should immediately go to the Lord to see if the source is demonic.

Painful joints are another common demonic problem. Sometimes the joint will be swollen or appear inflamed, but usually it will appear completely normal. Again, usually covering the entire joint with oil and commanding the

Chapter 6
Demonic Wounds

demons to leave is all that is needed. However, if that doesn't completely handle the problem, and a physical problem such as an infection, cartilage problem, etc. is not present, a mixture of DMSO with 10% Hydrocortisone is very effective. DMSO was finally approved by the FDA in 1988. It is available with a prescription. Use a cotton ball to gently pat on the solution three or four times per day. Usually the pain and/or inflammation will subside after one or two days. You should not use the solution more than one week, however.

I know that most of these things need prescriptions, but I write them here in hopes that the people who need them will be able to find a doctor somewhere to help them get what they need. There are essentially no side effects to any of these, so none of them are dangerous to use.

One last word to physicians. We must realize that demons are experts in handling viruses and bacteria. These infections are difficult to treat. The most common treatment error I came across while I was in practice was the use of too small a dose of antibiotics. Talk to your patients and pray with them. If you feel a patient is being afflicted by witchcraft, treat his/her infection aggressively. Anything less than 500 mg per dose of most any oral antibiotic in adults is too little in these cases. I would frequently use a gram per dose for the first 24 to 48 hours. I found through practical experience that this made the difference between handling an infection quickly and effectively and having to deal with a prolonged and complicated course or a low-level smoldering infection which is most bothersome. ALWAYS be sure to anoint with oil and command the interfering demons to leave in the name of Jesus. Demons are experts at hindering the body's attempts to fight infection.

If a person has a preexisting weakness or tendency to a particular illness, the demons will always strike in that area. For

Chapter 6
Demonic Wounds

instance, if a person has a seizure disorder, then the demons will try to give them seizures. If they have had kidney stones, that is where the demons will strike. It is easier for demons to create illness where there has been illness before. The same is true for those coming out of the craft. Usually the demons will strike in the same way they did to discipline while the person was in the craft. We need to be careful to pray for special shielding in such areas.

One last area that needs to be addressed is the problem of cancer. Demons are expert at causing cancer. However, I have seen too many people terribly disappointed when they have been promised healing from cancer by deliverance. This is just NOT so. I want to emphasize again that when demons start a physical process such as cancer, casting out the demon will NOT put a stop to the cancer. The process has already been set in motion. The only way the cancer can be healed is if it can be totally removed surgically, treated by radiation or chemotherapy (although few courses of chemotherapy are truly effective in bringing about cures) or if the Lord chooses to do a miracle and heal the person directly.

These are all things that have been revealed to myself and others by the Holy Spirit. All physicians should be much in prayer seeking guidance on how to treat their patients, especially those afflicted with demonic illnesses.

Our Lord is so very gracious. I have been privileged to see many, many miraculous healings. But the problem of demonically created wounds and illnesses is a very real one which will, I believe, become more and more common as we get closer to the end.

Evil is escalating at an amazing rate. Jesus Himself prophesied that the evil in the last days prior to His return would be worse than it ever has been on the earth except in

Chapter 6
Demonic Wounds

the days of Noah. I firmly believe we are living in those days. We, as Christians, and especially as Christian physicians, are going to see things "stranger than fiction" as Satan's kingdom grows in power and strength.

We MUST walk closely with the Lord because we are entering days when ONLY the guidance of the Holy Spirit will keep us alive.

Chapter 6
Demonic Wounds

CHAPTER 7

THE HOLY SPIRIT VERSUS DEMON SPIRIT GUIDES

I believe it is very important for those people coming out of the occult to gain a good understanding of the operation of the Holy Spirit in their lives. They are used to having one or more demon spirit guides. Once they accept Jesus Christ as their Lord and Savior, they are given the Holy Spirit to help and guide them. However, the Holy Spirit functions very differently from a demon spirit guide.

Christians who have never been involved in the occult need to know how demon spirits act as spirit guides. Why? Because the sad truth is that many Christians today are accepting a demon spirit guide thinking it is the Holy Spirit. Most of these errors could be avoided if Christians had a good basic understanding of how scripture describes the functions of the Holy spirit in our lives.

The following shows comparisons between the Holy Spirit and demon spirit guides

1. The Holy Spirit IS God almighty with unlimited power and knowledge. He has all the attributes of the Godhead.

Demon spirits are limited created beings. They have none of the attributes of the Godhead. Their knowledge and intelligence, though far superior to human intelligence, IS LIMITED.

2. The Holy Spirit values our individuality. He does not try to usurp our individual personality in any way.

Demons HATE human beings! They try to usurp the individual's personality and replace it with their own.

3. The Holy Spirit wants US to be in control and responsible for our own actions. He works in us to "will to do God's will." (Phil. 2:13)

Demons want total control. They will frequently knock the person unconscious and then use them in any way they want.

4. The Holy Spirit is gentle. When He comes into a person, He is so gentle that when you look inside yourself, you can't tell what is the Holy Spirit and what is you.

Demons are harsh. Because of their desire to take over, a person can always sense a difference between the demon spirit and themselves. This is true even if they think the demon is a "counselor" of part of their own subconscious mind. It is always an "entity" separate from their conscious mind.

5.The Holy Spirt is holy and pure. He brings purity into our lives. He gives us POWER to overcome sin.

Demons are totally corrupt. They will ALWAYS lead a person deeper and deeper into sin. Even the demons in the New Age Movement who try to present themselves as being "good" quickly lead the person into sin. Within the New Age Movement, the areas of sin to show quickly are sexual immorality and a desire to delve into the occult and increase contact with the spirit world.

**Chapter 7
The Holy Spirit Versus Demon Spirit Guides**

6. The Holy Spirit always uplifts and glorifies Jesus, thereby bringing humility into the life of the person He indwells.

Demons hate Jesus! They glorify the person in whom they dwell, always drawing attention to the person himself instead of toward Jesus. PRIDE is the hall mark of demons AND the people they inhabit.

7. The Holy Spirit NEVER blanks out our minds. He puts thoughts into our minds, but does NOT blank them. He wants us to "take every thought captive" (II Cor. 10:5) and to "will to do God's will." (Phil.2:13) He always wants us to ACTIVELY cooperate with Him. We do not have to blank our minds for the Holy Spirit to speak to us. He is so powerful that He can override our active mind at any time. THIS is the place where most Christians make mistakes and fall into deception, thinking they have to blank their minds for the Holy Spirit to operate through them or speak to them.

Demons frequently blank out a person's mind. They function best when the person passively lets them take over. That's why Eastern and occultic meditation ALWAYS involves relaxation techniques to blank the mind. Demons have difficulty overriding an active strong mind. They always encourage periods of mental passivity.

8. The Holy Spirit convicts us of our sins. BUT His conviction is nondestructive. He always leads the person to repentance, forgiveness, redemption and peace.

Demons do one of two things. They help the person justify his sins, or they bring destructive crushing guilt with NO hope of forgiveness or redemption. Demonic guilt always brings with it the message: "You cannot be forgiven."

Chapter 7
The Holy Spirit Versus Demon Spirit Guides

9. The Holy Spirit will NEVER give us any communication that contradicts God's word.

Demons will twist and turn God's word and take it out of context to justify sin.

10. We can NEVER control the Holy Spirit! He functions when and how HE pleases. We are the servants. HE is the Master. Example: We CANNOT control WHEN the Holy Spirit speaks to us, gives us a glimpse of the spirit world, makes us aware of God's presence, heals, or gives us discernment. The Holy Spirit never does the same thing twice. He refuses to allow us to depend on any routine or ritual. "And there are diversities of operations, but it is the same God which worketh all in all. But manifestation of the Spirit is given to every man to profit withal..,[lists various gifts]...But all these [gifts] worketh that one and the selfsame Spirit, dividing to every man severally as he will." (I Cor. 12:6-11) "God also bearing them witness, both with signs and wonders, and with divers miracles, and gifts of the Holy Spirit, ACCORDING TO HIS OWN WILL." Heb. 2:4

Demon spirits dupe the people they indwell into thinking they can control them. They will come whenever the person calls, heal when the person wants, etc. They love rituals and routines. They enable a person to see the spirit world more and more. The demonic counterfeits of the gifts of the Holy Spirit are usually under the control of the person, i.e. he can heal, prophesy, have "words of knowledge," etc., whenever he wants.

11. The Holy Spirit demands that we walk in faith -- NOT by sight OR emotions. Therefore, He does not frequently or routinely give us visions or emotions. The Holy Spirit does not satisfy carnal desires for emotional rewards. Because we must walk by faith and not by sight, the Holy

Spirit RARELY lets us see the spirit world, and certainly not on a routine basis, or when we want to.

Demons love to manipulate human emotions. They control MANY by giving them emotional "highs" or rewards. Demons also love to give humans emotional extremes. Demons FREQUENTLY help people see the spirit world, thus decreasing their need for faith. People with demon spirit guides frequently have visions and super-natural experiences.

12. We can grieve the Holy Spirit by disobeying Him. When we disobey Him, He withdraws and does not function in our lives. The Holy Spirit NEVER goes against our free will. God doesn't want puppets or robots.

Demons bring quick punishment to anyone disobeying them. They are quick to take over and control, ALWAYS trying to usurp the person's free will. Demons love puppets and robots.

13. The Holy Spirit loves us and brings us into eternal life in the presence of God.

Demons hate us and lead people into eternal destruction separated from God forever in Hell.

14. Jesus loved us enough to die for, and shed His OWN blood for us, paying the price for our purification from sins Himself.

Demons never shed any of THEIR blood for people. They are always demanding that people shed blood for them, teaching the people that they must do this for their purification so that Satan and the demons can "bless" them. Or, in the case of Christians, demons bring about all sorts of self-

Chapter 7
The Holy Spirit Versus Demon Spirit Guides

imposed punishment and/or rigid legalistic rules so that "God" can bless them.

15. Jesus paid the price for our sins ONCE and for all. (I Pet. 3:18)

Demons always demand more and more sacrifices. They are NEVER satisfied.

16. The Holy Spirit gives the desire to read the Bible.

Demons try to keep people from reading the Bible.

17. The Holy Spirit helps us to understand the scriptures. (John 14:26)

Demons bring confusion. They block a person from understanding the scriptures. "God is NOT the author of confusion." (I Cor. 14:33)

18. The Holy Spirit draws us to pray.

Demons hinder all true prayer.

19. The Holy Spirit is NOT a show-off.

Demons LOVE to make a show.

20. When the Holy Spirit "transports a Christian in spirit" He takes good care of the physical body. (See Rev. 4:1-2, II Cor. 12:2-3, etc.)

When a person astral-projects, the demon spirit left in his physical body to maintain it, could care less about that person's body. That's why astral-projection creates such a terrible physical drain on the person doing it. The hair of most people doing astral-projection turns gray quickly.

Chapter 7
The Holy Spirit Versus Demon Spirit Guides

21. The Holy Spirit is a spirit of truth. He NEVER lies.

All demons are liars, so are the people they indwell.

22. The Holy Spirit demands that we actively use our minds to learn. He is never willing to serve as an information bank independent from our minds.

Demon spirit guides are quite willing to serve as an information bank so that the person they indwell does not need to actually learn the information with their minds. Therefore, when a person accepts Jesus and kicks out his/her spirit guide, whatever information they allowed to reside in their spirit guide is immediately and forever lost.

23. Far too many Christians make the fatal error of thinking the Holy Spirit will come and "take control of them" so that they do not know what they are doing, or so that they do not control themselves. ONLY demons do this. The Holy Spirit always demands our active conscious cooperation with His will. Any time we give up the control of ourselves, we have opened the door for demons to come in and control us.

Demons LOVE to take over and control the people they indwell.

24. The Holy Spirit is NOT a fortune teller. Neither does he give us divination ability. (Matt. 6:34)

One of the most common deceptions of demon spirit guides is to give the person many false "words of knowledge" which is really simple divination. Demons also give many individual "prophecies" which is really fortune telling. Prophecy in the scriptures is usually for the whole body of Christ, rarely for individuals, and certainly not on a frequent basis.

Chapter 7
The Holy Spirit Versus Demon Spirit Guides

Chapter 8

THE SIN NATURE

As I travel about the country and around the world, I find that Christians everywhere seem to lack a good understanding of what I call our "sin nature." This spiritual warfare in which we are involved is very real, but, we must face up to our own responsibility before God. We cannot blame all of our sins on Satan or the demons. We are fully responsible before God to control ourselves and stop sinning.

I believe that when Adam fell into sin, all of his offspring inherited that fallen nature from him.

> "Wherefore, as by one man sin entered into the world, and death by sin; and so death passed upon all men, for that all have sinned." Romans 5:12

> "Therefore as by the offence of one judgment came upon all men to condemnation; even so by the righteousness of the one the free gift came upon all men unto justification of life. For as by one man's disobedience many were made sinners, so by the obedience of one [Jesus] shall many be made righteous." Romans 5:18-19

Exactly what is this "sin nature?" It is the almost continual desire to sin that saturates every part of us. Andrew Murray describes it like this:

> "The whole power of sin working in us is nothing but this - that as we inherit Adam's fallen nature, we inherit this tendency to disobedience. By our own choice we become 'the children of disobedience.' Clearly, the one work Christ was needed for was to remove this dis-

obedience - its curse, its dominion, its evil nature and
workings. Disobedience was the root of all sin and
misery. The first object of His salvation was to cut away
the evil root and restore man to his original destiny --
a life in obedience to his God." (*The Believer's Secret of
Obedience*, by Andrew Murray, Bethany House
Publishers, p. 25)

Paul described it as follows:

"For the good that I would I do not: but the evil which
I would not, that I do. Now if I do that I would not, it is
no more I that do it, but sin that dwelleth in me. I find
then a law, that, when I would do good, evil is present
with me. For I delight in the law of God after the in-
ward man: But I see another law in my members, warring against the law of my mind, and bringing me into
captivity to the law of sin which is in my members."
Romans 7:19-23

Clearly, the desire to sin is present even at the same time as
the mind desires to obey God. Sin is an integral part of us.
That is why I call it our "sin nature." Scripture refers to this
sin nature in different ways. Sometimes it is called our "old
man."

"Knowing this, that our old man is crucified with Him
[Jesus], that the body of sin might be destroyed, that
henceforth we should not serve sin." Romans 6:6

"But now ye also put off all these; anger, wrath, malice,
blasphemy, filthy communication out of your mouth.
Lie not one to another, seeing that ye have put off the
old man with his deeds; And have put on the new man,
which is renewed in knowledge after the image of him
that created him." Colossians 3:8-10

Sometimes scripture calls this sin nature our "flesh," or our
"carnal nature."

Chapter 8
The Sin Nature

"For the law of the Spirit of life in Christ Jesus hath made me free from the law of sin and death. For what the law could not do, in that it was weak through the flesh, God sending his own Son in the likeness of sinful flesh, and for sin, condemned sin in the flesh: That the righteousness of the law might be fulfilled in us, who walk not after the flesh, but after the Spirit. For they that are after the flesh do mind the things of the flesh; but they that are after the Spirit the things of the Spirit. For to be carnally minded is death; but to be spiritually minded is life and peace. Because the carnal mind is enmity against God: for it is not subject to the law of God, neither indeed can be. So then they that are in the flesh cannot please God." Romans 8:2-8

Sin is woven through our very being -- body, soul and spirit. Here are some scriptures that clearly show us the extent to which sin has taken us over.

BODY
"O wretched man that I am! who shall deliver me from this body of death?" Romans 7:24

SOUL
"The heart is deceitful above all things, and desperately wicked: who can know it? I the Lord search the heart, I try the reins, even to give every man according to his ways, and according to the fruit of his doings." Jeremiah 17:9-10

"Because the carnal mind is enmity against God: for it is not subject to the law of God, neither indeed can be." Romans 8:7

SPIRIT
"Do ye think that the scripture saith in vain, the spirit that dwelleth in us lusteth to envy?" James 4:5

"Having therefore these promises, dearly beloved, let us cleanse ourselves from all filthiness of the flesh and

Chapter 8
The Sin Nature

spirit, perfecting holiness in the fear of God."
II Corinthians 7:1

And finally:

"And the very God of peace sanctify you wholly; and I
pray God your whole spirit and soul and body be
preserved blameless unto the coming of our Lord Jesus
Christ." I Thessalonians 5:23

These scriptures clearly show that all three areas of us, body,
soul and spirit, are affected by sin. All three areas must be
cleansed by our Lord Jesus Christ. But we deal with sin on
a day-to-day basis mostly within our conscious mind. I don't
think we will ever have a full understanding of the terrible
down-drag this sin nature has been on us until we receive
our glorified bodies and are set free from sin forever!

Yes, demons tempt us to sin, but, ultimately, the decision is
ours. We CHOOSE to sin! Therefore, whether the demons
are inside of us or afflicting us from the outside, we are
squarely responsible before God for everything we do. You
may be sure the demons understand our sin nature through
and through. That is why they can manipulate us so well.
The whole Bible is full of verses strongly urging us to battle
against our natural desire to do those things which are
wrong.

"Wherefore seeing we also are compassed about with
so great a cloud of witnesses, let us lay aside every
weight, and the sin which doth so easily beset us, and
let us run with patience the race that is set before us."
Hebrews 12:1

"For consider him that endured such contradiction of
sinners against himself, lest ye be wearied and faint in
your minds. Ye have not yet resisted unto blood, striv-
ing against sin." Hebrews 12:3-4

Chapter 8
The Sin Nature

Have you ever stopped to wonder why scripture has so much in it commanding us to stop sinning? Well, for one thing, God is completely holy and just. He cannot allow sin to remain. That is why Jesus died on the cross -- to pay the price for our sins so that God would not have to give us the just punishment and destruction we deserve for our sins. The ultimate punishment for sin is to be banished from God's presence forever.

However, too many people fall into the trap of thinking that once we are saved our sins are not so important. Paul addressed this issue very plainly:

> "What shall we say then? Shall we continue in sin, that grace may abound? God forbid. How shall we, that are dead to sin, live any longer therein?" Romans 6:1-2

The real reason why it is so important for us to put sin out of our lives is because sin separates us from God. Do you want more abundance in your life? Then put sin OUT of your life!

> "Furthermore then we beseech you, brethren, and exhort you by the Lord Jesus, that as ye have received of us how ye ought to walk and to please God, so ye would abound more and more." I Thessalonians 4:1

> "For it is the will of God, even your sanctification [to be set apart for God, to separate from sin and the world] that ye should abstain from fornication: That every one of you should know how to possess his vessel [you] in sanctification and honour; Not in the lust of concupiscence [personal desires], even as the Gentiles which know not God." I Thessalonians 4:3-5

Scripture is clear. The ONLY way to have a close relationship with God and to live a life of abundance in Christ Jesus, is to STOP SINNING!

Chapter 8
The Sin Nature

In fact, there is a very unpopular concept that we must think about very soberly. We MUST prove ourselves to God. We must demonstrate obedience and faith. Jesus learned obedience through suffering. Can we do any less?

> "Though he were a Son, yet learned he obedience by the things which he suffered; And being made perfect, he became the author of eternal salvation unto all them that obey him." Hebrews 5:8-9

The hard facts are this: We CANNOT progress in our growth in the Lord without first proving ourselves obedient and faithful by putting sin out of our lives. This is one of the gravest errors in the current teachings about the Holy Spirit. Too many people promise instant access to great power in Christ. We receive this type of power ONLY as we prove ourselves faithful. I find it amazing, actually, the amount of power God does give to new Christians. BUT, we cannot sidestep the growing and refining process. This process will continue as long as we live, but we will reach a point where much of it is behind us. The parable of the man who went to a far country to be crowned king applies here. Let's look at it.

> "A certain nobleman went into a far country to receive for himself a kingdom, and to return. And he called his ten servants, and delivered them ten pounds, and said unto them, occupy till I come. But his citizens hated him, and sent a message after him, saying, We will not have this man to reign over us. And it came to pass, that when he was returned, having received the kingdom, then he commanded these servants to be called unto him, to whom he had given the money, that he might know how much every man had gained by trading. Then, came the first, saying, Lord, thy pound hath gained ten pounds. And he said unto him, well, thou good servant: because thou hast been faithful in a very little, have thou authority over ten cities. And the second came, saying, Lord, thy pound hath gained five

Chapter 8
The Sin Nature

pounds. And he said likewise to him, Be thou also over five cities. And another came, saying, Lord, behold, here is thy pound, which I have kept laid up in a napkin: For I feared thee, because thou art an austere man: thou takest up that thou layest not down, and reapest that thou didst not sow. And he saith unto him, Out of thine own mouth will I judge thee, thou wicked servant. Thou knewest that I was an austere man, taking up that I laid not down, and reaping that I did not sow: Wherefore then gavest not thou my money into the bank, that at my coming I might have required mine own with usury? And he said unto them that stood by, Take from him the pound, and give it to him that hath ten pounds. (And they said unto him, Lord, he hath ten pounds.) For I say unto you, That unto every one which hath shall be given; and from him that hath not, even that he hath shall be taken away from him. But those mine enemies, which would not that I should reign over them, bring hither, and slay them before me."
Luke 19:12-27

In this parable, the man who went to be crowned king is Jesus. We are His servants left behind waiting for Him to come back. Now the question is this. Are we going to be faithful and profitable servants for our King? It is only as we prove ourselves faithful that we are given more power and authority in Christ. Far too many Christians think only about what benefits they can GET from God. They never stop to think that they are here to be SERVANTS. The Lord Jesus makes it very clear that the servants must PROVE themselves before they are given more power and authority. The same is true today.

Unfortunately, too much of modern day teaching tries to sidestep this testing and growing time. We MUST not try to avoid the painful learning process! Every servant of God in the pages of scripture went through this process. I am convinced that this is the reason why so many in leadership fall.

Chapter 8
The Sin Nature

They were thrust into positions of leadership too fast. That is why Paul wrote to Timothy as he did.

> "Lay hands suddenly on no man, neither be partaker of other men's sins: keep thyself pure." I Timothy 5:22

> "A bishop then must be blameless, the husband of one wife, vigilant, sober, of good behavior, given to hospitality . . . Not a novice [new Christian], lest being lifted up with pride he fall into the condemnation of the devil." I Timothy 3:2-6

> "Likewise must the deacons be grave . . . And let these also first be proved [tested]; then let them use the office of a deacon, being found blameless."
> I Timothy 3:8-10

Scripture could not be more clear. Anyone who would come into a position of any authority in God's kingdom MUST first prove himself or herself faithful in obeying God and putting sin out of their lives. This takes TIME. Scripture does not specify how much time, it is different with each person, but it does take some time. In my own life I went through five years of fiery trials before the Lord called me to start into this ministry, and then I went through another five years of even more intense testing before my first book was published. That makes ten years in all of intense preparation and testing. I had to prove myself faithful and obedient. I am thankful for that testing time because it has given me a deep stability in the Lord I could not have obtained in any other way.

Our authority over Satan's kingdom increases as we prove ourselves steadfast and faithful. We must be faithful in little before we can be faithful in much. I believe every new believer is given authority in Christ over the demons inside of himself, BUT he should not jump into trying to deal with

Chapter 8
The Sin Nature

demons in others. He has not yet had time to grow or prove himself.

My heart grieves as I see this happening to those coming out of Satanism. All too often they are thrust into a position of publicly giving their testimony, etc. PRIDE crouches at the door! They come under such terrible attack that they cannot stand.

My advice is this: "Humble yourself under the mighty hand of God and in due time He will lift you up." (James 4:10) Walk quietly before the Lord and learn the lessons He wants you to learn. Prove yourself faithful and obedient. No matter how great the temptation, NEVER allow a new Christian to be put in a place of public prominence. You will contribute to his/her destruction if you do.

Our Lord is so gracious. He allows us to do some work for Him, especially in sharing the gospel, even as we are babes in Christ first learning to walk. He does this to encourage us. But we must be willing to go through the training and proving process. If we are not, then He can never fully use us as He wants. We can effectively teach ONLY those lessons we have ourselves learned!

You will NOT grow or prove yourself as long as you continue to allow active sin in your life. God so intensely desired us to be cleansed from SIN that He gave His very own life to provide for our purification. WE must also so intensely desire to be free from sin that we are willing to lay down ANYTHING, no matter how painful it may be, to put sin out of our lives!

O.K., so we know we must stop sinning. But we are still left with the terrible struggle Paul described (quoted earlier in this chapter) in Romans chapter 7. How then can we have victory in this struggle against our sin nature? The answer

Chapter 8
The Sin Nature

is simple. We must have more power than our sin nature has, or we can never overcome it. Where do we get such power? I believe the answer is in the following scriptures.

> "There is therefore now no condemnation to them which are in Christ Jesus, who walk not after flesh but after the spirit. [Holy Spirit] For the law of the spirit of life in Christ Jesus hath made me free from the law of sin and death." Romans 8:1-2

Jesus set us free from the power of sin when He died on the cross. Once we receive Him as our Lord and Saviour and Master, that power is available to us. We have not yet received everything God has promised to give us. In the future, at the return of Christ, each one of us will receive the rest of what God promised us in our redemption. We will receive a new and glorified physical body exactly the same as the one Jesus now has, AND, best of all, our sin nature will be wiped away so we will never have to struggle with it again!

> "For our conversation is in heaven; from whence also we look for the Saviour, the Lord Jesus Christ: Who shall change our vile body, that it may be fashioned like unto his glorious body, according to the working whereby he is able even to subdue all things unto himself." Philippians 3:20-21

This is our bright hope. One day, we will never again have the desire to sin, and we will be continually in the presence of the Lord and know Him face-to-face! How I look forward to that day! But, in the meantime, we must fight the battle against sin.

The way to victory over sin in our lives is really two fold. The first and most important way to victory is through the working of the Holy Spirit in our lives. The second is given to us

Chapter 8
The Sin Nature

in Romans. I want to deal with the second part of the answer first.

> "For they that are after the flesh [sinful desires] do mind the things of the flesh; but they that are after the Spirit [Holy Spirit] the things of the Spirit." Romans 8:5

Simply put, the more time we spend every day reading the Bible, thinking about God's word (the Bible), and thinking about God, the more victory we will have over our sin nature. King David learned this lesson even as did Joshua before him.

> "Wherewithal shall a young man [or woman] cleanse his way? by taking heed thereto according to thy word. With my whole heart have I sought thee: Oh let me not wander from thy commandments. Thy word have I hid in mine heart, [memorize] that I might not sin against thee." Psalm 119:9-11

God commanded Joshua:

> "This book of the law shall not depart out of thy mouth; but thou shalt meditate therein day and night, that thou mayest observe to do according to all that is written therein: for then thou shalt make thy way prosperous, and then thou shalt have good success." Joshua 1:8

You know, there is one thing about the Bible that makes it different from every other book in the world. It is literally alive! It is alive because it is God speaking to us.

> "For the word of God is quick, and powerful, and sharper than any two-edged sword . . ." Hebrews 4:12

No other book or printed page in the whole world has the unique power of the Bible. The more we saturate our entire lives and minds with the scripture, the more power we

Chapter 8
The Sin Nature

will have to live in obedience to it, thereby putting sin out of our lives. However, we must study the Bible to OBEY it.

> "If you accustom yourself to study the Bible without an earnest and very definite purpose to obey, you're getting hardened in disobedience. Never read God's word concerning you without honestly yielding yourself to obey it at once and asking grace to do so. God has given us His Word to tell us what He wants us to do, and to show the grace He has provided to enable us to do it. How sad to think it a pious thing just to read that word without any earnest effort to obey it! May God keep us from this terrible sin! Let us make it a sacred habit to say to God, 'Lord, whatever I know to be Your will, I will at once obey.' Always read with a heart yielded up in willing obedience." (*The Believer's Secret of Obedience*, by Andrew Murray, Bethany House Publishers, p. 46)

Have you ever noticed just how difficult it is to pick up the Bible and read it if you have let several days go by without reading it? Oh how quickly our sin nature gains strength if we do not keep it under control! The apostle Paul made a profound statement about this after many years in the ministry.

> "But I keep under my body, and bring it into subjection: lest that by any means, when I have preached to others, I myself should be a castaway." I Corinthians 9:27

I am so thankful the Holy Spirit had Paul write that statement. It has been very helpful to me to know that even the apostle Paul had a struggle against his sin nature all of his life.

Here's a little test for you. How many times in a day do you think about God or think about scripture, or talk to God? How often do you stop to compare what is happening to you, or what you are doing, to scripture? You should be doing

Chapter 8
The Sin Nature

this almost continually. If you will do this, you will find that your entire life will change.

There is such a PURITY in the scriptures. As I work with people coming out of Satanism, I hear and see such terrible things. The sin and perversions in these people's lives are incredible. I find that I have to continually turn my mind back onto scripture, and that as I do, God's word brings a wonderful purity into my mind. Those of us who have been called by God to work in areas where we must deal with people involved in terrible perversions, MUST be very careful to continually wash our minds with God's word. If we do not, we will be quick to fall.

Taking control of your mind is a real "key" to having victory over sin. That's the meaning of that scripture in Romans 8:5 The more we have our mind on the things of God, the less we will sin.

> "And be not conformed to this world; but be ye trans-
> formed by the renewing of your mind . . . " Romans 12:2

> "and bringing into captivity every thought to the
> obedience of Christ . . . " II Corinthians 10:5

It should be normal that a Christian should live so that he sins VERY RARELY! This is why the apostle John wrote as he did.

> "My little children, these things write I unto you, that
> ye sin not. . . " I John 2:1

If you have not done so, may I recommend that you carefully read the chapter entitled "The Double Minded Man" in my second book "*Prepare For war*" on this subject of taking every thought captive. We CANNOT have victory over sin

Chapter 8
The Sin Nature

in our lives unless we discipline our minds and take every thought captive to make them obedient to Christ.

However, saturating your life with God's word, helpful and necessary as this is, is not, in itself, the complete answer. We must also have POWER. That power comes to us from the Holy Spirit.

> "Nevertheless I tell you the truth; It is expedient for you that I go away: for if I go not away, the Comforter will not come unto you; but if I depart, I will send him unto you." John 16:7

> "For it is God which worketh in you both to will and to do of his good pleasure." Philippians 2:13

It is only with the help of the Holy Spirit that we can overcome our sin nature and stop sinning. Remember I just told you there were two parts to the answer of how to control our sin nature? Controlling our thoughts and saturating our minds with God's word is the first part, and the indwelling power of the Holy Spirit is the second part. We must have both equally. The longer I live in this walk with my Master, the more aware I become of my own utter helplessness to cope with or stop the sin in my life! But, praise God, the power of the Holy Spirit enables me to have the victory.

Look at John 16:7 quoted above. When Jesus was here on earth in bodily form, his disciples followed Him faithfully and Jesus ministered to each one of them every day. But they fell again and again. Why? Because no matter how faithful or diligent they were, they did not have POWER INSIDE OF THEM over their sin natures. Thus, even though they were in the very presence of God Himself, they fell into unbelief and sin, time and time again! That is why it was necessary for Jesus to leave earth. Once Jesus was no longer on earth in bodily form, He could send the Holy

Chapter 8
The Sin Nature

Spirit to work in His disciples from the inside. Jesus made this possible by paying the price for our sins on the cross. When we are washed clean from our sins, then God Himself in the form of the Holy Spirit can enter into us and bring the power we need to overcome sin!

If you have never gotten down on your knees and asked Father to completely fill you with His Holy Spirit to give you power to stop sinning, you need to do so. BUT, it is a two-way street. The more you saturate your mind with God's word and put sin out of your life, the more freedom the Holy Spirit has to operate in your life with POWER. Please don't fall into the trap of thinking that all you need is the Holy Spirit, that you don't need to do anything yourself. This just isn't true. James sums it all up very simply:

> "Wherefore lay apart all filthiness and superfluity [excess] of naughtiness, and receive with meekness the engrafted [planted] word, which is able to save your souls. But be ye doers of the word, and not hearers only, deceiving your own selves. For if any be a hearer of the word, and not a doer, he is like unto a man beholding his natural face in a glass: For he beholdeth himself, and goeth his way, and straightway [immediately] forgetteth what manner of man he was. But whoso looketh into the perfect law of liberty [the Bible], and continueth therein [lives in it] he being not a forgetful hearer, but a doer of the work, this man shall be blessed in his deed." James 1:21-25

> "Even so faith, if it hath not works, is dead, being alone. Yea, a man may say, Thou hast faith, and I have works: show me thy faith without thy works, and I will show thee my faith by my works. Thou believest that there is one God; thou doest well: the devils also believe, and tremble. But wilt thou know, O vain man, that faith without works is dead?" James 2:17-20

Chapter 8
The Sin Nature

We have, today, far too often fallen into the trap of looking only for signs and miracles. That is why there are so many books on Christian bookshelves on such things as "How to Heal," "How to Perform Miracles," etc. God is MUCH more interested in our DAILY obedience and faithful walk than He is in performing miracles and signs and wonders! All too often Christians of today are falling into deception and accepting demonic counterfeits as being signs and miracles from God. You CANNOT have true signs and wonders from the Holy Spirit in your life without walking a walk of obedience and discipline, putting sin out of your life.

The Holy Spirit is a wonderful help to us in fighting against sin. Ask the Lord to quicken to you those scripture verses that particularly apply to sins you commonly commit. Then memorize those verses and ask the Holy Spirit to flash them into your mind when you are about to commit a sin. The Holy Spirit knows everything we do before we do it. He monitors everything we do. He can help us to stop sinning.

Let me give you an example from my own life. A couple of years ago two young women came to live with Elaine and me for a few months. They were called by God to help us in our ministry, but they were unwilling for the rigid discipline necessary in our lives. They ended up turning against me, and ended up spreading lies about me to other people who knew me. I was becoming rather angry about the whole situation. One weekend during my quiet time with the Lord, I started reading the letters written by Peter. I reached I Peter 2:21-23. As I read those verses, the Holy Spirit spoke to me very plainly. "Memorize those verses!" He said. "And every time you are about to sin in this matter, I will bring them back to your conscious mind." Here are the verses I memorized:

> "For even hereunto were ye called: because Christ also suffered for us, leaving us an example, that ye should

Chapter 8
The Sin Nature

follow his steps: Who did no sin, neither was guile found in his mouth: Who, when he was reviled [slandered], reviled not again; when he suffered, he threatened not; but committed himself to him that judgeth righteously." I Peter 2:21-23

You see, this scripture told me that even though those two were telling all sorts of lies about me that I was not to defend myself, but forgive them and commit the whole matter into the Lord's hands.

Well, I asked them to move out, but the Lord completely blocked them from doing so for three very long months. Do you have any idea just how many times the Holy Spirit had to flash those verses into my mind during those three months? BUT, having those verses flashed into my mind kept me from sinning in the situation. Praise God! The Holy Spirit will be a great help to you if you will only obey Him.

There is a very important principle I want to give you. The root of all sin is SELF-CENTEREDNESS. Oh how we love to think about ourselves! The root of ALL mental illness is the sin of self-centeredness. The mark of someone who is "mentally ill" or has a lot of problems in their life is that they refuse to think about anything or anyone but themselves. Notice that I said "they refuse" rather than "they are incapable of." Mentally ill people choose to be mentally ill, for the most part. Oh, they use the excuse of past rejections and hurts. But stop to think for a minute. Has anyone suffered more rejection and hurt than Jesus? NO! What a terrible fix we would be in if Jesus chose to spend His time in self pity, dwelling on and reacting to the hurt and rejection He suffered!

Most people, whether they are classified as mentally ill or not, spend the bulk of their time thinking about themselves. This is especially true of people with what is called an "in-

Chapter 8
The Sin Nature

feriority complex." I should know, I was guilty of this sin for a number of years. It was one of the first things the Holy Spirit demanded I deal with after I had made Jesus the total master in my life.

I had experienced much rejection as a child growing up. As a result, I thought I was worthless, ugly and repulsive to other people. I had such an "inferiority complex" that I would never go into even a fastfood restaurant by myself to eat. I didn't want people looking at me. I will never forget the evening shortly after I had made Jesus the total master in my life when the Holy Spirit dealt with me on the problem. I was starting to drive through a drive-up window at MacDonald's when the Lord spoke to me with profound clarity and force. "No, you will go inside and sit down at a table and eat!"

"But Lord," I replied, "You know I can't stand doing that. What will all those people think of me eating alone?"

The Lord's answer was swift, clear and to the point. "That's just the problem. You never think about anything but yourself! You must confess your inferiority complex as SIN! It is the sin of self-centeredness. The fact is that you aren't important enough for other people to bother with you at all. They are all thinking about themselves."

I was shocked! But I knew immediately that what the Holy Spirit said was true. Paranoia, inferiority complexes, people reacting because of past rejection in their life, are ALL the sin of self-centeredness! It's time we stopped thinking about ourselves all the time and became the servants of our King that we should be. Has someone hurt you? Then, before God, you are required to forgive him. Do you know what it means to forgive?

Chapter 8
The Sin Nature

"Be ye therefore merciful, as your Father also is merciful. Judge not, and ye shall not be judged: condemn not, and ye shall not be condemned: forgive, and ye shall be forgiven." Luke 6:36-37

"And grieve not the Holy Spirit of God, whereby ye are sealed unto the day of redemption. Let all bitterness, and wrath, and anger, and clamber, and evil speaking, be put away from you, with all malice: And be ye kind one to another, tenderhearted, forgiving one another, even as God for Christ's sake hath forgiven you." Ephesians 4:30-32

If we refuse to forgive those who have hurt us, we grieve the Holy Spirit so that He cannot work in our lives. Most people coming out of Satanism have been horribly abused while in the craft. This is especially true of those who were raised by parents who were satanists, or who were recruited into the craft while very young. The abuses these people suffer are beyond anything most people can imagine. However, God's word applies to them and to YOU the same as to those of us who have not been abused in this way. They must FORGIVE those who have hurt them so that Father can forgive them of their own sins.

There are four basic steps in this matter of forgiving someone who has hurt you.

1. We do not forgive because we FEEL like it. We forgive as a pure act of our will in obedience to God's command.

2. When we forgive someone, we acknowledge that we no longer have any right to revenge on that person.

"For we know him [God] that hath said, Vengeance belongeth unto me, I will recompense, saith the Lord. And again, the Lord shall judge his people. It is a fear-

Chapter 8
The Sin Nature

ful thing to fall into the hands of the living God."
Hebrews 10:30-31

"Bless them that curse you, and pray for them which
despitefully use [mistreat] you." Luke 6:28

**3. When we forgive someone, we must do so following
God's example.** Once we have forgiven someone, we no
longer have any right to allow the memories or thoughts of
what they have done to hurt us, to stay in our minds. We
MUST discipline our minds and stop thinking about ourselves!

> "For I will be merciful to their unrighteousness, and
> their sins and their iniquities will I remember no more."
> Hebrews 8:12

4. Once we have taken these steps in obedience to God, we
can ask Father to control and change our emotions in the
situation. We human beings can do very little to control or
change our emotions. But the Lord can and will, as we obey
Him and forgive those who have hurt us.

Too often, Christians completely side-step the whole issue
of forgiving by repressing their emotions. We know that we
should not be bitter or angry when someone does something
against us. It is much easier to push the unacceptable emotions out of our conscious minds than to deal with the necessary forgiveness or confrontation in the situation.

If a brother or sister sins against us we are not only commanded to forgive him/her, we are also commanded to talk
to them and show them their sin. Then, whether they repent
or not, we are required to forgive them. Repressing the
anger and hurt is one way of avoiding the whole situation.
This is not God's will. He <u>always</u> demands honesty.

**Chapter 8
The Sin Nature**

As we forgive someone, we must also truthfully talk to the Lord, recognizing and admitting our true emotions in the situation. As we do this, we then have the right to ask the Lord to heal and change our emotions. He will do so as we walk in obedience to Him.

I know I will make many of you reading this passage very angry, but I must tell you as the Lord taught me. You DO NOT HAVE THE RIGHT to live your life reacting to past hurts. God DEMANDS that you forgive and forget and stop thinking about yourself and how you have been hurt. If you do not do so, you are living in active SIN!

Lastly, we must all come to a maturity in Christ where we make James 4:17 a reality in our lives.

> "Therefore to him that knoweth to do good, and doeth it not, to him it is sin." James 4:17

To put this in very simple terms, we must do the right thing simply because it IS the right thing to do, NOT because someone else demands it of us. If we would only reach this point, so many, many interpersonal relationship problems would simply disappear!

Chapter 8
The Sin Nature

Here in the United States, the Lord has very graciously given us a simple tool in just about every household to help teach us this principle. It looks like this: (Figure 8-1)

Figure 8-1

Chapter 8
The Sin Nature

When we don't obey this principle of James 4:17, it then looks like this: (Figure 8-2)

Figure 8-2

Come on now, be honest! How many times have you had a fight with someone over whose turn it was to take out the trash? God's word says that when we know the right thing to do and don't do it, we are sinning. If you see that the trash can is full, you KNOW the right thing to do is empty it! AND when you empty it, you DON'T go to your parent or spouse and say something like, "Honey, I emptied the trash for you."

Chapter 8
The Sin Nature

No you didn't. You are looking for a pat on the back. You should have emptied it simply because it was the right thing to do.

You see, when you do things just because someone else expects you to, you will have a lot of anger towards the other person. "I have to do so-and-so because my wife expects it!" Or, "I have to do so-and so or my mom will get mad!" How many times have you heard such statements? The sad thing is, we treat God in the same way. We become angry at God because we feel we "have to do" certain things because the Lord demands it.

NOT doing the right thing is sin. I believe greater than 75% of all the problems amongst church members would be solved if people would grow up and begin to operate as this one scripture tells us. DO the right thing!

I never cease to be amazed at how people can walk right past something that they can see needs to be done, and simply not do it! This is a mark of immaturity. It is because of this attitude in our lives that the Lord must chastise us so often. That's where the trouble starts in our relationship with Him!

I well remember one day when I was driving to work when the Lord spoke to me and told me that I must begin to bring some discipline into the lives of two young women who had come to live in my home about a month previously. I had been through the cycle many times, and I was tired and didn't want the hassle. I said, "Oh Father, I just don't think it is worth the hassle! Whenever I try to do such a thing people try to send me on such guilt trips! They say things like 'Who do you think YOU are? Who made YOU God!'"

The Lord's answer was clear and forceful. "Child, would you like a precise accounting of the number of times YOU have

Chapter 8
The Sin Nature

tried to send ME on guilt trips? For example 'Father IF You loved me, how could you let this happen to me?'"

Needless to say, I did NOT want such an accounting! How many times have YOU tried to send God on guilt trips? "God IF You loved me how could You let this happen to me? God IF You loved me You would give me so-and-so! How can a loving God allow such-and-such to happen?" ALL such questions are SIN and a mark of our terrible immaturity. It is time we Christians grew up! Paul said:

> "When I was a child, I spake as a child, I understood as
> a child, I thought as a child: but when I became a man,
> I put away childish things." I Corinthians 13:11

We MUST put all such childish things behind us. Let us face up to our responsibilities and commitments and fulfill them in righteousness before God. Let us fight this fight against our sin natures and WIN.

This is the way to an abundant life in Jesus Christ our Lord.

If the reader is convicted by this chapter to rise up and take control of his/her sin nature, a good place to start is by a thorough confession of all your past sins to God. Please see Appendix A for some helpful notes on how to approach such a confession.

Chapter 8
The Sin Nature

Chapter 9

DEFILEMENT OF GOD'S TEMPLE

"Nevertheless the foundation of God standeth sure, having this seal, The Lord knoweth them that are his. And, Let every one that nameth the name of Christ depart from iniquity. But in a great house there are not only vessels of gold and of silver, but also of wood and of earth; and some to honour, and some to dishonour. If a man therefore purge himself from these, he shall be a vessel unto honour, sanctified, and meet for the master's use, and prepared unto every good work." II Timothy 2:19-21

Over and over throughout the New Testament, we are exhorted to cleanse ourselves, to purge our vessel, us. Our Lord Jesus Christ paid a terrible price on the cross so that we CAN "depart from iniquity" and become a "vessel unto honour."

There are two areas in which this "purging" is needed. The first is in the area of our sin nature. We must bring our sinful nature under control and put active sin out of our lives. Secondly, we must put all defilement out of the temple of God (us). I believe God's temple is not only defiled by active participation in sin, but also by the presence of demons.

This brings us to the hotly debated question, "Can a Christian have a demon dwelling inside of him?" I believe scripture clearly shows us that he can.

Demons cannot just hop into people whenever they want. We are hedged about so that they cannot get in unless we break a hole in the hedge of protection. (Figure 9-1)

Figure 9-1 ("....whoso breaketh an hedge, a serpent shall bite him.")
Ecclesiastes 10:8

Figure 9-2 (Sin breaks a hole in hedge -- opens a doorway in our lives)

Chapter 9
Defilement of God's Temple

How do we break a hole in this protective hedge? By SIN.

I call such sins that permit the entrance of demons <u>temple defiling sins</u>. Why? Because the bottom line in this issue of demons in Christians is this: "Can the temple of God, us, be defiled, and if so, how does scripture define the term <u>defilement?</u>" To answer this we must first turn to the Old Testament.

In the Old Testament, God gave his people, the children of Israel, many "pictures" in their lives so that they would understand the coming of Christ and work He would accomplish. For instance, through the sin offerings, they were brought to understand the necessity of the shedding of innocent blood and the giving of life to pay the price for their sins. The sin offerings gave a poignant picture of what Jesus accomplished once and for all on the cross. In the same way, the temple of God, as built by King Solomon, was a picture of those of us who have come under the new covenant with Christ. We are the temple of God with the Holy Spirit dwelling in us just as the presence of God dwelt in Solomon's temple. (Figure 9-3)

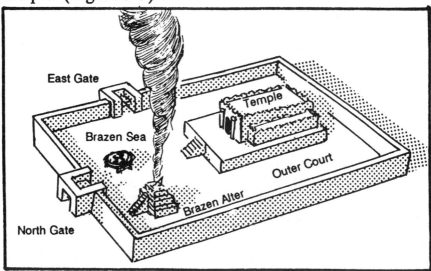

Figure 9-3 (Solomon's temple)

Chapter 9
Defilement of God's Temple

Let us go back now and look at the defilement of Solomon's temple. Here is a sketch of the temple. The temple itself faced north. (Ezekiel 8:14) It was surrounded by a wall which had two gates in it. One in the north wall and one in the east wall. The brazen altar which was used for the sin offerings and the sea sat in front of the temple. The temple itself was divided into two parts. The front part was called the inner court, and the back part was called the "holy of holies." The presence of God dwelt in the holy of holies over the mercy seat. The high priest could enter this part of the temple only once per year.

After Solomon's death, his son Rehoboam took the throne. But Rehoboam refused godly counsel and oppressed the people so that they rebelled and the nation of Israel was split into two parts. The city of Jerusalem was in the part called Judah, the other half of the country was called Israel.

The evil king Manasseh set up altars right inside the temple to his demon gods.

>"And he built altars for all the host of heaven in the two courts of the house of the Lord." II Chronicles 33:5

From that time, the Lord tarried nearly 100 years with prolonged periods of defilement of His house before removing His presence from the temple.

The Israel half was carried off into captivity before the Judah half. Ezekiel prophesied from captivity in Babylon contemporary with Jeremiah who prophesied in Jerusalem. In Ezekiel chapters 8-10 the Lord transported Ezekiel in spirit from Babylon to Jerusalem to show him the defilement of His temple. (Figure 9-4)

>"And he put forth the form of an hand, and took me by a lock of mine head; and the spirit lifted me up between

Chapter 9
Defilement of God's Temple

the earth and the heaven, and brought me in the visions
of God to Jerusalem, to the door of the inner gate that
looketh toward the north; where was the seat of the
image of jealousy, which provoketh to jealousy...Then
said he unto me, Son of man, lift up thine eyes now the
way toward the north. So I lifted up mine eyes the way
toward the north, and behold northward at the gate of
the altar this image of jealousy in the entry." Ez. 8:3-5

Figure 9-4 (Idol by brazen altar)

We do not know exactly what the idol looked like, but we
do know that demons are associated with ALL idols. Paul
wrote specifically about this:

> "What say I then? that the idol is any thing, or that which
> is offered in sacrifice to idols is any thing? But I say,
> that the things which the Gentiles sacrifice, they
> sacrifice to devils, ..." I Corinthians 10:19-20

Clearly then, demons were present by the brazen altar with
the idol. Next, the Lord showed Ezekiel the walls around
the temple. Verse 10 says:

Chapter 9
Defilement of God's Temple

"So I went in and saw; and behold every form of creeping things, and abominable beasts, and all the idols of the house of Israel, portrayed upon the wall round about." Ezekiel 8:10

Now, what is the purpose these occultic drawings that resemble our modern graffiti? It is well known within all forms of witchcraft that demons are placed at the spot of an occult drawing. Therefore, there were demons placed upon the walls around about the temple. Now, look again at the drawing of the temple. The next action takes place just inside the north gate. (Figure 9-5)

"Then he brought me to the door of the gate of the Lord's house which was toward the north: and, behold, there sat women weeping for Tammuz." Ezekiel 8:14

Figure 9-5 (Women weeping for Tammuz)

Most Christians do not realize the significance of this statement. First of all, you must understand that <u>the purpose of ALL occultic rituals is to bring demons to be present with the humans performing the ritual</u>. So why were the "women weeping for Tammuz?" The women were participating in a

Chapter 9
Defilement of God's Temple

common form of demon worship, practiced by the Babylonians. Tammuz was a demon god who was supposed to be Nimrod reincarnated. Who was Nimrod? Nimrod and his wife Semiramis, were human beings who were the leaders of the formation of demon worship after the flood. Nimrod is briefly referred to in Genesis 10:9-10. Ancient history shows us that Nimrod is the same as Ninus, the first Assyrian King, founder and builder of ancient Babylon where the tower of Babel was built. Nimrod was worshipped in Egypt as Osiris. It is from the Egyptian records that we find an account of Nimrod's death which was a violent one. Apparently he was put to death by Noah's son Shem, in judgment for his abominable practices of demon worship. (See *The Two Babylons,* by Rev. Alexander Hislop.)

"If there was one who was more deeply concerned in the tragic death of Nimrod than another, it was his wife Semiramis, who, from an originally humble position, had been raised to share with him the throne of Babylon. What, in this emergency shall she do? Shall she quietly forego the pomp and pride to which she has been raised? No. Though the death of her husband has given a rude shock to her power, yet her resolution and unbounded ambition were in no wise checked. On the contrary, her ambition took a still higher flight. In her life her husband had been honoured as a hero; in death she will have him worshipped as a god, yea, as the woman's promised seed. "Zeroashta," who was destined to bruise the serpent's head, and who, in doing so, was to have his own heel bruised. The patriarchs, and the ancient world in general, were perfectly acquainted with the grand primeval promise of Eden, and they knew right well that the bruising of the heel of the promised seed implied his death, and that the curse could be removed from the world only by the death of the grand Deliverer. If the promise about the bruising of the serpent's head, recorded in Genesis as made to our first parents, was actually made, and if all mankind were descended from them, then it might be expected

Chapter 9
Defilement of God's Temple

that some trace of this promise would be found in all nations. And such is the fact. There is hardly a people or kindred on earth in whose mythology it is not shadowed forth." *The Two Babylons,* by Rev. Alexander Hislop, (Loizeaus Brothers, New Jersey, 1916) pp.58-60.

So Semiramis proclaimed the dead Nimrod to be the "deliverer" promised by God to Adam and Eve in the garden of Eden. Shortly after her husband's death, she had a son who was called Tammuz. Semiramis proclaimed Tammuz to be Nimrod come back to life as promised by God in the great messianic promise given to Eve. Down through the ages and in every land around the world this false mother and child has been worshipped under various names. Semiramis became "the queen of heaven" and remains so to this day.

Therefore, "weeping for Tammuz" was for the purpose of bringing Nimrod back to earth, and the demon worshipped by that name, to be present with the people performing the ceremony. Therefore, we clearly see that demons were inside the north gate. (Figure 9-6)

Then the Lord told Ezekiel that He was going to show him the worst abomination of all.

> "And he brought me into the inner court of the Lord's house, and behold, at the door of the temple of the Lord, between the porch and the altar, were about five and twenty men, with their backs toward the temple of the Lord, and their faces toward the east; and they worshipped the sun toward the east." Ezekiel 8:16

Chapter 9
Defilement of God's Temple

Figure 9-6 (Worshipping "the sun toward the east")

Worshipping "the sun toward the east" is a form of Egyptian demon worship, because it is worship of the Egyptian sun god Osiris which, as previously stated, was the Egyptian name for Nimrod. Again, the purpose was to bring demons to be present with the people. So, demons were right in the inner court of the temple. II Chronicles 33:5, quoted earlier in this chapter, about Manasseh also clearly showed the presence of demons IN the temple of God, AND the presence of God had not yet left.

Demons AND the presence of God were together in the same temple. I believe this is a picture of what can happen to us. It was not until after the Lord had showed all these abominations to Ezekiel that Ezekiel then saw the glory of the Lord lift out of the temple and leave. But please remember, earlier I showed you how this condition of defilement

Chapter 9
Defilement of God's Temple

of demons being present in the temple had continued off and on over a period of almost 100 years. Finally, God brought judgment. He removed His presence from the temple and then the temple was totally destroyed!

Now, let's look at the New Testament.

> "Know ye not that ye are the temple of God and that the spirit of God dwelleth in you? If any man defile the temple of God, him shall God destroy; for the temple of God is holy, which temple ye are."
> I Corinthians 3:16-17.

These two verses are clearly addressed to Christians. Now, if it were not possible for the temple of God to be defiled, then this verse would not be in scripture. These verses carry a sober warning. Do NOT allow your temple to be defiled. If you do, eventually you will be destroyed.

It is interesting that the same Greek word is used in these verses for "defile" and destroy -- meaning to spoil, corrupt, destroy; to bring into a worse state; to deprave. (*A Critical Lexicon and Concordance to the English and Greek New Testament,* by Ethelbert W. Bullinger [Zondervan Publishing, Grand Rapids, MI 1975], p. 213.)

I believe the sense here is that the defilement a person permits into the temple (himself) will result in his destruction. For instance, if a person goes out and participates in a homosexual relationship, not only will he receive the defilement of demons, but he may also receive AIDS. The AIDS will destroy his physical body, thus destroying the temple. A born-again believer cannot expect God to protect him from AIDS if he participates in a homosexual encounter any more than he can expect God to protect him from receiving demons!

Chapter 9
Defilement of God's Temple

I have had many people ask if I thought the destruction mentioned here meant loss of eternal salvation. I don't have all the final answers, but, in my personal opinion, I do not think so. I think the physical body will be destroyed, but the spirit and soul will go on to be with the Lord. However, the believer will suffer loss of rewards in heaven. In the verses just prior to the above statement, Paul addresses this issue:

> "Every man's work shall be made manifest: for the day shall declare it, because it shall be revealed by fire; and the fire shall try every man's work of what sort it is. If any man's work abide which he hath built thereupon, he shall receive a reward. If any man's work shall be burned, he shall suffer loss; but he himself shall be saved; yet so as by fire." I Corinthians 3:13-15

We hear very few sermons on these verses. People don't like to think about suffering loss in heaven. We want to think that we will ALL receive the same reward no matter what we do down here on earth. This simply is not true. A person may not lose their salvation, but, if they permit defilement to continue in their life, they will not receive the rewards they would otherwise have received had they lived a life in complete obedience to the Lord.

One of the main arguments used against Christians having demons is "what communion hath darkness with light?" Now, let's look at that scripture in context:

> "Be ye not unequally yoked together with unbelievers; for what fellowship hath righteousness with unrighteousness? and what communion hath light with darkness? And what concord hath Christ with Belial? or what part hath he that believeth with an infidel? And what agreement hath the temple of God with idols? for ye are the temple of the living God: as God hath said, I will dwell in them, and walk in them: and I will be their God, and they shall be my people. Wherefore come out from among them, and be ye separate, saith the Lord,

Chapter 9
Defilement of God's Temple

and touch not the unclean thing: and I will receive you,
and will be a Father unto you, and ye shall be my sons
and daughters, saith the Lord Almighty."
II Corinthians 6:14-18

This passage was addressed to the Christians at Corinth, so obviously some of them were already unequally yoked. Paul was telling them to clean up their lives. Therefore, this scripture cannot be used as a proof text that Christians cannot have demons. Just the opposite. Paul goes on in chapter 7 to write:

"Having therefore these promises, dearly beloved, let
us cleanse ourselves from all filthiness of the flesh and
spirit, perfecting holiness in the fear of God."
II Corinthians 7:1

"....And, let every one that nameth the name of Christ
depart from iniquity. But in a great house there are not
only vessels of gold and of silver, but also of wood and
of earth; and some to honour, and some to dishonour.
If a man therefore purge himself from these, he shall
be a vessel unto honour, sanctified, and meet for the
master's use, and prepared unto every good work."
II Timothy 2:19-21

We MUST purge our vessels and cleanse God's temple -- US.

Clearly, the Spirit of God AND demons dwelt within the same temple at the same time in the Old Testament.

Clearly, scripture warns us about defiling the temple of God, us. Over and over again, we are exhorted to CLEANSE ourselves! The rest of this book has been written to help you obey God's word and cleanse yourself. Are YOU willing to allow a condition of defilement to exist in you?

Chapter 9
Defilement of God's Temple

Chapter 10

THE SPIRIT
AND
THE SPIRIT WORLD

I find it interesting, that in this time of unprecedented escalation of the occult and evil, there has probably never been a time when Christians, as a whole, believed LESS in the reality of the existence of the spirit realm and Satan and his kingdom.

It was not necessary for any of the writers of scripture to teach about the reality of the spirit realm because the population as a whole already believed in it and KNEW about the occult. During the time of Moses, for instance, the Lord had no need to define, or describe, occult practices because the people generally knew very well what was being spoken about. The Israelites had just spent 400 years living in the Egyptian culture steeped in occultism and demon worship. But, today, few Christians have any idea what a wizard, or necromancer, is or what it means "to divine."

> "When thou art come into the land which the Lord thy God giveth thee, thou shalt not learn to do after the abominations of those nations. There shall not be found among you any one that maketh his son or his daughter to pass through the fire, or that useth divination, or an observer of times, or an enchanter, or a witch, or a charmer, or a consulter with familiar spirits, or a wizard, or a necromancer. For all that do these things are an abomination unto the Lord: and because

of these abominations the Lord thy God doth drive
them out from before thee. Deut. 18:9-12

The Lord did not have to define the terms given in these
verses because the people KNEW what He was talking
about. Just as in the times of Jesus and the writing of the
New Testament, knowledge about the occult and demons
was widespread.

In fact, it was widespread knowledge that demons could do
all sorts of things.

> "So general at the time of our Lord was the belief in
> demons and in the power of employing them, that even
> Josephus (Ant. viii.2,5) contended that the power of
> conjuring up, and driving out demons, and of magical
> cures had been derived from King Hezekiah, to whom
> God had given it. Josephus declares himself to have
> been an eyewitness of such a wonderful cure by the
> repetition of a magical formula. This illustrates the
> contention of the Scribes that the miraculous cures of
> our Lord were due to demoniac agency." (*The Life and
> Times of Jesus the Messiah*, by Alfred Edersheim, Vol.
> II, Eerdmans Pub. Co., © 1947, p. 762)

> "We must here bear in mind that the practice of magic
> was strictly prohibited to Israelites, and that -- as a mat-
> ter of principle at least -- witchcraft, or magic, was sup-
> posed to have no power over Israel, if they owned and
> served their God (Chull. 7b: Nedar. 32a). But in this
> matter also -- as will presently appear -- theory and
> practice did not accord. Thus, under certain cir-
> cumstances, the repetition of magical formulas was
> declared lawful even on the Sabbath (Sanh. 101a).
> Egypt was regarded as the home of magic (Kidd. 49b:
> Shabb. 75a). In connection with this, it deserves notice
> that the Talmud [writings for Jewish made laws by the
> Rabbis] ascribes the miracles of Jesus to magic, which
> He had learned during His stay in Egypt, having taken
> care, when He left, to insert under his skin its rules and

Chapter 10
The Spirit and The Spirit World

formulas, since every traveller, on quitting the country, was searched, lest he should take to other lands the mysteries of magic (Shabb. 104b).

"Here it may be interesting to refer to some of the strange ideas which Rabbinism attached to the early Christians, as showing both the intercourse between the two parties, and that the Jews did not deny the gift of miracles in the Church, only ascribing its exercise to magic." (*The Life and Times of Jesus the Messiah*, p. 172)

How different it is amongst the Christians of our day! The average Christian has NO idea of what occultism is all about! This is why so many Christians are falling into Satan's traps. Through ignorance!

Today, we need to come to a basic understanding of occultism so that we do NOT fall into the trap of accepting it as being from God. Occultic practices are rampant throughout Christian churches! Far too many Christians are turning more and more to occultic alternative forms of medicine, forms of divination, fortune telling and many other occultic abominations.

Scripture is clear. If you have ANY dealings with the occult, **YOU WILL BE DEFILED!** (Leviticus 19:31)

Hosea 4:6 says

"My people are destroyed for lack of knowledge: because thou hast rejected knowledge, I will also reject thee, that thou shalt be no priest to me: seeing thou hast forgotten the law of thy God, I will also forget thy children." Hosea 4:6-7

Dear ones in Christ, let us wake up and CLEANSE ourselves from all such defilement! The purpose of this book

Chapter 10
The Spirit and The Spirit World

is to help you understand the rapidly expanding world of the occult so that you can not only cleanse yourself from any involvement in it, but also so that you can avoid its traps.

In order to understand the occultic world, it is essential that the Christian understand the human spirit and the existence of the spirit world. Within the spirit realm, there are only two masters, two sources of power -- Jesus Christ or Satan. Satan's power is limited. The power of Jesus Christ is the absolute, unlimited power of Almighty God.

The central purpose of ALL occultism is to achieve and maintain contact with the spirit world and the spirits therein. The occultist maintains this contact with the spirit world to gain POWER. Every human being on the face of this earth desires power. It is at the very root of our sin nature. Satan is only too happy to supply people with a false power to do what they want. He does this to keep them from turning to the one true God, Jesus Christ. Unfortunately, Christians, being human with sin natures, also desire power. Satan has brought massive deceptions into the Christian churches, making Christians think they are experiencing and using the power of God when, in some cases, they are actually using demonic power. If the Christian is going to stand firm in God's word against this last great onslaught by Satan, he must have a good scriptural understanding of the human spirit and the spirit world.

How is it that we, as physical creatures, are able to maintain contact with the nonphysical spirit realm? The answer is found in scripture. It is because God made us in His image. He created each one of us in three parts just as He is a Trinity. We have a physical body, a soul and a spirit. It is through the spirit part of us that we can experience the spirit realm. This is true for both Christians and non-Christians.

Chapter 10
The Spirit and The Spirit World

> "And the very God of peace sanctify you wholly: and I pray God your whole spirit and soul and body be preserved blameless unto the coming of our Lord Jesus Christ." I Thessalonians 5:23

Paul teaches us here that we humans are tripartite beings. That is, we have three parts -- the body, soul and spirit. He plainly states that all three must be cleansed and committed to Jesus, and that Jesus Himself must enable us to keep all three parts "blameless" until His return.

I believe that in the beginning, before the fall, God created man a trinity (three parts) in perfect unity even as God Himself is in perfect unity. In other words, body, soul and spirit were perfectly united.

> And the Lord God formed man of the dust of the ground, [physical body] and breathed into his nostrils the breath of life [spirit]; and man became a living soul [the self which manifests as our mind, will and emotions.]" Genesis 2:7

I believe the unfallen Adam and Eve had many abilities that we fallen humans do not have today. Why? Because of the perfect unity of their body, soul and spirit. Where can we find an example of another perfect man? In Jesus Christ. Jesus Christ was without sin. He is called the "second or last Adam" in many places in scripture. Even after His resurrection, Jesus still had a physical body. However, it was a glorified physical body such as we will have one day. Scripture tells us that we will one day have a body just like Jesus now has. In that day, we will be restored to an unfallen state and human beings will once again be a perfect unity. What were some of the characteristics of the perfect unified unfallen state? We see them in Jesus -- especially after His resurrection. He could, with His physical body, do those things a spirit can do, such as walk through walls.

Chapter 10
The Spirit and The Spirit World

I believe there was a terrible severing at the fall. Body, soul and spirit were no longer in their original relationship with each other. Stop to think a minute. What is one of the first characteristics you think of in someone that is totally demon possessed? Unnatural strength. This strength is the result of the control over the physical body by a spirit, in this case a demon spirit. Those involved in the martial arts strive to achieve unnatural abilities with their physical bodies -- abilities that come only with the control of spirit over the physical.

Since the fall, we human beings do not naturally have conscious control over our spirits. BUT, the occultist MUST achieve this control in order to maintain their vital contact with the spirit world.

There are many lies in the whole area of occultic activities. Satan and his demons do not want human beings to understand what they are doing. So, they invent lies and perform false miracles to back up the lies. One of these is the "third eye."

The "third eye" dates back into antiquity. "Third eye" ability is the ability to "see" or gain contact with spirits.

You see, our brain is like a computer with two channels of input. When we "see" something in the physical world, the image goes from the retina of our physical eye through special nerves back into our brain. The image of the physical object is then created in our brain and we "see." The same is true of objects or spirits in the spirit world. Only, the information does not come through our physical eye. It comes through our spirit. Our brains are capable of receiving two sets of images at once, images from the physical world, and images from the spirit world. (Figure 10-1)

Chapter 10
The Spirit and The Spirit World

However, the demons do not teach people about their spirits. Instead they teach about a "third eye." Sometimes, demons actually create a false physical third eye in the center of the forehead. (Figure 10-2)

INPUT FROM PHYSICAL EYE WHICH SEES PHYSICAL WORLD.

INPUT FROM SPIRIT EYE FROM SPIRIT BODY WHICH SEES SPIRIT WORLD.

Figure 10-1

Occultists believe it is this third eye that gives them the ability to see the spirit world. They do not realize that they are actually using their spirit. Third eye abilities are also called "psychic abilities." Now, we have the massive influx of the New Age Movement with a whole new set of terminologies. Because the third eye is located in the center of the forehead, the New Agers call it "centering" instead of the "third eye." "Centering" is the New Age term which means the process of gaining contact with the spirit world.

Figure 10-2 (Third eye)

In fact, as Satan adds deception to deception, the old occult terms are no longer used. We now have new and scientific sounding words. One of the most important things a Christian can do is DEMAND A DEFINITION OF TERMS! Exactly WHAT do words mean? Let's look at some examples.

Chapter 10
The Spirit and The Spirit World

REMEMBER, there are only four different types of spirits:
> demon spirits
> angels in God's service
> human spirits
> and God Himself.

NEW AGE TERMS

Words that refer to one of the four types of spirits:
> energy
> vibrations
> electromagnetic vibrations
> inner man -- human spirit
> counselor -- demon spirits that used to be called "spirit guides" or "familiar spirits"
> entity
> force
> higher powers
> atman -- specific in Hinduism for the human spirit
> prana -- a form of breathing, used in yoga, to bring about the flow of spirit power.

Words that refer to contact with the spirit world:
> Self-realization -- the ability to control your own spirit so that you can achieve contact with the spirit world.
> Higher State of Consciousness -- contact with spirits and the spirit world.
> God consciousness -- contact with the spirit world because the new ager thinks God IS the entire spirit

world. They make no difference between created spirits and the creator God.

> Alpha or Theta level -- used in Silva Mind Control and other places. A trance state where contact with the spirit world is achieved. In such a trance state, these brain waves predominate on an EEG, thus the pseudo-scientific term.

> Left-brain, right-brain -- this whole theory is used to slide into contact with the spirit world.

> Higher State of Consciousness -- contact with spirits and the spirit world

Once you begin to define terms, you begin to understand that you are dealing with the God-forbidden contact with the spirit realm.

NOTE: There is NO such thing as impersonal vibrations or energies that people can use and control! ALL spiritual energy is VERY personal. It resides in a spirit of one of the four groups mentioned -- demon, angel, human or God. Human beings CANNOT control God or His power in any way! Therefore, if you are controlling an "energy" from the spirit world, you are using demons.

I have written in detail about the human spirit and the occultist's use of it in *"Prepare For War,"* Chapter 16. I will not repeat that information here.

Down through the ages, Satan has consistently used three methods to get people into contact with the spirit world:

> 1. Drugs

> 2. Meditation, hypnosis and trance states -- all involve a blank mind

> 3. Visualization and guided imagery

The mind altering drugs have been used all around the world in every culture by the wise men or shamans or witch doctors to gain contact with spirits. It is interesting that the hard-core Satanists of the Western world have no interest in taking such drugs as LSD. Why? Because they don't trip on them. They see the spirit world most all the time anyway. They don't need a drug such as LSD to enable them to do this. The "trips" taken on such drugs are nothing more or less than experiences in the spirit realm.

Demons are masters of deceit. They have the ability in the spirit realm to "switch the sets" just the same as men do in the movie making industry. If you visit Universal Studios, where many of the movies are made here in America, you can walk down one street and be in the "Old West," turn the corner, and you are in 18th century England, turn another corner, and you are in a different time and country. Demons can do the same thing in the spirit world and create all sorts of illusions for the humans under their control.

The Eastern religions center around gaining contact with the spirit world. To do this, they have developed forms of "meditation" which involve relaxation techniques to blank the mind. Scripture tells us that WE are responsible to control our minds at all times. (II Cor. 10:5) Once our minds are blank, the demons are free to take over and control them.

Lastly, visualization and guided imagery is a very old technique for gaining contact with the spirit world. This one technique alone is responsible for thousands of Christians falling into the trap of using occultic techniques. (See "*Prepare For War*," Chapter 16).

But, what are people actually doing when they gain contact with the spirit world? They are, in reality, gaining conscious control over their spirit. I don't know what to call this con-

Chapter 10
The Spirit and The Spirit World

trol so I have called it establishing a "link" between soul and spirit. In some way, the conscious mind gains control over the spirit so that the person can use their spirit to "look" into the spirit world and communicate with spirits in the spirit world. Remember, our physical bodies cannot "see" or communicate with the invisible spirit realm in any way. This communication must come through our spirits. We cannot normally communicate with the spirit world. This linking together of soul and spirit was lost at the fall.

The three techniques mentioned are used by occultists the world around to establish such control over their spirits. It is interesting that once a person comes to Jesus Christ out of the occult, they do not lose this ability until they specifically ask the Lord to sever between their soul and spirit according to Hebrews 4:12. Also, with those that do not come to Christ, on very rare occasions, I have asked the Lord to sever between their soul and spirit. When the Lord grants my request the person instantly loses their ability to communicate with the spirit world.

Clearly, it is NOT the Lord's will for His people to have this control over their spirits. Our spirits are to be directly under the control of the Holy Spirit, NOT our minds.

This is the basic difference between the occult and Christianity. Occultists control their contact with the spirit world, and they control to a large extent the power they use. Christians, on the other hand, are never in contact with the spirit world except on the brief occasions the Holy Spirit allows such contact, and Christians do NOT control the power of their God in any way. Christians are servants, nothing more. The Lord works through his servants as HE chooses, not as they choose. Demons cooperate with humans to give them power when the people want it to draw them ever farther away from the Lord.

Chapter 10
The Spirit and The Spirit World

Let us be careful to walk in faith and obedience to our Lord. Do not let sinful desire for power draw you into Satan's traps.

Chapter 10
The Spirit and The Spirit World

Chapter 11

DOORWAYS

What is a doorway? The Bible says that we are the temple of the Holy Spirit. I use the term "doorway" as a sin that defiles the temple. Through that doorway of sin demons can enter and cause havoc in our lives. I believe there are only three areas of sin which fall into this category. They are:

> 1. Inheritance

> 2. Sexual sins

> 3. Any involvement in the occult

I have written in detail about many doorways in both of my first two books. I do not wish to repeat all of that information here. Rather, I am going to briefly list the most common doorways, and briefly describe only those I have not written about in the other two books.

First, inheritance. Demons are inherited. This fact is very well known in the occultic world. It is also known within the Asian religions. Please see *"Prepare For War,"* p. 131-133 for a more in-depth discussion of this doorway.

SEXUAL SINS

Demons are passed from one person to another through sexual sins. These sins fall into eight basic categories:

> 1. Sex with the opposite sex outside of marriage

> 2. Sex with the same sex

> 3. Incest

> 4. Sex with children

> 5. Sex with animals

> 6. Sex with demons

> 7. Sado-masochism

> 8. Pornography

ANY of these sexual sins will allow demons to come into the person committing the sin. Sexual molestation is one of the most common childhood doorways. It is ALWAYS followed by a cycle of early sexual involvements on the part of the child with ever increasing involvement in sexual sins as the person grows older. This is because of the demons placed into the child at an early age.

<u>ANY</u> INVOLVEMENT IN THE OCCULT

The occult has a multitude of activities in which people become involved. It would take pages to list them all. I am going to break the occult up into categories and list the more common problems.

Classic occult activities

Scripture lists these as:

> Divination

> Astrology (star gazing)

> Wizard, necromancer, or sorcery (forms of witchcraft)

> Consulter with familiar spirits (calling up the spirits of the dead or performing seances is the most common of these)

Chapter 11
Doorways

Divination:

DIVINATION: The art that seeks to foresee or foretell future events **or** discover hidden knowledge. (Webster's Dictionary)

Most Christians realize that divination includes fortune telling, but it is the second half of the definition that gets people into trouble. Here is a list of common forms of divination:

> palm reading

> crystal ball reading

> water witching

> pendulum

> divining rod

> tarot cards or some form of card reading

> tea leaf reading

> numerology

> study of animal entrails (as in the Santeria religion)

However, there are modern forms of divination that are presented as scientific. Satan takes various procedures that will give a small amount of legitimate knowledge and then expands them to give very large amounts of knowledge. This is where divination comes in. Here is a list of some of these:

GRAPHOANALYSIS

Hand writing analysis. A few facts can be discovered through hand writing analysis such as if the person is male of female, or if the article is a forgery. However, when they start telling you such things as "you were involved in a painful accident at the age of 11 which causes you to have difficulty relating to people," look out. They are getting into divination. Most large corporations are now having graphoanalysis done on prospective employees. Unfortunately, many churches are falling into this trap.

IRIDOLOGY
The iris is the colored part of the eye. It is claimed that by merely looking into the iris any illness in the body can be diagnosed.

KINESIOLOGY
Please note that there is a science called, "kinesiology." The word comes from the Greek word "kinesis," which means, motion. Therefore, kinesiology is the study of human motion. It deals with the study of which muscles are involved with various movements of the body. I am not referring to this science.

I am referring to alternative types of kinesiology such as, Applied Kinesiology and Behavioral Kinesiology. Although such disciplines offer valuable insights into the function of our bodies, some practitioners have ventured far beyond the realm of science. I refer to such things as the diagnosing of illness through muscle testing. Some practitioners even claim to be able to diagnose the illness of a person at a distant location by proxy -- testing your muscle strength while you simply think about your sick friend who lives many miles away.

You will also find that books relating to alternative types of kinesiology promote the concepts of life energy, life force, acupressure holding points, acupuncture meridians, etc.

CYTOTOXOLOGY
Diagnosis of any illness from the supposed study of blood cells. Much information can be legitimately obtained by studying the blood, but it is impossible to diagnosis all illnesses by studying one type of blood cell.

Chapter 11
Doorways

REFLEXOLOGY
Diagnosis of illness from reflexes.

HYPNOTISM
Hypnotism is basically a demonic trance. It is in direct violation of God's word. We are commanded to take every thought captive (II Cor. 10:3-5) and to be sober and vigilant (I Peter 5:8). We must always be alert. God holds us directly responsible for ourselves and our minds. Hypnotism requires submission of the person being hypnotized. Demons are ALWAYS placed into a person through hypnotism. Anyone using this technique also has demons. God's people MUST stay clear of this trap.

ACUPUNCTURE
Acupuncture originated in Asia. It is an integral part of the Asian religion. The needles are supposed to tap into the "chi" or spirit. Acupuncture provides a demonic healing.

ACUPRESSURE
Acupressure works on the same principle as acupuncture.

COLOR ANALYSIS
By this I do not mean fashion. I am talking about the type of analysis where you are told that certain colors affect your energy level, etc.

HAIR ANALYSIS
Diagnosis of illness by analyzing hair. Hair is protein very similar to finger nails. Other than a protein deficiency, illnesses cannot be diagnosed from hair.

For an in-depth discussion of these techniques, I recommend a book called, *Healing At Any Price? The Hidden Dangers of Alternative Medicine,* by Samuel Pfeifer, M.D., (Word Publishing, © 1988).

Chapter 11
Doorways

Occultic Games & Toys

Occultic games and toys have saturated our stores. Such games as Dungeons and Dragons are a crash course in witchcraft. ALL role playing games involve intense visualization which quickly brings the players into contact with the spirit world.

Parents need to be extremely careful about the toys they buy for their children. The various monster toys are actually accurate replicas of demons as they appear in the spirit world. Children naturally go through a developmental stage where they use a lot of imagination and visualization. It is an easy step for demons that look like the toys to make contact with children playing with them.

Nearly all the children's cartoons have occultic teachings in them. And, there is a massive move in our public schools to train children to become spiritualist mediums in the lower grades. If you have not already done so, I would strongly recommend that you obtain and read "*Like Lambs To The Slaughter,*" by Johanna Michaelson. This book is an excellent expose of the occultism being taught in our schools. Every parent with a child in school should read this book.

Martial Arts

It is very well known in the occultic world that demon spirits are the power used in the martial arts. However, there is a great deal of confusion concerning such things as self-defense. I think a good "rule of thumb" is that if you reach the point where you can do those things which would normally rend flesh and bone without getting hurt, then you are using demon spirit power.

Chapter 11
Doorways

Seances

Seance: A spiritualist meeting to receive spirit communications. (Webster's Dictionary).

There are many forms of seances other than the old fashioned seances around a table in a dark room. Remember, a seance is anything that calls up a spirit to receive communication from it. Here are some other seances:

> Ouija Board

> Bloody Mary -- a game played by children in which a demon appears in a mirror to them.

> Meditation -- to speak with a counselor or spirit guide as in Silva Mind Control and many other techniques.

> Roman Catholicism -- calling upon the "saints" and Mary for help.

Other Occultic Doorways

> Yoga

> Eastern Meditation

> Visualization & guided imagery

> Rock Music

> Use of crystals

> ESP

> Astral-projection

> Blood contracts of ANY kind -- including becoming "blood brothers"

> Sacrifices of any kind

> Idols of any kind

> Chants of any kind

The list is almost endless. I would recommend the reader to the chapter entitled "Doorways" in *"Prepare For War."* I have discussed these doorways in detail in that book so I will not repeat that information here.

Chapter 11
Doorways

Chapter 12

DELIVERANCE

This book is written for all those children of God who hunger and thirst after a close personal relationship with HIM. It is for those who long to "hear" His voice in their innermost being, who will not be satisfied with anything less than the experience of His presence and glory. It is for those who value such a relationship with our wonderful Creator enough to be willing to pay the price in their own lives to achieve it -- the pain of daily carrying the cross. This book is for those who are willing to strive for holiness in obedience to our beloved master, JESUS.

> "Having therefore these promises, dearly beloved, let us cleanse ourselves from all filthiness of the flesh and spirit, perfecting holiness in the fear of God."
> II Corinthians 7:1

There is a desperate need for God's people to wake up and bring holiness into their lives! The professing Christian church of the Western world today has settled down into a gospel of compromises with the world. Doctrines of prosperity and satisfaction of the fleshly desires are uppermost throughout the churches. No one wants to pay the price for living a truly separated and holy life.

The consequent poverty in the average Christian's personal relationship with the Lord is astounding. The most common question I get from pastors over the phone is, "Is it really possible for the Lord to communicate with me directly?" How tragic this is! Truly we are living in a church age characterized by the church of Laodicea.

"And unto the angel of the church of the Laodiceans write; These things saith the Amen, the faithful and true witness, the beginning of the creation of God; I know thy works, that thou art neither cold nor hot: I would thou were cold or hot. So then because thou art lukewarm, and neither cold nor hot, I will spew thee out of my mouth. Because thou sayest, I am rich, and increased with goods, and have need of nothing: and knowest not that thou art wretched, and miserable, and poor, and blind, and naked: I counsel thee to buy of me gold tried in the fire, that thou mayest be rich; and white raiment, that thou mayest be clothed, and that the shame of thy nakedness do not appear; and anoint thine eyes with eye-salve, that thou mayest see. As many as I love, I rebuke and chasten: be zealous therefore, and repent." Revelation 3:14-19

The glitter of "Christian" TV stars and "Christian" entertainment has blinded the eyes of God's people to their terrible poverty. The emotional highs induced by repeated choruses and emotional music in many church services completely drown out that still quiet voice of the Holy Spirit calling us to repentance and holiness.

I believe A.W. Tozer summed it all up best in his book *The Pursuit of God.*

"Shallow lives, hollow religious philosophies, the preponderance of the element of fun in gospel meetings, the glorification of men, trust in religious externalities, quasi-religious fellowships, salesmanship methods, the mistaking of dynamic personality for the power of the Spirit. These and such as these are the symptoms of an evil disease, a deep and serious malady of the soul." (*The Pursuit of God,* by A.W. Tozer, Christian Publications, Inc., 1982, p. 69.)

Those of us who have accepted our Savior's gracious offer to wash away our sins by His precious blood shed on

Chapter 12
Deliverance

Calvary's cruel cross, must put sin and defilement out of our lives. Let us purge ourselves so that we may become a vessel unto honor. (II Timothy 2:21) The choice is yours. Will you become a vessel of honor or of dishonor?

There is a little book by Phillip Keller which I strongly urge everyone to obtain and read. In it, Keller beautifully describes a visit to a potter's home in Pakistan. He watched an expert potter making a vessel:

> "Once more the stone began to turn. But just as suddenly it stopped a third time. The potter's shoulders slumped disconsolately. An abject look of dismay welled up in his tired eyes. In despair he pointed to a deep, ragged gouge that cut an angry gash in the body of the beautiful goblet. It was ruined beyond repair.

> "In a gesture of frustration and utter futility he crushed the clay down upon the wheel. Beneath his hands it was again a formless mass of mud lying in a dark heap upon the stone."

> 'And the vessel that he made of clay was marred in the hand of the potter' (Jeremiah. 18:4...)

> "What will the potter do now? . . . Then the potter turned to look at me from his wobbly stool. His eyes were clouded, sad, like deep wells filled with remorse. He spoke softly, hesitantly. 'I will just make a crude peasant's finger bowl from the same clay!'" (*In The Master's Hands,* by Phillip Keller, Vine Books, 1987, pp. 28-31.)

> "Let every one that nameth the name of Christ depart from iniquity. But in a great house there are not only vessels of gold and of silver, but also of wood and of earth; and some to honour and some to dishonour. IF a man therefore purge himself from these, he shall be a vessel unto honour, sanctified and meet for the

Chapter 12
Deliverance

master's use, and prepared unto every good work."
II Timothy 2:19-21

The choice is ours. Will we resist our Master and thus become a vessel of dishonor? If we harden our hearts and resist the Holy Spirit as he convicts us that we need to cleanse ourselves, then we most surely end up a vessel of dishonor.

Purging ourselves, is what this chapter is all about. We MUST purge OURSELVES. The responsibility is on US. Over and over again in scripture we are exhorted to cleanse ourselves.

> "Having therefore these promises, dearly beloved, let us cleanse ourselves from all filthiness of the flesh and spirit, perfecting holiness in the fear of God."
> II Corinthians 7:1

> "Wherefore, my beloved, as ye have always obeyed, not as in my presence only, but now much more in my absence, work out your own salvation with fear and trembling." Philippians 2:12

Jesus paid the price for our sins on the cross, but it is OUR responsibility to take up the power and authority available to us in the name of Jesus to cleanse our temples, that is, us.

> "Know ye not that ye are the temple of God, and that the Spirit of God dwelleth in you? If any man defile the temple of God, him shall God destroy; for the temple of God is holy, which temple ye are."
> I Corinthians 3:16-17

Because the Holy Spirit dwells in those of us who have made Jesus Christ our Lord and Master and Savior, we must be careful to keep ourselves pure. That not only means that we

Chapter 12
Deliverance

must stop sinning, but we must also cleanse all filth out of the temple. That means demons.

The more we come to know God, the more aware we will be of our sinful condition! It is my prayer that the Holy Spirit will show each individual something of the awesome greatness of our God.

> "The fear of the Lord is the beginning of knowledge:
> but fools despise wisdom and instruction." Proverbs 1:7

It is only as we come to a reverent appreciation of the greatness and utter holiness of our God that we will fall on our faces and cry out:

> "Woe is me! For I am undone; because I am a man of
> unclean lips, and I dwell in the midst of a people of un-
> clean lips: for mine eyes have seen the King, the Lord
> of hosts." Isaiah 6:5

Let us humble ourselves and get on our faces before the Lord and repent of our sins! Let us be careful to cleanse ourselves in order that we may become vessels that our Master can use. Oh how I want to be a profitable servant for my Master! It is my total heart's desire to please Him. I cannot do this if I am careless about sin and careless about defilement in my temple (me).

I have spent the last several chapters of this book talking about areas of sin that bring about defilement, or the dwelling of demons, in us. If you have been involved in any of these areas, then you need to cleanse yourself. It is my belief that the average Christian can cleanse himself through the power and authority given to him by the Lord Jesus Christ. I am writing this chapter so that Christians can do just this. Unless you have been deeply involved in the occult, you do not need someone else to help you cleanse yourself. It is

Chapter 12
Deliverance

helpful if you have someone else who can pray with you, but, YOU need to get onto your face before God and do business with Him one-on-one. Jesus is our mediator. We need no other. I urge you to cleanse yourself NOW! Do not delay. The time is short. I am convinced that our Lord's return is near.

Will you "purge your vessel" in obedience to our Lord's commands? Or will you persist in rebellion and living a life of comfort and ease and become a "vessel unto dishonor?"

The choice is YOURS.

"And these signs shall follow them that believe; in my name shall they cast out devils . . ." Mark 16:17

"Behold, I give unto you power to tread on serpents and scorpions, and over all the power of the enemy: and nothing shall by any means hurt you." Luke 10:19

Jesus gives His servants authority over demons in His name. Unfortunately, deliverance has gotten a very bad name in Christian churches because of the unscriptural practices many use in a deliverance. We all go through a learning process. I regret that I did not make a clear enough statement in my first book, "*He Came To Set The Captives Free,*" that the struggle I had with the demons in Elaine was because I was ignorant as to how to approach deliverance. The Lord demanded that I write my mistakes as well as my successes. I wish to emphasize that I do NOT speak with demons or allow the physical manifestations of demons now, that I did in those early days of this ministry. If I had known then what I know now, it would not have taken so many hours to deliver Elaine.

Chapter 12
Deliverance

As soon as I started my medical practice, I began to see people daily who were coming out of Satanism. Obviously, I could not spend many, many hours with each one in deliverance. Quickly I sought the Lord for the answer. My prayer went something like this: "Lord, why is it that when Jesus commanded a demon to come out it came out immediately and I am spending an hour arguing and fighting just to get one to come out?" The Lord's answer was short and to the point: "Exactly!" You see, the fact that I was talking to and arguing with the demons WAS the problem. Not only was it the problem, it was SIN. Why?

First, because I was allowing the person being delivered to fall into the sin of becoming a "medium." What is a medium? A medium is a person who allows spirits to speak through them. (See Webster's Dictionary.) God strictly forbids this! (Deut. 18:10-12) Far too many times, deliverance workers will ask the person being delivered to just relax and let the demons speak through them. They are directly asking the person to sin!

Secondly, scripture strictly forbids the practice of "familiar spirits." (See Deut. 18:10-12) What does it mean to consult a familiar spirit? It means to speak to a demon to obtain information from it. Witches have special demons that they use all the time to gain information from. When the deliverance worker relies on gaining information from the demons themselves about who they are and how they got in, etc., the worker is himself falling into the sin of having a familiar spirit, or consulting with a demon spirit!

Lastly, we Christians are a temple of the Holy Spirit.

> "And what concord hath Christ with Belial?"
> II Cor. 6:15

Chapter 12
Deliverance

The Holy Spirit of Jesus Christ has NO concord or fellowship or agreement with Belial or ANY demon spirit. Therefore, any Christian who allows a demon to take over and control his body in any way is sinning! The book of James, especially chapters 3 and 4, teaches us that WE are responsible to control our bodies.

> "For in many things we offend all. IF any man offend not in word, the same is a perfect man, and able also to bridle [control] the whole body." James 3:2

James 4:8 tells us to cleanse our hands and hearts. There are many scriptures that make reference to our responsibility to control our bodies.

The major hindrance to deliverance is SIN! We must NOT sin by obtaining information from demons, neither must we allow the people we work with to sin by becoming a medium or channel for demons to speak through. These practices are condemned by God's word.

The Lord then showed me that deliverance must be a step in faith. Our whole Christian walk is based on faith. Everything we receive from the Lord we receive by faith. Deliverance is no different.

How does faith operate in deliverance? It is like this:

FAITH = absolute acceptance, as fact, that God always performs His word.

Therefore, deliverance is based upon God's word. We accept as FACT, that, when we comply with God's commands, He will always keep His promises. Deliverance is based upon the following scriptures:

**Chapter 12
Deliverance**

"If we confess our sins, he is faithful and just to forgive us our sins, and to cleanse us from all unrighteousness."
I John 1:9

"Behold, I give unto you power to tread on serpents and scorpions, and over all the power of the enemy..."
Luke 10:19

IF we repent and confess our sins, God will cleanse us. It is just that simple.

THE ONLY BASIS FOR DELIVERANCE IS TRUE REPENTANCE.

REPENTANCE =

1. to turn from sin and dedicate oneself to the amendment of one's life.

2. to feel sorrow, regret, or contrition for
 (Webster's Dictionary)

You CANNOT deliver someone who is continuing in active sin, or who doesn't want to be delivered.

THERE ARE FOUR SIMPLE STEPS IN DELIVERANCE:

Step 1 : Define the doorways or temple-defiling sins.

Step 2: REPENT and confess those sins asking God for forgiveness and cleansing.

Step 3: Command the demons that came in through those sins to get out of you forever.

Step 4: Stop sinning! Saturate your life with God's word.

Chapter 12
Deliverance

WHEN DELIVERANCE IS DONE AS A STEP IN FAITH, DEMONIC MANIFESTATION WILL NOT BE PERMITTED.

This was a major "key" in helping me to understand how the Lord wanted deliverance to be done. No wonder I had such a terrible time trying to get the demons out of someone. As I permitted the demons to speak through a person, I was, in reality, asking that person to sin, and I was sinning too! It is most difficult to get a demon to come out of someone while they are engaging in active sin.

Once I realized this and started approaching deliverance as a step in faith, there were no more fights with the demons! Deliverance became very simple. We human beings make things so complicated. God makes everything simple. Deliverance then is like this:

> > Repent for the sin that allowed demons to come in.

> > Command the demons to leave that came in through that sin.

> > Accept by **FAITH** that God **ALWAYS** performs His word. IF a person truly repents for his/her sin, God **WILL** cleanse, and the demons have to leave. Once confession of sin and commanding the demons to leave is accomplished, the person accepts in faith that they are gone.

Now, let us look at each of the four steps in deliverance one by one.

STEP 1 : Define the doorways or temple-defiling sins.
As I stated in Chapter 11, I do not believe that demons can come into a person through just any sin. I believe that what I call "templedefiling sins" fall into the three categories:

Chapter 12
Deliverance

> 1. Inheritance

> 2. ANY involvement with the occult

> 3. Sexual sins

I have written about many specific sins within these three areas in the preceding chapters. The first step is to sit down with a pen and paper in hand and carefully go through your life from birth to present. Ask the Holy Spirit to bring to your memory any sins you may have forgotten. Make a list of them on the paper. I have found that it is helpful to make the list of sins in chronological order -- that is, start with birth, and list them as you committed them down through the years to the present time.

If you are counseling someone, ask them to tell you about their life from their earliest memories on. Look for sins that fall into these three areas. Do not fall into the trap of mistaking symptoms for doorways.

People will frequently come to the deliverance worker complaining of such things as depression, anger, violent temper, etc. These are just symptoms. The underlying cause is the sin that allowed the demons to come into the person. ALL demons will cause depression, anger, rebellion, hatred, etc. Always look for the root cause.

Next, BE METHODICAL. I find that one of the most common reasons for an incomplete deliverance is because people were not methodical. That is why everything must be written down on a piece of paper. If you do not write it down, the demons will confuse your mind and make you forget.

It is not necessary for the deliverance worker to ask a person to give them details, especially in the area of sexual sins.

Chapter 12
Deliverance

If you do, you will be opening the door for all kinds of temptation through lust. For example, there are eight areas under sexual sins. I simply ask people if they have been involved in one or more of these areas. If so, then I ask them to write down the names of the specific people with whom they have been involved so that they can confess each sexual contact individually. But I do NOT ask them for any details. Here are the categories of sexual sins:

> 1. sex with the opposite sex outside of marriage

> 2. sex with the same sex

> 3. incest

> 4. sex with children

> 5. sex with animals

> 6. sex with demons

> 7. sadomasochism

> 8. pornography

As you help someone make up a list of the doorways in his life, it is important to try to get an understanding of just how much passivity the person practices. People involved in the occult, and especially with problems of depression and suicide, usually have very lazy and passive minds. People in the occult have become used to blanking out their minds, thereby giving control of their entire mind and body to the demons. These people must be carefully taught how to regain control over their minds before a deliverance can be successful, and also to enable them to keep the demons out after deliverance.

I have also found it most helpful to question the person to see just how much control the demons have over them. As the years have passed, the Lord has steadily shown me that the less passive a person is in their deliverance, the more

Chapter 12
Deliverance

likely they are to remain free of demons once they are set free.

It is also helpful to find out just how much control the person has established over his spirit, and/or how much control somebody else has established over that person's spirit.

You should keep two lists of sins. One list is for the sins that allowed demons to come into a person (temple-defiling sins), the other list is of sins that are not demonic doorways, but are still sins that need to be confessed. Please see Appendix A for help with the second list.

The deliverance worker must always be much in prayer. If the Holy Spirit does not give you a peace that the person you are helping has been completely honest with you in making the list of doorways, do not proceed beyond this step. I never cease to be amazed at the way people can lie. Over and over again I have had people look at me so innocently and tell me that they have told me about ALL of their doorways when they have deliberately left out major areas of sin! Don't be afraid to wait. NEVER go into a deliverance unless the Lord specifically tells you to do so.

STEP 2: REPENT and confess those sins asking God for forgiveness and cleansing.
I think it is very unfortunate that so little repentance is preached these days. RARELY do Christians sit down and make out a list of every sin they can think of and SPECIFI-CALLY confess those sins to God. I find that those people who do this at the time of initial salvation have very little trouble believing that they are saved. Too many Christians struggle with assurance of salvation. If Christians would be. more diligent in confessing their sins, I believe that few would have this struggle.

Chapter 12
Deliverance

When confessing sins, the person should confess every sin he can think of. But he needs to command demons to leave only when confessing those sins that allowed demons to come into him. (See Appendix A) I believe that a specific listing and confession of sins as I am advocating is one way of fulfilling James 5:16

> "Confess your faults one to another, and pray for one another, that ye may be healed. The effectual fervent prayer of a righteous man availeth much." James 5:16

Sins were committed one-by-one. They should be confessed one-by-one as much as possible. As a person repents for his sins and asks the Lord to forgive and cleanse him, he takes away any legal ground the demons have to cling to. That is why deliverance done in this manner is so much quicker and easier. It took ten hours to completely deliver Elaine. Since the Lord taught me this approach to deliverance, I can now help someone as deeply infested with demons as Elaine was to a complete deliverance in a couple of hours.

If you do not feel a person is truly repentant for his sins, then do not go any further. Wait for the Holy Spirit to bring conviction into their lives. This may take days, weeks, months or years. Again, you must be very sensitive to the guidance of the Holy Spirit in each case.

STEP 3: Command the demons that came in through "temple-defiling sins" to get out of you forever.
Many people ask why they, themselves, should command the demons out when Jesus clearly commanded the demons to leave people. I believe it is because we have the Holy Spirit available to us now. The Holy Spirit was NOT available to people during the time Jesus walked and taught on this earth. After Jesus ascended to the Father and left this earth, we entered into a whole new dispensation. Scripture now exhorts Christians to cleanse themselves and "work out

their own salvation." (Phil 2:12) We have a responsibility now that those people did not have in the days before the giving of the Holy Spirit.

I have also found that once a person establishes authority over the demons within himself, the demons have to go. This is particularly true for those who have been involved in the occult. People in the occult are used to obeying the demons and letting them do pretty much whatever they want to do. It is a big step for them to realize that once they serve Jesus Christ they now have more power in Jesus than the demons have. It is absolutely necessary that people establish authority over the demons within them in the name of Jesus. If they do not, they will not be able to keep the demons out after deliverance.

IT IS NOT NECESSARY TO KNOW THE NAMES OF ALL THE DEMONS. It is NOT necessary to command the demons to come out one by one. Command the demons to come out by the sins that let them in. The ONLY time you should deal with specific demon names is with people involved in the occult who work with familiar spirits. These familiars must be rebuked individually and commanded to leave by name. BUT, the people already know the names of these demons. If they tell you they do not, they are lying.

It is NEVER necessary to allow a demon to manifest or speak through the person. The more the person being delivered controls the demons inside of himself, the quicker and easier the deliverance will be.

The most common question is, "If the demons don't manifest, then how do we know they have left?" The answer is simple. "Because the Holy Spirit tells you." Remember, demons are spirits, and as such, we cannot see them. If you are relying on physical manifestations to let you know the demons have left, you will be fooled because the demons

Chapter 12
Deliverance

can easily fake physical symptoms of leaving. ONLY the Holy Spirit can see the demons. You must rely upon Him for guidance. Also, IF the person has truly repented and confessed his sins, the demons have to leave. So you accept in faith that they are gone because God ALWAYS performs His word.

STEP 4: Stop sinning! Saturate your life with God's word. However, there is a most important point in all of this that many people over look. That is Step 4 in deliverance -- STOP SINNING. You MUST be a true believer in Jesus Christ to have authority over demons. But, you cannot be a BELIEVER without also being an OBEYER.

> "If ye love me, keep my commandments ... He that hath my commandments, and keepeth them, he it is that loveth me: and he that loveth me shall be loved of my Father, and I will love him, and will manifest myself to him." John 14:15 & 21

> "Not everyone that saith unto me, Lord, Lord, shall enter into the kingdom of heaven; but he that doeth the will of my Father which is in heaven." Matthew 7:21

There is no substitute for obedience. If you think you believe in and are serving Jesus, but are not also obeying His commands as given in the Bible, you are lying to your-self. You are not a believer unless you are also an obeyer.

> "Submit yourselves therefore to God. Resist the devil, and he will flee from you." James 4:7

Unfortunately, usually only the second half of this verse is quoted. I cannot emphasize enough the necessity of the first half. If we are not submitted to the Lord and obeying His commands, we cannot hope to have any power over demons. It is not uncommon for me to stop counseling with someone because they are unwilling to put active sin out of

Chapter 12
Deliverance

their life. It is simply a waste of time to try to deliver some-one who is living in active sin. Many times I have simply prayed with a person and asked the Holy Spirit to convict them of their sins. I also ask the Lord to work in their life in whatever way is necessary to bring them to a place where they are willing to give up their sins. Too often people seek deliverance only to gain relief from their problems, NOT because they want to serve the Lord and live a life pleasing to Him.

POST DELIVERANCE PROBLEMS:
I have found that there are five general areas of problems people experience after deliverance:
> 1. Fear that the demons are back in
> 2. Demands for emotional rewards
> 3. Passive mind
> 4. Unwilling to put up with demonic harassment which is part of the reaping period
> 5. Discipline of the "flesh" or sin nature

1. FEAR THAT THE DEMONS ARE BACK IN
This is the most common problem of all. People are continually afraid that the demons have gotten back into them. There are only two ways that demons can get back into a person after deliverance:
1. If the person commits a "temple-defiling sin"
2. If the person directly asks the demons to come back in

Remember, the demons can cause the same physical symptoms from the outside that they did from the inside. Physical symptoms, or thoughts, are NOT proof that the demons are back inside. The person must stand in FAITH that they are gone.

IF the person commits a temple-defiling sin thus opening a doorway, the demons will all come back in and many more besides. People who have been in the occult are particularly tempted with doing "just one more incantation" to get their own way. If they do, they have just asked all the demons to come back into them. Also, remember, scripture says rebellion is the same as the sin of witchcraft. You CANNOT rebel against the Lord's commands. If you persist in walking in disobedience and rebellion, you will be unable to keep the demons from returning.

Often I have people tell me that they don't "feel any different" after deliverance. That's O.K. There is no feeling in faith. The fruits of their life will show that they are clear. You cannot rely upon feelings when dealing with the spirit world.

2. DEMANDS FOR EMOTIONAL REWARDS.

Oh how we human beings love emotional rewards. People always want to FEEL something. They want to feel the demons leave. They want to feel the love of God. They want to feel good.

This walk of ours is in FAITH. There are no feelings in faith. One of the first things the Lord does is wean us away from emotional rewards. You OBEY regardless of how you feel. You function regardless of how you feel.

Demons are only too happy to give us emotional highs to get us into bondage to them. People after deliverance should not seek emotional highs thinking these are "spiritual experiences."

One of the most common complaints I get is that someone doesn't think he is clear from the demons because he doesn't FEEL like reading his Bible or praying. Our sin nature will keep us from "feeling like" doing the things God

Chapter 12
Deliverance

requires. We cannot use that as an indication that demons are inside of us or outside of us.

People who have had demons living in them for long periods of time get very addicted to the emotional rewards the demons give them. It is a matter of self-discipline to begin to walk in obedience and faith to our Lord without the emotional highs we desire.

3. PASSIVE MIND.

This is an area of great difficulty. The mind is like a muscle. If you don't use it for a period of time it becomes weak and flabby. It is PAINFUL to rebuild a muscle that has not been used. It is a hundred times more painful and difficult to regain the use of a passive mind.

If someone has been used to blanking out his mind, he will tend to do this after deliverance. Every time someone allows his mind to go blank, he has directly opened a doorway for demons to come back inside of himself. As soon as he realizes that he allowed his mind to go blank, he must confess that sin and then command all the demons to leave him immediately that came in while he was blanked out.

I have found that the best way to rebuild a passive mind is through intensive scripture memory and plain old mathematical tables. One reason why most people hate math is because of the mental discipline it takes to memorize the addition, subtraction, multiplication and division tables. That is why the companies who make calculators make so much money! Because people are basically lazy. I often have people who have been involved in Eastern forms of occultic meditation drill on mathematical tables in addition to scripture memory. This is very helpful in overcoming a passive mind.

Chapter 12
Deliverance

4. UNWILLING TO PUT UP WITH DEMONIC HARASSMENT WHICH IS PART OF THE REAPING PERIOD.

Jesus told us in a parable that when a demon is cast out that it will get seven others stronger than himself and come back to try to get in. (Luke 11:24-26) I always tell people that the battle to stay clear after deliverance is always seven times worse than it was to get clear in the first place.

Many people are simply unwilling to put up with any discomfort whatsoever. They DEMAND that their problems be taken care of so that they do not have any difficulties at all. This just is not possible.

Galatians 6:7-8 tells us that we will reap what we sow. If we have sown in sin, allowing demons to come into us, then we are going to reap. Part of the reaping is the demonic torment that comes as the demons try to get back in after deliverance.

Physical symptoms are common. Remember, the demons can cause the same physical symptoms from the outside as they do from the inside.

One of the common forms of demonic torment after deliverance is a noise in the ears. People are unwilling to put up with this, saying that they have not been delivered. They refuse to accept the reaping process and fight the demons. People become weary if they have to rebuke demons or demonic thoughts more than two or three times. In the battle to stay clear after deliverance, they will have to rebuke the demons thousands of times! They will have to be consistent in their stand for the Lord.

Demons never wear out with repetition. People wear out very quickly. In the case of demonic thoughts, rebuke the demons once or twice, then force your mind onto scripture and ignore the demons. The most common thing the demons will do is flash thoughts into the person's mind telling him that he is not delivered, that the demons are back inside. The person MUST stand in faith that this is not so!

In the case of physical torment, you must rebuke the demons, and then stand.

> "Wherefore take unto you the whole armour of God, that ye may be able to withstand in the evil day, and having done all, to stand." Ephesians 6:13

Just standing is the hardest thing of all for us to do. Please read Chapter 4 of "*Prepare For War*" for a more complete discussion of the reaping period.

5. DISCIPLINE OF THE "FLESH" OR SIN NATURE.
People who have allowed demons to dwell inside them rarely discipline their sin nature. This is especially true for those who have been involved in the occult.

Please see Chapter 10 of this book for a discussion of the sin nature. It is imperative that people put sin out of their lives after deliverance. They cannot stay clear if they do not do so.

CASE HISTORIES

I am going to give a series of case histories to try to help demonstrate how to look for doorways. All of these are true case histories, but I have changed the names of everyone to protect those involved.

I am dealing with the deliverance of people involved in Satanism in a separate chapter.

Chapter 12
Deliverance

Case #1. Susan (not her real name), 33 years old

Susan knew nothing about her father because he left her mother before she was born. However, there was a long line of mental illness in her mother's family and many of her mother's relatives were deeply involved in the Masons and the Shriners.
(Doorways: inheritance, Masons, Shriners, mental illness)

Susan was raised as a so-so Catholic. She rarely attended church, but she was baptized in the church, was confirmed and received communion occasionally.
(Doorways: Roman Catholicism, baptism, confirmation, communion)

When Susan was three years old her mother remarried.. Her step father started abusing her when she was four years old. He forced her into sexual relations and beastiality.
(Doorways: incest, beastiality)

As is typical for children who have been sexually molested, Susan became involved in multiple sexual contacts by her early teens.
(Doorways: multiple sexual partners)

Susan was an apt pupil and quickly learned to read tarot cards, play with the ouija board, and how to become a spiritualist medium. She also participated in hypnosis, voodoo, and finally, astral-projection.
(Doorways: witchcraft)

Susan was an apt pupil and quickly learned to read tarot cards, play with the ouija board, and how to become a

spiritualist medium. She also participated in hypnosis, voodoo, and finally, astral-projection.
(Doorways: tarot cards, ouija board, hypnosis, voodoo, astral-projection)

However, during Susan's sixteenth year, she had a horrifying experience while she was astral-projecting. Because of this experience, she decided to give up formal witchcraft. But, as she looked for something to take its place, she knocked on all the wrong doors.

Susan left the foster home and became involved in Transcendental Meditation and drugs and alcohol. As she frequented the various bars, she became attracted to the gay bars and entered into a lesbian life style.
(Doorways: TM, drugs, alcohol, lesbianism)

Susan was a bright student and continued on to college. She graduated with a degree in psychology and sociology and became a counselor for a government program. However, demons of sexual perversions seem to have a twin that walks hand in hand with them. That is violence. Susan found that she was growing more and more violent. She had many fights with her various lesbian partners as bitter jealousy is a common part of all lesbian and/or homosexual relationships.
(Doorways: violence, multiple lesbian partners)

In 1982 Susan got in a terrible fight with her lesbian partner and killed her. She went to prison. The killing was ruled involuntary manslaughter, so she only spent 25 months in jail.
(Doorways: murder)

While Susan was in jail, she did some serious thinking. She decided that her life had to change. She withdrew from everybody. She totally put alcohol and drugs out of

Chapter 12
Deliverance

her life and withdrew from an active lesbian life style as well. She was released early on good behavior. But, the parole board demanded that after her release she regularly attend the Gay A.A., and join the Metropolitan Community Church. The Metropolitan Community Church is not a Christian church, because they do not accept the complete word of God as it is written in the Bible. It is a church of all gay people.

Because of her enforced association with gays, Susan quickly fell back into lesbian relationships and violent fights. It was with one of her partners that a turning point in her life came. One night, while quarreling with her partner, Susan saw a demon surface and manifest through the other girl. Because of her experience in witchcraft years before, she recognized the demon for what it was. That frightened her. She told her partner that she "needed help." They did not know where to turn for help with a demon, but a few days later saw an advertisement on TV for a Christian tent meeting being held in their area. Susan talked her partner into going to see if someone at the tent meeting could get rid of the demon.

Both girls went to the tent meeting, but Susan's partner freaked out and left within the first five minutes of the service. Susan stayed, interested to see what would happen as she had never been in a Christian service of any kind. She told me that the only thing that got through to her mind during that service was the statement the preacher made that "narrow is the way and few there be that find it." She did not know what this narrow way was, but she became determined to find out.

After the service she went forward to stand in the prayer line hoping to have an opportunity to ask somebody about this "narrow way." As the preacher came down the line, he stopped before Susan to pray. He did not give her a

Chapter 12
Deliverance

chance to ask any questions, but reached out to put his hand on her forehead. She was told later by people who were there that the instant the preacher's hand touched her, her body jerked back and flew into the air, doing two back flips and landing on the ground more than twenty feet away from where she had been standing. Susan never felt the impact because she was unconscious.

It so happened that this was a charismatic tent meeting, so several people gathered around Susan, laid their hands on her and prayed over her in tongues. Susan regained consciousness speaking in tongues. The people all rejoiced and told Susan that she was saved, delivered and filled with the Holy Spirit. Unfortunately, Susan had ab-solutely NO idea how to get saved or what it meant to be saved. She did not know who Jesus was or what He had done. The people at that tent meeting had made a very serious error. They thought that the Holy Spirit works in some sort of magic way, knocking people unconscious and setting everything right while they are out. This just is not so! The demons knocked Susan out, and she most certainly was not saved or delivered!
(Doorways: false tongues)

The one good thing that came out of that experience was that Susan decided that now that she was "saved and filled with the Holy Spirit" that she should get a Bible and find a church. She did get a Bible, but never spent any time reading it as she could not understand it.

She joined a charismatic Episcopal Church and decided to "go straight." She attended the church less than three months when she was invited to join their counseling staff. Susan still wasn't saved! But, because of her experience

Chapter 12
Deliverance

with T.M. and hypnosis, she quickly became expert at their counselling techniques of inner healing via visualization and self-hypnosis.
(Doorways: TM, hypnosis, inner healing, visualization, self-hypnosis)

Because Susan decided to "go straight," she was encouraged to get married as a solution to her lesbian problem. She married a young man who was also on the counseling staff of the church. That marriage lasted only six months because Susan soon found out that this man was a hard-core satanist and she was scared to death by the things he did.
(Doorways: demons from husband who was a satanist)

After her divorce, she left the church and quickly fell back into her old pattern of lesbian relationships and violent quarrels. Six months before I met her, Susan came across my first book. It was as she read the book that she accepted Jesus Christ as her Lord and Savior and severed her relationship with her current lesbian partner. She came to me six months later for help. That is when Susan was finally and completely delivered.

You may think this story is unusual, but let me tell you that this type of history is COMMON! I cannot begin to count the number of People I have counselled with who have very similar stories.

From Susan's history, I not only gained a list of doorways, but I also knew that she had the link established between her soul and spirit because of her contact with the spirit world. This was first established at the age of fourteen when she started to train in witchcraft, mediumship and astral-projection.

Chapter 12
Deliverance

Susan had a severe problem with a passive mind because of her extensive practice of Transcendental Meditation and self-hypnosis. By the time I saw her, she was having difficulty holding a steady job because she could no longer control when her mind would blank out. She would go blank at crucial times and lose her job as a result. The problem of a passive mind proved to be the worst thing Susan had to deal with after deliverance.

Here is a list of her doorways, and here is how we approached her deliverance.

Doorways:
> inheritance -- Masonry, Shriners, mental illness, and inheritance from father unknown. However, because of the history, there is sure to be some inheritance from her father, so that was broken as well.
> Roman Catholicism -- baptism, confirmation,
> communion
> incest
> beastiality
> multiple sexual contacts in her teens
> witchcraft
> mediumship
> tarot cards
> voodoo
> hypnosis
> ouija board
> astral-projection
> T.M.
> drugs

Chapter 12
Deliverance

> drunkenness

> lesbianism -- multiple partners

> violence & murder

> demon of false tongues

> visualization

> inner healing practices including self-hypnosis

> demons from husband who was a satanist

Deliverance Procedure:

STEP 1: Susan reaffirmed her acceptance of Jesus Christ as her Lord and Savior. She prayed specifically asking the Lord Jesus Christ to become her total Master as well.

Then she made a statement out loud telling Satan and his demons that she was now a servant of Jesus Christ and would never serve them again as long as she lived.

STEP 2: Susan worked through the list of doorways. She checked off each one as she finished it. Closing the doorways is a two step procedure. Here are samples.

PRAYER: Father, in the name of Jesus, I humbly ask you to cleanse me from everything I have inherited from both my father and mother. I refuse to have anything from Satan in my life. Please break those lines of inheritance forever. I thank you for it in the name of Jesus.

STATEMENT: In the name of Jesus Christ my Lord, I now command every demon that came into me by inheritance to leave me at once! In the name of Jesus Christ, I break any and all oaths taken by my relatives in Masonry and Shriners that are binding upon their offspring. I command every demon associated with Masonry and the Shriners to leave me at once in the name of Jesus Christ my Lord!

PRAYER: Heavenly Father, in the name of Jesus Christ, I ask you to forgive me for my involvement in Roman Catholicism. Please cleanse me from all of those sins. I ask you for it and thank you for it in the name of Jesus.

STATEMENT: In the name of Jesus Christ my Lord, I renounce all of my involvement in Roman Catholicism. In the name of Jesus I command every demon that came into me through Catholic baptism, confirmation and communion and any other practices that I may have participated in to leave me at once!

PRAYER: Father, in the precious name of Jesus Christ Your Son, I ask you to forgive me and cleanse me for the sin of incest with my stepfather. I thank you for forgiveness, in the name of Jesus.

STATEMENT: In the name of Jesus Christ, I command every demon that came into me through all the sexual relationships I had with my stepfather to leave me now!

PRAYER: Father, in the name of Jesus, I humbly ask you to forgive me for participating in beastiality. Please cleanse me completely for this terrible sin. Thank you so much for cleansing me in the name of Jesus.

STATEMENT: In the name of Jesus Christ my Lord, I now command every demon that came into me through the practice of beastiality to leave me at once!

PRAYER: Father, in the name of Jesus, I ask you to completely cleanse me from all the many sins I committed in the many sexual contacts I had during my teenage years. I now recognize all of that to be an abomination to you and repent for those sins. Thank you for your cleansing in the name of Jesus Christ. She also repented of specific relationships by name as much as she could remember.

STATEMENT: In the name of Jesus Christ, I now command every demon that came into me through the many sexual contacts I had in my teenage years to leave me at once!

PRAYER: Father, in the precious name of Jesus, I humbly ask your forgiveness for all of my involvement in witchcraft. I renounce all of that and repent for it and will never do it again. Please, Father, cleanse me from all of that sin. I thank you for it in the name of Jesus Christ.

STATEMENT: In the name of Jesus Christ, I completely renounce all of my involvement in witchcraft. I command every demon that came into me through my practice of witchcraft to leave me at once in the name of Jesus!

PRAYER: Father, in the name of Jesus, I ask your forgiveness for allowing my body to be used as a medium for demons to speak through. I humbly ask you to completely cleanse me from my sins of functioning as a spiritualist medium. I thank you for it in the precious name of Jesus.

STATEMENT: In the name of Jesus Christ my Lord, I hereby renounce all of my involvement as a spiritualist medium. I command every demon who came into me as a result of my functioning as a medium to leave me at once! etc., etc.

In this way, Susan worked through every doorway she had opened. She confessed her sin and repented for it, asking God the Father for cleansing. Then she commanded the demons that came into her through that sin to leave.

Chapter 12
Deliverance

STEP 3: Because Susan had been involved in witchcraft, mediumship, astral-projection, hypnosis, T.M. and visualization, we knew that she was very much in communication with the spirit world. She had learned to control her spirit body, thereby establishing that demonic link between her soul and spirit. In people who have developed communication with the spirit world, I then have them do a final general clearing after closing all the doorways.

GENERAL CLEARING:
> spirit
> sever between soul and spirit
> mind
> will
> emotions
> physical body

PRAYER: (Spirit) Father, in the name of Jesus, I ask you to forgive me for my sinful use of my spirit and to completely cleanse my spirit of any remaining demons. I ask you to seal it so that no one can ever control it again except You. I thank you for this in the name of Jesus.

STATEMENT: Now, in the name of Jesus Christ my Lord, I command every demon remaining in, or afflicting my spirit, to leave me at once! Never again will my spirit be used to serve Satan or any of you demons.

PRAYER: (Sever between soul and spirit) Father, in the name of Jesus, I ask you to completely and forever take away my ability to communicate with the spirit world in any way, except what the Holy Spirit wants me to receive. Therefore, I am asking you to once and for all sever between my soul and spirit as in Hebrews 4:12 and remove all demons that give me the ability to control my spirit and communicate with the spirit world.

STATEMENT: In the name of Jesus Christ, I command all demons linking my soul and spirit which give me the ability to communicate with the spirit world and astral-project to leave me at once!

PRAYER: (mind) Father, in the name of Jesus Christ I ask you to completely cleanse and heal and renew my mind. I ask your forgiveness for all those times I deliberately gave up the control of my mind. I want to use my mind to serve and honor YOU. Please help me to regain the control of my mind. I thank you for it in the name of Jesus Christ.

STATEMENT: In the name of Jesus Christ, I command every demon left in my mind, or afflicting my mind, to leave me at once!

PRAYER: (will) Father, in the name of Jesus Christ, I ask you to forgive me for using my will to participate in so much sin. I also ask you to forgive me for allowing my will to become so passive to allow the demons to control me. Please cleanse my will and send your Holy Spirit to work in my will to help me to will to do your good pleasure. (Phil 2:13)

STATEMENT: In the name of Jesus Christ my Lord, I command every demon in my will or afflicting my will to leave me at once!

PRAYER: (emotion) Father, in the name of Jesus, I ask you to forgive me for all my hatred and bitterness and lust and every other sinful emotion. Please forgive me for living to please my own emotions. Please cleanse my emotions and heal them so that they will be pleasing to you.

Chapter 12
Deliverance

STATEMENT: In the name of Jesus Christ my Lord, I command every demon in my emotions or afflicting my emotions to leave me at once!

PRAYER: (physical body) Heavenly Father, I humbly and sincerely repent for all the terrible things I have done with my body, sinning against you. In the name of Jesus, I ask you to completely cleanse my body and heal it. Please, Lord, help me to use my physical body to glorify you and to honor you in everything I do. I thank you for it in the precious name of Jesus.

STATEMENT: In the name of Jesus Christ, I command every demon left within my physical body to leave me at once!

COMMENTS: Susan had great difficulty in kicking out the demons that came into her though T.M., hypnosis and visualization. She had spent many hours blanking her mind in her extensive use of T.M. As she tried to command those demons to come out, she would lose consciousness or become very confused. She struggled for an hour or more, binding those demons over and over again until at last she established authority over them. She prayed and asked the Lord to help her and strengthen her as she exerted her will against blanking out her mind for the first time in her life.

Post Deliverance Follow-up:

After deliverance, Susan continued to have a struggle with her mind. She had allowed her mind to become extremely passive. She forced herself into a scripture memory program. During the first few weeks, she fell repeatedly by allowing her mind to go blank. Each time she realized that her mind had blanked for a period of time, she immediately confessed that as sin and commanded the demons that had come back into her during the time she was blanked

Chapter 12
Deliverance

out, to leave at once in the name of Jesus Christ. The struggle was intense, but over a period of months, Susan gradually regained more and more control of her mind. As she did so, she was again able to hold a steady job.

Susan also had a struggle learning to walk by faith rather than feelings. She was used to living with many emotional extremes. Emotional highs, lust and many emotional lows as well. She wanted to feel God's love and experience emotional highs by feeling God's love. She wanted to feel joy and desire to read the scriptures, rather than doing so out of obedience in spite of how she felt. Over the months, as she set her will to walk in obedience to God's commandments in the Bible in spite of her feelings, her emotions began to smooth out so that she did not experience such great emotional swings.

Anyone who is infested with demons for so many years like Susan was, must understand that it takes a minimum of one year to stabilize after deliverance. It takes time and persistence AND OBEDIENCE to God's word to develop a walk with the Lord in faith. Be patient. The Lord WILL make big changes in your life, but it does take time.

Case #2. Ron (not his real name), 30 years old

Ron came to me with the chief complaint that he could no longer read his Bible or pray, except in tongues. He had almost continual abdominal pain, difficulty sleeping and much depression. He had been seeking help from various churches for the past year without success. His mother came across my books and asked Ron to read them. After reading them, he called and asked to see me. I agreed, and counselled with Ron with a pastor who works with me. I wish to emphasize again that I NEVER counsel with men alone. I always work with another brother in Christ who leads the session.

Here is Ron's story as we began to question him about his life.

Ron was born to Christian parents who were missionaries in Mexico. He did not know of any problems of inheritance as both of his parents came from a long line of Christian families.

All went well until Ron turned sixteen. At that time, his folks came back to the U.S. for a year. During that time, his mother fell into adultery and the marriage split as a result. In the emotional struggle Ron went through over his parent's divorce, he sought the Lord personally for the first time. He accepted Jesus Christ as his Lord and Savior. He had a deep experience with the Lord and became very enthusiastic to serve the Lord. Reading his Bible and praying was his joy.

About six months after his salvation, Ron was asked to go to a Christian camp for a youth revival. He went and greatly enjoyed the weekend. The camp was a good one except for one thing. They taught wrongly about the baptism of the Holy Spirit. At the end of the last service at the camp which was a very emotional one, an invitation was given to all those who wanted to receive the baptism of the Holy Spirit. Of course Ron wanted it, so he went up to the altar for prayer. Unfortunately, the people at the altar were told to close their eyes and hold up their arms and hands. Then they were told to shake their arms and hands, relaxing them, and then to completely stop controlling their arms and hands, to clear out their minds and give up the control of their mind and body to the "Holy Spirit." They were told that, as they did this, that the Holy Spirit would then be free to come into them and completely take them over. Ron was too young a

Chapter 12
Deliverance

Christian to realize the error in this teaching, so he tried to follow the instructions completely.

Ron said that, as he began to relax his arms and hands and try to clear his mind of thoughts, he suddenly felt something take hold of his hands. Then he felt a charge of energy go down his arms into his stomach with such force that it knocked him over backwards. He felt like a ball of fire was in his stomach which spread up into his chest and he began to speak in tongues. He was overjoyed and went home thinking that he had been baptized by the Holy Spirit. Unfortunately, Ron had fulfilled the conditions to receive a demon by blanking his mind and giving up the control of his body.

Shortly after the camp, someone gave Ron a book on how to hear the Lord speak to you. This book taught that a Christian must blank out his mind or clear his mind of all thoughts and wait quietly on the Lord so that the Holy Spirit can speak to them. This is, of course, completely in error, but Ron accepted it as truth because that is how he started speaking in tongues at the camp meeting. As Ron practiced, he learned to blank out his mind quickly and experienced many times of emotional ecstasy which he interpreted as experiencing the presence of the Lord. Through these times of meditation, Ron obtained three spirit guides. What do you suppose they called themselves? "Father, Son and Holy Spirit" of course. What else would demon spirit guides call themselves to a Christian. Of course Ron did not realize that these were demon spirit guides. He thought he was hearing from the Lord. He had long conversations with the "lord" and received many directions from these spirits. However, Ron should have realized that he was not hearing from the true Lord when the spirits began to lead him into sin. They told Ron that he was "special" and twisted and turned scripture to condone all sorts of sin that went directly against God's commandments.

Chapter 12
Deliverance

Ron went to a Christian college and then on to seminary. While he was in school, his three spirit guides quickly lead him into pornography, multiple sexual relationships, and, finally, homosexuality.

Ron finished school and became an associate pastor in a large charismatic church in Texas. He was the youth pastor. While in this church, he became involved in inner healing using visualization and guided imagery. Because of his ability to blank his mind and contact the spirit world, he became expert at these techniques and was much in demand on the counselling staff of the church. He steadily drew more and more of the young boys into a homosexual experience, all the time justifying his sins by his three demon spirit guides.

After about three years working as a youth pastor, God, in His mercy began to work in Ron's life.A Christian brother came to Ron's church and challenged him, telling him that his experiences in the spirit world were NOT of God. Ron was shocked and could not accept the possibility that he was being deceived. Then, as a result of this brother's challenge, Ron began to get convicted that his homosexual encounters were sin. He decided to go straight and get married. Ron began to date a young woman who was also on the counselling staff at the church. However, this girl was a witch. She wanted to marry Ron, and began to bring him under her control. Ron got scared when he realized that this girl was controlling his whole life. He tried to break off their relationship and that's when the trouble began. Every time Ron was not physically in this girl's presence, he experienced severe abdominal pain. He quickly reached the point where he could not read his Bible at all nor could he pray, except in tongues. Frightened and depressed, Ron ran. He quit his job as associate pastor at that church and went north to another state seeking help to get free from the incantations the witch had placed on him. He went from

Chapter 12
Deliverance

church to church for a year without any help. That's when he came to us.

We talked to Ron extensively, making up a list of doorways. Ron had great difficulty accepting the fact that the three spirits he heard from so regularly were actually demon spirit guides. We showed him from scripture that these spirits proved their nature by the fact that they had led Ron into all sorts of sexual sins. For the first time, Ron had to squarely face the fact that God did NOT make any special exceptions to His commandments as the spirit guides had told Ron.

Ron was particularly hesitant to give up his tongues. He argued that the only way he could pray was in tongues. That in itself was proof that his tongues were not from the Holy Spirit. The demons had Ron in so much bondage that he literally could not pray in English. He could do so only under the control of the demon in a demonic tongue.

We spent several hours with Ron helping him to pray through all the doorways to repent and close them and command the demons to leave. As Ron prayed, the Lord did a remarkable work, steadily revealing to him more sins that he had forgotten to tell us about. After Ron had closed each doorway individually, he went through and also did a general clearing of spirit, severing between soul and spirit, soul and body, as I described in Case #1. After it was all over, we were all exhausted.

We heaved a big sigh of relief and sat back on the floor from where we had been kneeling. "Wow, Ron," I remarked, "the Holy Spirit really did a powerful work in you. Wasn't that wonderful how He kept showing you areas you had forgotten to tell us about?"

Chapter 12
Deliverance

Ron shook his head saying, "Yes, I guess so, but I don't think anything happened."

"What do you mean?" I asked.

"I mean, I don't think any of the demons left because I didn't feel anything."

It was only the grace of the Lord that kept me from wringing Ron's neck right there on the spot. It was very late and we had all just spent about five exhausting hours with him, and he didn't think anything had happened because he didn't FEEL anything! This is a very good demonstration of the trap so many thousands of Christians have fallen into. If they don't FEEL something, they don't think anything has happened !

THERE IS NO FEELING IN FAITH!

FOLLOW-UP:

Ron had a very difficult year after his deliverance. He continually demanded emotional rewards, and felt that the Lord was not interested in a relationship with him because He did not give Ron the feelings he wanted. Ron also continued to have the abdominal pain though not as severe. I told him that the demons could and would create the same symptoms from the outside as from the inside. But Ron refused to accept any discomfort at all. I urged him to go for a complete medical evaluation, which he did. The doctors were unable to find anything physically wrong. The pastor that helped me with Ron continued to counsel with him and eventually got Ron established in a good Christian church. I urged Ron to spend much time in Bible study and scripture memory. I also counselled him to ask the Lord to speak to him ONLY through the scriptures for a period of time because Ron was so used to receiving communication from demons.

It was a very rough year, but Ron began to grow spiritually and accept a walk in faith. He experienced an immediate release in prayer after deliverance and could read his Bible without difficulty. He obtained a secular job and brought discipline into his life. I lost contact with him after a year, but by that time his abdominal pain had stopped and he was actively growing in the Lord.

It grieves my heart as I see such terrible damage being done through wrong teaching to young people who are on fire to serve the Lord. How many Rons are there in our churches today? I think we would be amazed if we knew. How these things must grieve the heart of our Lord. I cannot praise the Lord enough for His patience and marvelous grace in our lives and the lives of such people as Ron. Truly, Jesus did come to set the captives free!

Case #3 - Sam (not his real name), 18 years old

Sam was 18 years old when we first saw him. He heard about my books through a Bible study he was attending, but had not read them by the time he came to me. He came to me because of a horrifying experience he had two weeks previously. He was seeking an explanation for the experience.

Sam was in his bedroom one evening when suddenly he smelled a terrible odor like burning sulphur. Suddenly two huge demons came up through the floor of his bedroom and appeared to him. The demons told him that he was not the Christian he thought he was. They said that he was actually serving Satan and that Satan was demanding that Sam sign a contract in his own blood selling himself body, soul and spirit to Satan. They went on to say that Sam must demonstrate his absolute faithfulness and submission to Satan by killing the teacher of his current Bible study.

After telling Sam all of this, the demons vanished as suddenly as they had come. Sam wondered at first if he had been dreaming, but the whole experience was far too real to be a dream. He talked to his Bible study teacher about the episode and she referred him to me.

To say that Sam was shaken up is to put it very mildly. Prior to that visit by the demons, Sam had not even believed they existed and certainly never believed they could come to see him!

Quite obviously, there had to be a lot more to Sam's story than this one visit by demons. I want to emphasize again that you must not get side tracked looking at symptoms or one occurrence. There is ALWAYS a root cause.

I asked Sam to tell me about his life in as much detail as he could remember. This is his story.

Sam was born to Christian parents. He was raised in a very strict Christian home and attended only Christian schools. At the age of five, Sam had a visitation by Jesus and was called to preach the gospel. As a result, all of his life, Sam had planned to become a pastor.

All went well until Sam turned thirteen years old. Suddenly, to his horror, Sam began to experience very strong homosexual desires! Sam had never been sexually molested or participated in pornography or homosexuality of any kind. He did not listen to Rock music, go to movies, or even watch TV except on rare occasions. Sam knew from God's word that homosexuality is an abomination to the Lord. He did not dare talk with anyone about the problem because

Chapter 12
Deliverance

he did not know anyone who would understand. Sam struggled alone with the homosexual urges. He did not participate in any homosexual act of any kind. The more he struggled to put the urges and desires out of his mind, the worse they seemed to get.

At the age of fifteen, Sam entered a Christian high school. The homosexual desires grew steadily in intensity such that Sam fell into a deep depression over the problem which seemed to have no solution. His grades began to suffer as he had always made very high grades. By the end of his first year in high school, Sam was so depressed that he tried to commit suicide by taking a large overdose of pills. He was rushed to the hospital unconscious, but his life was saved.

Sam went to the pastor of his church for counseling, but could not bring himself to tell the pastor his true problem. The whole suicide attempt was passed off as a reaction to the stress of a new school and the first year of high school.

When Sam entered his second year, he started drinking alcohol to try to cope with his depression. As the alcohol took away Sam's inhibitions, he began to experiment with homosexual contacts. He hated what he was doing and knew it was wrong, but could not stop himself. His life became an endless cycle of repentance and crying out to God to help him, then depression because no help came, then drinking to cope with the depression, then homosexual experiences and back to guilt and repentance. Over and over the cycle continued throughout his last three years at high school. Sam noticed that immediately after his first physical homosexual encounter, he suddenly had a violent temper and had trouble controlling blind rages. Sam had never had a problem with a violent temper before. He found that thoughts of murdering someone filled his mind much of the time. This was something Sam had never experienced

Chapter 12
Deliverance

before. This increased his guilt, depression, drinking, and the whole vicious cycle.

After graduation from high school, Sam was enrolled in a Christian college where he planned to study to become a pastor. He cut off his contact with his homosexual partners during the summer before college and started attending the extra Bible study in an effort to put an end to his problem. It was in August, one month before Sam was due to leave for college, that the demons appeared to him.

After listening to Sam's story, I knew we were facing two major problems. Demons had come into Sam through the suicide attempt, drunkenness, and homosexual acts, of course. But, WHERE did the homosexual urges come from in the first place? Clearly from a demon within Sam, but what was the doorway?

The second problem was this. Sam clearly had a special calling by God. But from all Sam said, I was not convinced that he was even saved. I cannot count the number of people who come to me for counseling who have been raised in Christian homes and attended Christian churches all of their lives who are NOT saved. They just assume that they are!

First things first. I challenged Sam. "Sam, if you were to drop dead this very moment, where would you go -- heaven or hell?" He paused a moment and said soberly, "Well, I HOPE I would go to heaven." There was my answer. Sam wasn't saved, just as I suspected.

I went on to question him further. "Tell me Sam, did you give an answer to those demons?"

Chapter 12
Deliverance

Sam shook his head. "No, I wanted to tell them to get lost that I would never serve Satan, but I just couldn't. I don't understand why."

Clearly, Sam was demonically bound. The Christian brother with whom I was working on this occasion had never seen a case of demonic bondage preventing salvation, so I pushed Sam a bit more to clearly show this brother what was going on.

"Sam," I said, "choose right now who you are going to serve. Are you going to serve Satan, or are you going to serve Jesus Christ?"

Sam moved restlessly. "Rebecca, I want to choose, but I just can't. I really can't."

I got up and handed Sam a marker for the black board which was in the office. I went to the board and drew a line down the center. I wrote "Satan" on one side, "Jesus" on the other side. Then I asked Sam. "Here, you know scripture better than any eighteen year old I have ever met. I want you to write down the pros and cons of serving Satan and serving Jesus. Then make your decision.

Sam went to the board and wrote down scripture after scripture. It didn't take him long to fill up the board. When he was finished he turned to us and said, "The answer is obvious. There is NO benefit at all in serving Satan."

"O.K.," I said, "then make your decision, Sam. WHO are you going to serve!"

Sam sat down in defeat. "I want to decide for Jesus, but I just can't. Oh, it is useless. I am unable to make a decision."

Chapter 12
Deliverance

"No it isn't, Sam. What you don't realize is that the demons within you are literally binding you from accepting Christ. In fact, they have bound you from infancy. You know you are called by Jesus Christ into a ministry, but you have never been able to actually make Jesus your Lord and Savior, have you?"

Sam nodded. "Yes, that is correct. I couldn't tell anyone in my family or at church. They all knew I had been visited by Jesus at the age of five. They all knew I was called to preach. How could I tell them that I wasn't even saved? I just couldn't!"

Pastors, just how many people are in YOUR congregations with this terrible problem? I urge you to get on your face before the Lord and find out. Then talk to your people. Let them know these sorts of problems exist so they won't be afraid to talk to you about it.

I then asked the Christian brother working with me to anoint Sam with oil and take authority over the demons inside of him and bind them in the name of Jesus Christ. He did so.

Before Jack had completely finished his prayer Sam scrambled out of his chair and fell onto his knees on the floor, tears streaming down his face. He cried and cried and prayed asking Jesus to forgive him and wash away his sins with His precious blood. He asked Jesus Christ to become his Lord and Savior and Master and completely committed his life to Christ. Sam spent some time weeping before the Lord and confessing his sins. He got up off that floor a different boy, I can tell you.

Once Sam was really saved, then we started looking for the root cause of his problem. It has been my experience that demons of sexual sins that are either inherited or placed in

Chapter 12
Deliverance

children at a very young age, raise their ugly heads at puberty. When the hormones begin to flow as youngsters reach the age of 12 to 14 years old, the sexual demons rise up to take over. This is what had happened with Sam.

Sam did not have any childhood doorways that we could discover. We then turned our attention to the possibility of inheritance. Sam's mother was from generations of Christians. But his father's story was different. Prior to marrying his mother, Sam's father had been a man with a multitude of sexual encounters, although Sam did not know of any homosexuality in his father. Sam's mother became engaged to his father knowing that he was not a Christian. Finally, the night before their wedding, his mother told her husband-to-be that if he did not accept Christ that night that there would be no wedding the following day. Sam's father made a profession of faith that night, but one wonders just how sincere it was. Sam said that their marriage was not a particularly happy one, but that to his knowledge, his father had never had any sexual encounters outside of the marriage. He attended church regularly, though not very enthusiastically. There was the source of Sam's inheritance -- His father.

Sam then went through and confessed all the doorways and kicked out all the demons that had come into him through those doorways. To review, his doorways were:

> inheritance

> suicide attempt

> drunkenness

> homosexual acts

> violence

Chapter 12
Deliverance

It has been my experience, as I remarked earlier, that violence and murder go hand in hand with demons of homosexuality. I don't know why that is, it just is a fact.

After Sam finished kicking out all the demons, I said to him, "Sam, you now have one piece of unfinished business to take care of."

He looked at me questioningly. "What is that?"

"You have not yet given those demons and Satan a direct answer to their demand that you serve them."

A big grin came on Sam's face. He jumped to his feet. "You're right!" he exclaimed. "Satan and you demons! I will NEVER serve you as long as I live! I am NOW a servant of Jesus Christ and will serve Him forever. In the precious name of Jesus Christ my Lord, I command you to leave me forever and ever!"

I have remained in contact with Sam for two years following his deliverance. He continued to have a struggle with homosexual urges in his thoughts. The demons placed these into his mind from the outside. He put himself on a scripture memory program and vigorously disciplined his mind to take every thought captive to make it obedient to Jesus. (II Cor. 10:5) The battle has not been easy, but Sam in growing in the Lord and has not fallen into drunkenness or homosexuality since his deliverance. I praise God for His wondrous work in Sam's life!

★★★★★★★★★★★★★★★★★★★★★★★★★★★★★

I could write a book of case histories alone. However, I believe these three will give you a good example of how to approach a deliverance. I have written a separate chapter on the deliverance of those who have been involved in Satanism. I will briefly touch on a few other areas here.

Chapter 12
Deliverance

Deliverance of those involved in Asian religions.

This is an area of deliverance in which I will freely admit that I have more questions than answers. Those people who become involved in Asian religions and Eastern forms of meditation develop EXTREMELY passive minds. The other major problem is the massive use of brainwashing techniques and hypnosis. There are deep demonic "hooks" left in their minds. These "hooks" can be a sight, a word, a gesture, or just a smell which will trigger a trance and complete demonic control. I do not, at this point, know how to go about removing these demonic "hooks." Such a person can seem to be completely delivered, but will suddenly go into a trance (a state where their mind goes blank and they lose control) for no known reason. This state, of course, allows the demons to come flooding back into them. I am seeing a very great deal of this in people coming out of various involvements in the New Age Movement.

Those people who come under the control of the various gurus take an additional very dangerous step. You see, the Western world satanists KNOW they are doing wrong, but they are willing to do it to gain power. Those people who come completely under the control of a guru, LOSE the ability to distinguish wrong from right and accept evil as being good. I have never yet seen anyone in such a state delivered.

The major problem with EVERYONE coming out of an Eastern form of meditation and Asian religions is overcoming their passive mind! Beware. The one thing that hinders demons from freely operating through a human being is their free will. God has given each one of us the precious gift of free will. The goal of all Asian forms of religion is to get the human being to TOTALLY give up their free will. This enables the demons to take them over and use them however they want.

Chapter 12
Deliverance

I believe that it is a serious sin to give up our free will. God himself does not override our free will. Scripture tells us that the Holy Spirit works in us to enable us to will to do God's will. (Phil. 2:13) I frequently have people ask God for forgiveness for giving up their free will and ask Him to restore their free will to them. This seems to be a key to helping them establish dominance over the demons within them.

Deliverance of Children

I cannot emphasize strongly enough the need to deliver children at a very early age. Parents, if you have had to close doorways in your own lives, then you MUST sever the lines of inheritance in your children and command the demons to leave which they inherited. I wrote about the deliverance of children in "*Prepare For War*," so I will not repeat that information here. I just want to add a few notes.

The deliverance of children who have been raised by parents involved in the occult is VERY difficult. This is another area in which I have more questions than answers. Once a child reaches the age of about four years, he/she quickly learns to control the demons within them. It is at this point where the terrible trouble starts! Little children have great difficulty being consistent. But, more than that, it is very difficult to persuade a small child that he/she should NOT do something that benefits them. Once you kick the demons out, the first time the child wants something he cannot get, he will ask the demons to come back in so he can use them to get what he wants! The cycle seems to be endless!

Don't ever under estimate the demonic strength children can wield. I had one little six year old boy live in my home for four months. He had been raised in a satanic coven. He was so very powerful in his use of witchcraft that he killed

Chapter 12
Deliverance

one of our pets just by looking at it, broke one of my bones with one of his incantations, and nearly killed two other people. This child had been specially birthed for a high position in the craft and was given very powerful demons at birth. We tried to bring him to Christ, but he refused to leave the demons out for more than a day or so at a time because he always wanted to use them for his benefit. He controlled every kid in his class at school and the teachers as well. When he started first grade, he was reading at third grade level within two days. Of course, his demon spirit guide did the reading for him. We could always tell the few days when this boy did not have his demons because he flunked every paper he did at school that day. He would make perfect scores on everything the other days.

Parents, be alert for symptoms of demonization in your children. Any signs of sexual maturity or function or interest in children beyond what is normal for their age should be a very strong warning signal. Attempts to kill -- either humans or animals is a sure sign. Frequent nightmares with demonic contents, and the many symptoms I gave in the chapter on "Ritualistic Child Abuse" in "Prepare For War" should never be overlooked.

I strongly recommend Dr. Dobson's book "The Strong Willed Child." This book does not deal with demon possessed children, but the principles in the book will be most helpful to any parent with such a child. Parents MUST be absolutely consistent in their discipline of such children. The child must be taught that life is much more pleasant when they keep the demons out than when they let them in.

Parents must command the demons within the child to be bound before punishing the child, or the child will use his demons so that he will feel no pain at all. (See next chapter for additional information on deliverance in cases of ritualistic abuse.)

Chapter 12
Deliverance

Parents, be alert to the toys and cartoons your children play with and watch. One of the most common spirit guides I am finding in children is She-Ra, princess of darkness from the He-man cartoon. When I ask the child how he/she knew She-Ra was a spirit, the answer always is, "as I played with her and watched the cartoon she came and told me so."

Deliverance of those involved in Roman Catholicism

The basic problem of Roman Catholicism is the idolatry that is practiced. I would urge the reader to look at the chapter on Catholicism in *"Prepare For War."* I find four common symptoms in people who have come out of Roman Catholicism and accepted Christ but were never delivered.

> An almost continual struggle to gain assurance of salvation.

> A strong, tormenting desire or compulsion to go back and partake of Catholic communion.

> A tendency towards self-mutilation because of the penance that is commonly practiced within the church.

Some have frequent visions or experiences in the spirit world. This comes from the occultic communication and prayers to the spirits of dead people such as Mary and the various saints. Establishment of the link between the soul and spirit is rather common.

Symptoms which occur with the link between soul and spirit:

> Frequent visions or communication with the spirit world.

> Ability to control when a person will receive a vision or communication from the spirit world.

> Ability to see auras. Auras are various types and colors of light around people and things.

Chapter 12
Deliverance

> Ability to "see" demons frequently.

History of involvement in any of the following:
> Astral-projection or other out-of-the-body experiences
> Visualization and guided imagery
> Any form of Eastern meditation or anything that blanks the mind.
> Ability to see spirits in a mirror, or changes in a reflection in a mirror.
> Ability to "see" the game in D&D or other fantasy role-playing games.
> Sexual contacts with spirits -- always be alert to these, they are common!
> Ability to levitate objects.
> Ability to see and/or hear demon spirits.
> Anyone who has served as a spiritualist medium or channel
> Involvement in the martial arts.
> Involvement in biofeedback.
> Hypnosis -- especially the ability to hypnotize somebody else.
> Contact with UFOs or extraterrestrials.

Sex with demons

This is an area that very few people are willing to write about because they are afraid of the ridicule it will bring. Most Christians laugh at the very thought and say it is impossible. But the occultists know the reality of it, and so does the world.

Chapter 12
Deliverance

Just two months before the publication of this book CBS put a two hour film on prime time TV called "The Entity." "The Entity" is a film telling a true story that happened in Los Angeles in 1976 and was researched by people from UCLA. It is the story of a young woman with three children who is divorced and raising her children alone. Suddenly, she was attacked and raped by an unseen being one evening. The attacks continued and involved the children and eventually the researchers. That film broke my heart! How accurately it portrayed the utter helplessness of any human being in the face of demonic power! If only that woman had been a Christian and had known the power available through the name of Jesus Christ! At the end of the film, it said that she had moved to Texas, but now, more than ten years later, was still suffering from these attacks, though not as frequently. How I pray that our Lord will bring this woman across the path of some Christian who will not laugh at her or say that what she is experiencing is impossible, but will share with her the answer -- the power in our wonderful Lord Jesus Christ!

If you want to read another book that deals briefly with these problems, it is *Earth's Earliest Ages*, by G.H. Pember. It is available through Kregel Publications, Grand Rapids, Michigan. Genesis 6:8 and other scriptures leave us little doubt of the validity of these people's experiences. Such sexual sin is an abomination to our Lord! But, we Christians MUST be able to help people be set free from captivity to this form of sin.

People in all forms of witchcraft, Satanism and eastern religions ALL experience sexual intercourse of various sorts with spirits. In Asian countries this is called "astral-sex." How does it occur? The physical partner experiences all the physical sensations of sex although the partner is a spirit and not physical at all.

Chapter 12
Deliverance

People involved in Satanism commonly have sex with demons. The problem is, once they turn to Christ, the demons are unwilling to give them up. There is a very real struggle after deliverance to fight off the demons who would come and rape the person time after time.

The only way is to FIGHT! I remember one young woman in her thirties I worked with who had been extensively used and abused sexually, in the craft. After salvation and deliverance, she had a terrible time with demons coming at night to rape her. At first, she gave in because of the terrible physical pain involved if she tried to resist them. Every time she gave in, many demons would be placed into her through the sexual encounter.

We talked extensivey about the problem. Finally, I showed her the scripture in Hebrews:

> "Ye have not yet resisted unto blood, striving against sin." Hebrews 12:4

I told her that she must ask the Lord for extra grace to bear any pain involved in resisting the demonic onslaught to the bitter end. She finally did this. The next time a demon came to have sex with her, she started rebuking it in the name of Jesus and commanding it to be bound and leave at once. The demons created very severe pain in her, but she hung on and continued to rebuke it and command it to leave in the name of Jesus. No matter how much pain the demon inflicted, this woman had made up her mind that she would resist to the end. This she did, and the demon finally left without being able to complete the sexual act. It only took about three times of such battling and she had the complete victory.

Another common tactic is for demons to come to rape someone and hit them while they are asleep. If the person

Chapter 12
Deliverance

will pray before going to sleep and ask the Holy Spirit to wake them up and alert them just before the demon attacks, they can start rebuking and commanding the demon to stop and leave just before it hits. In this way, it is possible to have the victory. Many times sexual encounters with demons will be interpreted as being "dreams", but the person awakes sexually aroused. This can be the cause of frequent "wet-dreams" in men. The sin of masterbation frequently leads to sex with demon spirits because of the intensive visualization involved. Jesus taught that if a person "lusted" in his/her mind, that they had already committed the sexual sin. I believe this applies to masterbation also.

These problems are very real, brothers and sisters in Christ. We as Christian workers must have much patience and love to help people to have victory in these areas.

Over and over again I have emphasized the need for the Christian to purge or cleanse himself. At the time this book was being prepared for printing, I received a beautiful letter from a young lady who took the information given in *Prepare For War* and completely cleansed herself through the power of Jesus Christ. I want to print a portion of that letter here to encourage the readers that you CAN cleanse yourself.

> "When I first read your book, there was so much valuable information that I read it once, then went back to take notes. The Holy Spirit really opened my eyes and heart to dealing with some things. I had been trying to cast the demons out of myself for about a year prior to reading your book. One thing the Holy Spirit showed me was that I was actually trying to name and cast each and every demon out - oops. Your book helped me to cast out the head demon and his underlings and all their doorways. Much easier of course.

Chapter 12
Deliverance

"All this time I was casting out 'surface' demons -- at least the ones I knew about. Many times the Lord would bring something else to my attention to cast out. NONE of this was easy, it was terrible. But they actually left and then there would be worse and deeper ones to cast out. The Lord was very gracious to me during this time as He wouldn't give me too much to handle and always gave me rests. AND, gave me a beautiful Christian husband that would be there with the Bible and prayer whenever I needed it (which was A LOT). We kept going deeper and deeper to the demons that I could handle (sounds easy in this letter, eh? It WASN'T.) But I got to a stop and knew I wasn't completely delivered. Then I got your book *Prepare For War* and did what you told me to. Later, I did everything you wrote about in Chapter 17.

"Because I was never involved in the occult like Elaine, I didn't think I could have a guiding spirit, or a demon that connected me to the spirit world. But the Lord kept bringing that section of your book to my attention and several things happened. One night I saw a 'Christian' girl that went to a church we had attended for awhile and didn't like. I kept telling my husband it wasn't a dream that I had actually seen her and that she must be a witch. That didn't go with your claim that the Lord doesn't want us to see in the spirit world (only Jesus will let us see if it's His will). So I realized I must have a demon that connected me to the spirit world.

"Finally one afternoon I went into a deep sleep and had a dream. In this dream was a man who was 'dark' and I had known him a long time and I 'trusted and loved' this man. He had kept me safe during my life! We were in a building and he put me in a boat and was driving the boat back to Egypt when we soared into a fog and hit a rock and the boat burst apart. Then I saw him laying like he was dead with candles around and other people (people? I couldn't see their faces) were weeping and saying that if I didn't want him to go he wouldn't. That I was responsible for his death.

Chapter 12
Deliverance

"Whew! When I awoke and told my husband about the dream he said it sounded like something he learned in art history. Because the water we were on wasn't a lake or ocean, but more like a river, my husband compared it to the burial practices of the pharaohs in Egypt. That they would actually build a boat for the dead person's journey on the river to the other side. I realized I did indeed have a guiding spirit because he drove the boat and the whole time always had me in something. I never got out by myself, he always directed everything! And the connecting demon was the river for the boat to go back and forth. I knew I had to cast them out.

"I sort of put it off because I was scared. I prayed and prayed. Then the day I was going to cast them out, I suddenly began to get tears in my flesh which started to bleed. It was scarey. My husband said I better get busy and cast them out because this was the worst I had ever been. So, we cast them out, then cast out all their underlings.

"This wasn't easy and the next day I was exhausted. Then I couldn't stop crying and later kept throwing up -- you know, a general terrible mess. We kept praying and reading the Bible and then I understood what it was. One of my major demons was what I will call 'Snatch.' He was put in me when I was a baby and he has snatched things away from me all my life. Memories, insight, the Lord Jesus trying to speak to me -- anything. Just 'POOF' and it was gone. That's why I couldn't remember anything and that's why other people such as a Christian counselor had such control over me. They would just have Snatch make things disappear so I wouldn't remember. He would also snatch any sound I would hear and many times I would be confused as if the things I heard were in my imagination or what.

"After casting him out, I suddenly saw a demon that I had actually bowed down to and given my soul to! We cast him out and I immediately fell asleep, but the

Chapter 12
Deliverance

dreams and visions were horrible so I prayed and the Lord commanded me to get rid of visions and all of his underlings and Imagination and all of his underlings and all of their doorways.

"I am exhausted. But, I have tears of real joy finally. Finally, I can have a conversation with Jesus and not have something snatch it away. Finally, I can memorize scriptures! Now Bible reading is such a joy. During the time I was casting out the demons, I was in terrible torment. But I claimed a sound mind because Jesus promised and I asked the Holy Spirit to restrain the demons so I could cast them out.

"A couple of days before the Lord revealed to me that I did indeed have those demons, I was given a decision. I could stay this way for the rest of my life or I could have the Lord clean them out. I decided to let Him clean them out because they were interfering with my walk with Jesus. I also understood it wouldn't be easy. it's like our walk with Jesus is a series of 'yes's' because He won't push or force.

"Rebecca, it's important for people to understand that, if you were born into the occult and even if you didn't have anything to do with them and was always forced, you still receive demons. Because of my parents they had legal ground. And casting out the demons is not a pleasant experience but it is worth it! A thousand times worth it so we can actually have the assurance that Jesus is real. Now, I have the assurance of an abundant life -- whatever He has in store for me. "

I extend my heartfelt thanks to the writer of this letter! I pray that many Christians will follow her example and step out boldly in faith to purge themselves. Let us ALL seek to become vessels of honor!

Chapter 12
Deliverance

Chapter 13

DELIVERANCE OF THOSE INVOLVED IN SATANISM

Satanism is a problem in our land that isn't going to just "go away." It is vast beyond anything that has been portrayed in the press. Every city and town has covens or groups of people who directly worship and serve Satan. Just about every junior high and high school has its own coven, IN-CLUDING some Christian schools. In addition to this, our country is being flooded with Asian religions which are another form of Satanism, and Egyptian and Caribbean cults (such as the Santeria), all forms of Satanism. EVERY religion that worships and serves demons is a form of Satanism, no matter what the demons are called -- energies, vibrations, pagan gods, spirit entities, etc.

At a police conference in February of 1986 in Las Vegas, it was estimated that there were approximately 40,000 - 60,000 "ritual homicides" (human sacrifices) in the U.S. in the previous year. I consider that estimate to be extremely conservative.

Recent press coverage of the human sacrifices performed at Matamoros, Mexico, in 1989, will shortly become daily events in the media. Everywhere, law enforcement depart-ments are beginning to try to educate police officers in the field of occult related crimes. Psychologists and psychiatrists are holding medical conferences to try to edu-cate themselves about how to deal with people involved in Satanism. Ritualistic child abuse is becoming a household word these days. Rock music stars and their albums are ped-dling blatant Satanism in their concerts, all through our music stores and on the popular MTV, every day. More and more hue and cry is being raised that we've got to stop the spread of Satanism amongst our teens. Unfortunately, the world, and many Christians, are turning to the psychiatrist and psychologist for the answers. Most do not realize that the field of psychiatry and psychology has probably the highest saturation of practicing satanists in it of any field of endeavor. The founding fathers of the whole field of psychology were deeply involved in the occult themselves!

We MUST turn our attention back to God's word for the answers. Jesus predicted that this would happen, so did Paul and many others. We are living in the "last days." Paul wrote in the second letter to Timothy this accurate description of the days in which we live.

> "This know also, that in the last days perilous times shall come. For men shall be lovers of their own selves, covetous, boasters, proud, blasphemers, disobedient to parents, unthankful, unholy, without natural affection, trucebreakers, false accusers, incontinent [no self control], fierce, despisers of those that are good, traitors, heady [conceited], highminded, lovers of pleasures more than lovers of God: having a form of godliness [religion], but denying the power thereof; from such turn away." II Timothy 3:1-5

That one simple paragraph describes in a nutshell any person who worships and serves Satan. Then Paul goes on to say:

> "Yea, and all that will live godly in Christ Jesus shall suffer persecution. But evil men and seducers shall wax worse and worse, deceiving and being deceived. But continue thou in the things which thou hast learned and hast been assured of, knowing of whom thou hast learned them; And that from a child thou hast known the holy scriptures, which are able to make thee wise unto salvation through faith which is in Christ Jesus.

Chapter 13
Deliverance of Those Involved in Satanism

All scripture is given by inspiration of God, and is
profitable for doctrine, for reproof, for correction, for
instruction in righteousness: That the man of God may
be perfect, thoroughly furnished unto all good works."
II Timothy 3:12-17

I believe that within a year or so of the publishing of this
book Christian churches will come under direct and open
attack by satanists. Recently, we were in South Carolina and
picked up a local newspaper. On the front page was a picture of a small local country Christian church. Across the
front of the church sprayed in black paint were the words
"Satan is God!" It won't be long, and those of us who serve
Jesus Christ will have to directly face those who serve Satan
in face-to-face confrontations.

In the month of May, 1989, I spoke with a pastor who is a
traveling evangelist. He told me of six churches that he personally knew of in the states of Texas and Oklahoma who's
doors were closed because of threats from the local
satanists. Neither the pastors nor the members of the
church were willing to stand up to the satanic death threats.
This same evangelist also told me of a church in Texas where
the pastor was approached by the high priest of the local
satanic coven who demanded the use of the church building. In this case the pastor told the high priest that he
couldn't have the building. The prompt response was a
death threat. The pastor answered, "In life or death, I will
serve Jesus. I am not afraid of death. You CANNOT use
this building!"

About two weeks later, the satanists broke into the church
and sacrificed a baby on the altar in the front of the church
and desecrated it, leaving the dead baby for the church
members to find. Still the pastor and some of the church
members stood for Christ. As a result, about three weeks
later, a revival broke out in that town, and many have come

Chapter 13
Deliverance of Those Involved in Satanism

to Jesus. I also know of a church in South Carolina that was closed down and several people in the church were killed in strange accidents. They had received threats from the local satanists. This will, I believe, become a very common occurrence within the next couple of years.

Ever since the publishing of my first book in the fall of 1986, letters have poured in to me from people who have suffered every kind of atrocity imaginable at the hands of Satan's servants. My heart breaks as I read these stories. One human being cannot touch another's sorrow. Only the Lord can help a person cope with all the terrible hurt that comes into his life. But through it all, we must remember that Jesus loved and died even for such as these. It has been my custom for years to petition the Lord for the souls of every servant Satan sends to try to hurt me. I figure that if Satan is going to use his servants against me, that I should at least have the opportunity to share the gospel with them. I have seen many hardened satanists who were sent to harm us become completely broken and turn to Jesus. This must always be our goal.

I have recently come under much criticism because I do not give specific names and places in my books or report the incidents to secular authorities. I want to make one thing very clear. My calling from the Lord is to bring people out of captivity to Satan into the kingdom of Jesus Christ. I deliberately left those details out of my books. If I had wanted them known, I would have published them. Satan is a spirit and his kingdom is in the spirit world. My battle is not against "flesh and blood." (Eph. 6:12) But more than that, I have been specifically called by God to use ONLY weapons with divine power, NOT the weapons of the world.

> "For though we walk in the flesh, we do not war after
> the flesh: For the weapons of our warfare are not car-

Chapter 13
Deliverance of Those Involved in Satanism

nal, but mighty through God to the pulling down of
strong holds . ." II Corinthians 10:3-5

The ONLY answer to Satanism and the crimes associated
with it is in the power of the gospel of Jesus Christ and His
finished work on the cross at Calvary. My calling is to bring
people out of Satanism and to set them free through a total
commitment to Jesus Christ.

I applaud the police efforts, but they are severely hampered
by two things. One, they do not believe in the reality of the
spirit world or that the satanists have any real power at all.
Two, they cannot begin to cope with what is going on
without the power of Jesus Christ and the discernment of
the Holy Spirit. Our jails are full of satanists. According to
a recent TV News documentary, here in California our jails
are so full that most of the criminals are back out on the
streets in a few days because there simply isn't enough space
in the jails to house them all. What in the world is the solution to this terrible state of affairs? It is time we Christians
rose up and started obeying Christ's command -- to share
the gospel with every man WITH POWER.

This is the whole issue of Satanism -- power. Every person
who becomes involved does so for one central purpose -- to
gain power. This is as old as the garden of Eden itself. Why
did Adam and Eve disobey God? Because they thought they
would gain special knowledge and thereby power to become as God Himself.

REBELLION is at the core of the lives of EVERY person
involved in Satanism. This is also true of those in Satanism
who have been very abused. No matter how abused they
have been, or how passive they seem, every one of them has
a hard core of rebellion so strong that I never cease to be
amazed by it.

Chapter 13
Deliverance of Those Involved in Satanism

> "For rebellion is as the sin of witchcraft, and stubborn-
> ness is as iniquity and idolatry." I Samuel 15:23

This tendency towards rebellion is something we all have to deal with, but especially those involved in Satanism. Always remember, passivity is the very worst form of rebellion possible. God hates passivity more than anything else. He made this very clear in Revelation 3 in the letter to the church of Laodicea. Because the Laodiceans were "lukewarm," that is, passive, the Lord said He would "spue them out of His mouth." (Rev. 3:15-16) Some of the most difficult satanists to work with are the breeders. The breeders are the women used to have children for sacrifice. They are so difficult to work with, because they have chosen to rebel through passivity. They have refused to do anything against the terrible sins they are told to commit.

One of the first things I must do when I am approached by anyone who says he or she wants to come out of Satanism, is pray! I must seek the Lord in prayer to be sure that it is HIS will that I work with that person. I must also talk to the person not only to see if he is willing to make Jesus his total master, but also to see if he is willing to pay the price involved in such a commitment. The majority of people involved in Satanism are not willing to pay the price involved in a total commitment to Jesus. They simply want relief from their current torment. They are typical of all human beings, we Christians included. About the only thing that makes any of us want to turn away from the sin in our lives is the fact that we finally become so miserable that we are willing to give up that sin to obtain something better. The prodical son in the parable given by Jesus is a typical example of this. He had to get down to eating with the pigs he fed before he was willing to give up his life of sin.

Many times in counseling situations, I have to come to the point of simply praying with the person and asking the Lord

Chapter 13
Deliverance of Those Involved in Satanism

to deal with them however He feels is necessary to bring them to the point of being willing to give up Satanism completely. As long as they feel that Satanism will benefit them more than it will hurt them, they will be unwilling to give it up. Perhaps this sounds harsh, but it is the truth. Most people come out of Satanism ONLY when they realize that they will most likely lose their life if they stay in any longer. In the case histories given in this chapter, you will find that this is almost always the turning point.

Working with people coming out of the occult is not easy. I have made just about every mistake possible to make. I must warn Christian workers in this field of two very real problem areas. First, the hard fact is that most people are looking for a "free ride." That is, they want someone else to fight for them and provide for them. Most people get into the occult in the first place because they think they can gain a lot without having to work. I have learned the hard way that it is necessary to place firm time limits on how long you will help and support someone. You cannot support people indefinitely. And, as long as you will support someone, usually that person will make no effort to support himself. Paul directly addresses this issue in II Thessalonians.

> "For even when we were with you, this we commanded you, that if any would not work, neither should he eat. For we hear that there are some which walk among you disorderly, working not at all, but are busybodies. Now them that are such we command and exhort by our Lord Jesus Christ, that with quietness they work, and eat their own bread." II Thessalonians 3:10-12

Secondly, there is a growing number of people pretending to be exsatanists, or pretending to have been ritualistically abused as a child. This is a problem which will no doubt increase as the amount of press exposure of satanism increases. These people come requesting support and attention. I am sometimes amazed at how much information they can pick up by reading and from the demons they allow to come into them through their claims to be demonized and to have been satanists.

Sometimes the Lord seems to deliberately with hold discernment in these cases. I can only suppose this is so that the person will have an unconditional chance for salvation. However, in the long run, they will reveal their deception through refusing to work and their continual attempts to gain attention, most often through faked illnesses and demonic attacks. NO ministry is safe from these problems. Anyone can be infiltrated. I can testify that such people bring untold grief and trouble. But, I dare not allow myself to become bitter. I must always remember that Christ loves even such as these.

FEAR. The Christian worker must always understand that people who are truly coming out of satanism are ruled by fear. FEAR is Satan's number one tool. Satan's kingdom is run on the principle of absolute competition. Satanists cannot trust anyone, it is every man for himself. They cooperate together only as they are forced to do so by the demons, through fear. The world of Satanism is also a world of lies. Satanists are accomplished liars and actors. That is the only way they survive. When they come out of Satanism, they will be extremely fearful, and habitual liars. It takes time for them to see that the power of the Lord is greater than anything Satan or his demons have. It takes time as well for them to break the habit of lying about everything. It takes MUCH loving, patience and endurance on the part of the Christian worker helping them.

Satanists reject everything and, consequently, feel rejected by everything and everyone. In the nine years that I have had a steady stream of people living in my home who have come out of Satanism, I have found continually that they interpret EVERYTHING as rejection. If I ask one of them to swat a fly on the wall, he/she will interpret that as rejection. It takes much love and patience to help them recognize and overcome this.

CONVICTION does not come to those coming out of Satanism immediately. Our Lord is so very merciful and gracious. He knows very well that, if He dumped the conviction of the terribleness of their actions on them all at once, they would lose their mind. As the person grows stronger in the Lord, the Holy Spirit brings to them the conviction of their deeds. We Christian workers MUST understand that these people have been through such terrible things, they cannot remember them all at once. It is normal for people coming out of Satanism to have significant amnesia. Total deliverance is usually not possible immediately because there is so much they will not remember. This is especially true in the case of the various inserts and episodes of ritual sex. We are weak human beings. Our minds can take only so much. Our Lord knows that. He does not push any of us beyond what we can stand. As they grow stronger and more secure in Christ, He will then release more and more of their memories.

I have found that it takes a minimum of one year for anyone coming out of satanism to stabilize. During that year, the Lord will bring back to their memory more and more of the rituals and contracts in which they have been involved. Most of their demons can be kicked out at the beginning, but more and more will be revealed as they remember more of what they have participated in. It is important that, as these things are remembered, the people repent of them, confess them as sin and ask the Lord's forgiveness and cleansing.

Much healing comes when we repent and confess our sins. These people are wounded lambs in the Lord's flock and must be tended with gentle firmness and great love.

Chapter 13
Deliverance of Those Involved in Satanism

I am going to give two complete case histories in this chapter to try to show more clearly my approach. I still kick out the demons by the sins through which they enter. But in the case of someone involved in any form of demon worship, you must also deal directly with their "familiar spirits," or those demons with whom the people worked closely. The people involved ALWAYS know the names of the demons with whom they worked. If they try to tell you they do not, they are lying. You must ask them for the names of their familiar spirits. Usually, there are several, not just one or two, as you will see by the case histories.

It is not necessary to know the names of any of the other demons within these people. You should NOT ask the demons themselves for their names. Talk to the person about his life, looking for doorways. In these cases, I have given first the histories and shown the doorways. Next I have listed their familiar spirits. Then, lastly, I have given our approach to their deliverances. You must list five categories for deliverance:

> Familiar spirits
> Blood Contracts
> Episodes of ritual sex
> Inserts
> Doorways

Case #1. MARIE (not her real name)

Marie was 21 years old at the time she came out of the craft and turned her life over to Jesus Christ. Her story is as follows:

Marie's mother was in Satanism, and, in fact, reached a high position. She married a fellow satanist, but the two were separated and divorced a month before Marie's birth.

Marie's father was considered to be mentally retarded, although he was able to work. He never reached a position of any rank within the craft. He left Marie's mother for another witch within the group. At the time of Marie's birth, Satan told her mother that she would be mentally retarded like her father. Unfortunately, Marie's mother accepted this lie from Satan without question.

Interestingly, Marie was not only dedicated to Satan as an infant, but also to Jesus Christ. This was because at the time of her birth, her mother held a significant position in the Christian church she had infiltrated. I have no doubt at all that the Lord took that dedication seriously, and, 21 years later, fulfilled it by bringing Marie to Himself.

At the age of four, Marie was taken to a special coven meeting, by her mother, where she signed her first contract in blood, selling herself to Satan. Marie very clearly remembers that, at the time of signing that contract, Satan appeared to her and gave her a demon named Komaer. Satan told her that Komaer would give her the ability to play the part of being mentally retarded which would enable her to get her mother to do anything she wanted. Sadly, Marie used that demon to perfection for the next 17 years. She is actually a very intelligent girl. But she continually flunked everything in school, tested out mentally retarded in all psychiatric evaluations, and convinced everyone that she actually WAS mentally retarded. Now she faces life with NO education to speak of and little in the way of job opportunities.

Marie's mother took her to some coven meetings, but mostly kept her away from them, always fearing that Satan would demand her sacrifice. Marie was an incredibly pampered child. No one ever said "No" to her, and neither did her grandparents. She had everything money could buy. Both sets of grandparents tried to make up to Marie for the abuse they had given to her mother as a child. She was almost completely undisciplined.

When Marie was 11 years old, her mother left the craft and accepted Jesus Christ. That's when the trouble began. As is usual with people coming out of the craft, Marie's mother lost everything. Eventually, she moved to another state as well, leaving the grandparents behind. Suddenly, Marie found that she was no longer worshipped by her mother, that someone else had taken that position in her life -- Jesus. And Marie hated Jesus and the Christians helping her mother with all of her heart! She rebelled against everybody and everything continually.

When they moved out of her home state, Marie stayed in touch with the high priestess who took her mother's place. She worked with that woman until she was 21 years old.

Marie associated with the kids who were into Satanism at the various public schools she attended. She participated frequently in animal sacrifice, and as she got older, attended human sacrifices as well -- climbing the ladder within the craft even as her mother had done before her.

Marie also trained in palm reading, tarot card reading, and recruited many kids into the craft by showing them how to play with the ouija board. She became fascinated with horoscopes and followed her's faithfully.

At the age of 17, she became involved in a gang which quickly lead her into drugs, drinking and multiple sexual contacts. She showed off to the other kids by cursing God every chance she got. At the age of 17, she had a baby out

Chapter 13
Deliverance of Those Involved in Satanism

of wedlock. Her mother would not permit her to have an abortion and, because she was a minor, forced her to give up the baby for adoption. It was most fortunate her mother did this, because Marie would probably have sacrificed the child had she been permitted to keep it.

Although she was not allowed to have Rock Music in the home, Marie listened to it constantly when she was away from home. At the age of 18, after the birth of her baby, Marie went back to her grandparents for a visit, and also visited her father. While there, she and her father had sex.

Marie lied about everything she did. She delighted in going to every occultic and horror movie she could. She also got involved in Dungeons and Dragons and occultic video games.

Finally, at the age of 19, after she had finished high school in a special-ed program for the mentally retarded, her mother sent her back to her grandparents as she could no longer have Marie in the house. Marie repeatedly tried to kill her mother, both by witchcraft, and physically. She persisted in believing that Satan was stronger than Jesus Christ in spite of everything her mother said or did to try to persuade her otherwise. Marie hated the whole world, and felt that the whole world hated her. She bitterly hated her mother most of all for leaving the craft and their change in circumstances.

Once Marie returned to her home state, her formal training in a satanic coven began. She was given a new and powerful spirit guide called Malachi, and a "gatekeeper" or "power demon" by the name of Gosser. Marie herself chose to call this particular demon Gosser. She chose to become what is known as a "huntress," which is a professional assassin. She was taught how to use all kinds of weapons, stars, poison darts, spears, swords, etc. She

Chapter 13
Deliverance of Those Involved in Satanism

started school in the martial arts -- Kung fu and Karate. However, she was too lazy to stand any kind of really rigorous physical training, so she mostly just acquired the various demons. She both used and peddled drugs.

Marie refused to work, and was placed into a governmental welfare program for the mentally retarded. She came under the care of two psychiatrists working for the government who were satanists. These men taught her much in the occult arts, especially in the area of hypnosis, astral-projection and yoga. She lived in a group home run by the government. This did not hinder her activities as most of the people working in the social services programs in that area were satanists in her own large coven.

It was during that two year period that she entered more and more into human sacrifice and cannibalism, along with frequent animal sacrifice. Finally, at the age of 21, she was given a big assignment. She was promised the position of high priestess (of a local coven) if she succeeded, and promised death if she failed. In reality, Marie was a loser, both in the craft and without. She never completed her craft training because of her laziness. She was always looking for the easy way out and a "free ride." She was sent out here to California to infiltrate and kill me.

Now I have, for years, had the policy of petitioning Father for the souls of every servant Satan sends to harm us. I figure that if Satan is going to send them to hurt us, that I should at least have equal time to share the gospel of Jesus Christ with them. Father seems to agree with my point of view as He usually allows me to share the gospel with them. Satan must send his servants against us at his own risk: the risk of losing them to Jesus Christ, MY master! After all, that seems only fair to me.

Chapter 13
Deliverance of Those Involved in Satanism

On the Lord's command, I took Marie into our home. She was with us for two weeks before she broke and confessed the whole plot to us. She realized that the power of Jesus Christ was too strong, and realized that she would never be successful in killing me. She feared for her life -- with good cause. Just prior to being sent out here, she was forced to watch the brutal killing of a 17 year old boy who had failed in a similar assignment for her coven. She was told that, if she failed in killing us, that she, too, would be sacrificed in the same manner.

Fearing for her life, Marie became willing to commit her life to Jesus Christ and give up her demons. However, her walk has been a most difficult one. She continues to be lazy and rebellious. Marie quite simply does not want to work or take responsibility for herself. She does not want to serve Jesus on His terms. She wants everything her own way. Marie lived with me for six weeks. Then I forced her to move out and go to work. The struggle for Marie's soul continues at the time of the writing of this book. But, here is how we approached her initial deliverance.

In addition to the doorways listed above, I asked Marie to make a list of the demons she knew well and worked with frequently. The Lord has shown me that people involved deeply in the craft must rebuke by name and cast out those demons with whom they worked closely. Those demons are listed below with their function. Not all of their names may be spelled correctly as Marie was not ever interested in how they were spelled, just how their names sounded. As is common within the craft, many of the demons she named herself. Demons do not care much what names people call them. They just want to enter into and control the people.

MALACHI
spirit guide

Chapter 13
Deliverance of Those Involved in Satanism

GOSSER
"gatekeeper or power demon" which gave her the ability to astral-project.

DOZZER
"Keymaster" This demon opened up any doors on houses, cars, or safes. She also sent him out to confuse and blind drivers to cause car and truck accidents.

DEATH
A demon placed in every person who signs a contract with Satan. This demon's function is to bring about the physical death of the person he inhabits in the event that person turns away from Satan to Jesus Christ.

KONEE
Gave Marie the ability to "pass out" but still know what was going on around her.

KEFFLAY
Received through first sexual contact. Functioned greatly in lust and seduction of sexual partners.

SYMUSE
Gave her the ability to drink as much as she wanted to without passing out. Also, this demon could affect the equipment so that she could have high alcohol levels and still pass the breathalyzer tests.

KEUMMA
Used to influence drug sellers so she could bring down their prices. Thus she could obtain drugs far below the street rate and then make a greater profit.

Chapter 13
Deliverance of Those Involved in Satanism

SUSKY

Received from the psychiatrist the first time he hyp-notized her. This demon placed "pink light" around her to protect her silver cord when she astralprojected.

SELUMEA

Came in through a suicide attempt. His purpose was to remain in her so that, if she ever decided to commit suicide again, he would perform the following: 1. Hold off all of her other demons so they could not stop her from taking her life. 2. Notify other satanists so that her suicide would become a sacrifice "Ninja style." A "Ninja style" suicide is for her to hang upside down, take a sword or dagger and carve out her heart and guts. If she didn't want to do this at the last moment, the other satanists would do it for her. Once Selumea was set in motion, nothing could stop him, not even Marie herself. She was promised that, if she decided to sacrifice herself in this manner for Satan, that she would be given a higher ranking in Hell -- Satan's kingdom.

LANERKER

Used in all forms of fortune telling. A demon of divina-tion.

DESAE

Received the first time she blasphemed God. This demon made a mantra out of swear words, and gave her some knowledge of Spanish so that she could swear in Spanish in front of others who did not speak the language. That way she would not "get in trouble" for swearing. This demon made her use extremely foul language almost con-tinually.

DEMEE

Came in through the first "Nightmare on Elm Street" movie she saw. He and other demons gave her the ability to watch all sorts of horror and torture without feeling any emotions except a sort of a "high." These films also became training films as she was learning the skills of an assassin.

KIMLUMLU

Demon of Rock music. Head demon that came in while she listened to Rock music. This demon, and those under him enabled her to understand the lyrics, the backmasking, and to listen to the music at very loud levels without hearing damage.

LABUE

Received in a special ceremony to give her strength and to guide her hands in ritualistic killings. (Many people get what is called a "blood lust" through sacrifices. Once they have killed, they have an overwhelming desire to shed blood again and again.)

CONVENO

Energy vampire demon. Marie could, with this demon, draw the strength out of any person she chose. Unless I bound this demon in her, Marie could sit down beside me and, within less than 10 minutes, I would be so weak I could not sit up. She received this demon at the age of four and used him extensively to afflict others all of her life.

SILENCER

Demon of quietness used in martial arts training. He would have enabled Marie to move with absolute silence had she continued in martial arts training.

KEASEME

Demon of runaways. She pulled him out of some other kid at the group home. He helped her to escape and run away from the group home whenever she wanted, and she

Chapter 13
Deliverance of Those Involved in Satanism

could use him to afflict other kids to make them want to run away from their parent's home.

KOMAER

Demon of mental retardation. Marie acted mentally retarded with great expertise. She is actually very intelligent and has normal reading skills.

KEELMA

Marie frequently sent this demon out to destroy a person's job. Anyone who made her angry usually ended up losing his/her job within a few months because of this demon. She received him at the age of six and used him regularly thereafter.

DOVA

Demon of illness. Came into Marie at the age of six. She very frequently used him to afflict other people and animals with all sorts of illnesses.

JERMONA

Received as a part of her training to become a huntress. He gave her skills with all sorts of weaponry. Once again, because of her laziness, she did not progress very far with her training and did not learn to use this demon well.

OUKA

Demon of emotional control. Came in through practicing yoga positions. She asked him in because she had a violent temper. This demon helped her to control her temper when she needed to for her benefit so she could keep a clear head in situations in which she would not otherwise have done so.

KAFA

Marie asked this demon in to give her the ability to win at any game especially video games. Since her

Chapter 13
Deliverance of Those Involved in Satanism

deliverance, she is unable to play any type of video game with skill.

LEGION

Marie invited this demon in at one of the gang rituals while she was a member of "Satan's Demons" in high school. The picture of this demon as he appears in the spirit world is on the back of the jackets worn by these particular gang members. He is sort of the "mascot" of the gang and inhabits all the members.

IN SUMMARY:

We approached Marie's deliverance as follows:

(1.) She got down on her knees and asked Jesus Christ to forgive her of her sins and become her Lord and Savior.

(2.) She renounced her involvement in Satanism and made a clear announcement to Satan and his demons that she would never serve them again as long as she lived, that she was now a servant of Jesus Christ.

(3.) She asked Father for His forgiveness for using a spirit guide. Then she commanded Malachi to leave her at once in the name of Jesus. This demon caused her great pain in spite of all commands for him to be bound. Marie had to be willing to suffer this pain to be set free. She rebuked this demon and commanded him to come out over and over again for about five minutes before he finally left.

(4.) Marie asked forgiveness for her contact with the spirit world and then kicked out Gosser, the gatekeeper.

(5.) Marie kicked out the death demon so he could not interfere with the rest of the deliverance. I usually always approach a deliverance of people involved in Satanism in this manner. The death demon must come out very early in the deliverance or he will cause much physical damage and distress.

After kicking out her spirit guide, Malachi, and her gatekeeper, Gosser, and the death demon, Marie was then ready to deal with all the other familiar spirit demons with whom she had worked so often. Each specific demon in the list of familiar spirits was rebuked individually and kicked out. Marie prayed first, asking the Lord to forgive her for allowing that particular demon to live in her and work with her. Then she commanded the demon to leave.

The demon that gave her the most trouble was Komaer. That was because she allowed Komaer so much control of her mind to act mentally retarded. Komaer knocked her unconscious twice, and made her very confused a number of times. Each time, we would help her gain control, and then demand that SHE control that demon with the power and authority given to her by Jesus Christ. Once Marie gained the upper hand and was able to bind Komaer, in the name of Jesus, and was able to stop him from controlling her mind, he had to come out.

Then, after the specific demons were kicked out, we went back and started on the doorways. Again, Marie prayed first for forgiveness, and then commanded every demon to leave her at once that came in through each doorway.

The Doorways were:

* inheritance
* Dungeons &Dragons
* general occult games
* animal sacrifices
* murder

* horoscopes
* blood contracts
* witchcraft
* drugs
* Kung fu

Chapter 13
Deliverance of Those Involved in Satanism

* Karate
* human sacrifices
* drinking blood
(animal & human)
* hypnosis
* incest
* palm reading
* yoga
* rock music
* occult & horror movies

* rebellion
* drunkenness
* multiple sexual
relationships
* cannibalism
* astral-projection
* blasphemy
* tarot cards
* ouija board
* ritual sex

Lastly, we did a final and general clearing of the following areas with the following prayers.

SPIRIT
SEVER BETWEEN SOUL AND SPIRIT
MIND
WILL
EMOTIONS
PHYSICAL BODY

SPIRIT: Father, in the name of Jesus, I ask you to forgive me for my sinful use of my spirit and to completely cleanse my spirit of any remaining demons. I ask you to seal it so that no one can ever control it again, except You. I thank you for this in Jesus' name.

STATEMENT: Now, in the name of Jesus Christ my Lord, I command every demon remaining in, or afflicting my spirit, to leave me at once! Never again will my spirit be used to serve Satan or any of your demons.

SEVER BETWEEN SOUL AND SPIRIT: Father, in the name of Jesus, I ask you to completely and forever take away my ability to communicate with the spirit world in any way, except what the Holy Spirit wants me to receive. Therefore,

I am asking you to once and for all sever between my soul and spirit as in Hebrews 4:12 and remove all demons that gave me the ability to control my spirit and communicate with the spirit world.

STATEMENT: Now, in the name of Jesus Christ, I command all demons linking my soul and spirit which give me the ability to communicate with the spirit world and astral-project to leave me at once!

MIND: Father, in the name of Jesus Christ, I ask you to completely cleanse and heal and renew my mind. I want to use my mind to serve and honor YOU. Please forgive me for living the lie of mental retardation and for using my mind to serve Satan.

STATEMENT: In the name of Jesus Christ, I command every demon left in my mind, or afflicting my mind, to leave me at once!

WILL: Father, in the name of Jesus Christ, I ask you to forgive me for rebelling against you for so many years. Please cleanse my will and send your Holy Spirit to work in my will to will to do your good pleasure. (Phil 2:13)

STATEMENT: In the name of Jesus Christ, I command every demon in my will, or afflicting my will, to leave me at once!

EMOTION : Father, in the name of Jesus Christ, I ask you to forgive me for all my hatred and bitterness and lust and every other sinful emotion. Please cleanse my emotions and heal them so that they will be pleasing to you.

STATEMENT: In the name of Jesus Christ my Lord, I command every demon in my emotions, or afflicting my emotions, to leave me at once!

Chapter 13
Deliverance of Those Involved in Satanism

PHYSICAL BODY: Father, in the name of Jesus Christ, I sincerely repent for all the terrible things I have done with my body, sinning against you. Please forgive me and cleanse me and heal my physical body.

STATEMENT: In the name of Jesus Christ, I command every demon left within my physical body to leave me at once!

After Marie was finally delivered, we had her pray and ask God the Father to fill her with the Holy Spirit. She was placed on an intensive Bible study and memorization program. Unfortunately, she quickly began to refuse to continue the study because she did not want to discipline herself. She lived with us for six weeks and then moved out. We are still in touch with her, but Marie has not yet decided once and for all that she will serve Jesus Christ totally. She is in a VERY dangerous position. You cannot sit on the fence with God for very long. Scripture says "It is a fearful thing to fall into the hands of the living God."
(Hebrews 10:31)

Case #2

Jane (not her real name) was fourteen years old when I first saw her. Her story is a very sobering one. It clearly demonstrates the power of the ouija board which most people consider to be just a game. It is even more sobering when you stop to think about the fact that just about every high school and junior high school here in the U.S. has an ouija board club. In fact, the ouija board has become the #1 best selling "game" here in the United States.

I have talked with many, many teens who are involved with ouija boards. Frequently, I ask them if they ever want to stop playing, but the spirits want to continue. Over and over again I am told that yes, this does sometimes happen, and if they disobey the spirits, the spirits get really mean and throw the board around the room or hurt the kids in some way. My next question is always, "Then why do you mess around with these spirits?" They always tell me that they have "good spirits" to protect them from the "mean or bad spirits." What a tragedy!

Jane was brought to me by her aunt who was, fortunately, a true Christian. The aunt, whom I will call Deborah (not her real name), found Jane and her 14 year old friend trying to sacrifice their niece, Deborah's 10 month old daughter. Praise God, instead of running to the police, Deborah ran to the Lord and brought Jane to a commitment to Jesus Christ! She then brought Jane to me for help in clearing out the demons.

JANE'S STORY:

Jane knew very little about inheritance. Her father and mother were divorced when Jane was young. As is so common, Jane was raised in a one-parent household, by her mother.

> Her mother was not a Christian, but sporadically attended the Christian Science church (not a Christian church). To Jane's knowledge, her mother was not involved in the occult directly.

(Doorways: inheritance-- father-- unknown, mother-- Christian Science)

> Heavy metal rock music was played in Jane's home from infancy. She and her mother attended rock concerts and watched MTV. Jane demonstrated the typical pattern for a youngster who's life is saturated with rock music. By the

time Jane was ten and eleven years old, she was sexually active with multiple partners, all boys.
(Doorways: multiple sexual partners)

In her eleventh year, Jane began to do drugs. In that year, she experimented with PCP (crystal), LSD (Acid), bennies, speed, marijuana, and cocaine. I asked her how she got these drugs. Her reply was, unfortunately, very common. "Oh, that was easy. I just got them at school. ALL the schools have drug pushers. You can get anything you want."
(Doorways: street drugs)

When Jane was thirteen, she got a boy friend who was sixteen years old. His name was Bobby. Jane and Bobby were very much "in love." However, Bobby was a fourth generation Satanist. But, for some reason, Bobby did not want to be involved in Satanism. He strongly warned Jane to never get involved in Satanism. He also warned her to be very careful not to call up demons, that demons could be very dangerous. Six months after they met, Bobby was murdered by the local Satanists. Jane was devastated.
(Doorways: demons of occultism from Bobby)

By this time, Jane was in high school. Because of her grief over Bobby, she did not become sexually involved with any other boys, and decided to "go straight" and stopped taking drugs because Bobby had told her these were bad for her.

However, as is so very common here in the U.S., Jane's high school English teacher was an occultist. She had the students do research papers on witchcraft under the guise of studying "medieval culture." Jane went to the school library and found many books on the occult. She felt a great drawing from inside of herself to study the occult. (This came from the demons she had received from

Chapter 13
Deliverance of Those Involved in Satanism

having sex with Bobby.) She found books with all sorts of incantations in the high school library. But, she also found much information on ouija boards. This really caught her interest as she wondered if she could contact Bobby through the ouija board. The books she read told her that ouija boards are often used to contact spirits of dead people.
(Doorways: ouija board, spirit guide, Bobby)

She asked her mother to buy her an ouija board. Her mother did so, thinking it was just a game!

Because of the demons already inside of Jane, she learned to use the ouija board very quickly. She contacted spirits directly through the board. Quickly she contacted a spirit that said he was Bobby. However, within a few months, Jane figured out that this spirit was not the Bobby she had known, but simply a demon masquerading as Bobby. She accepted this spirit as a spirit guide. She then obtained two other spirit guides called "Black" and "Caa." She was so enthusiastic about the ouija board that she got her friend Susan (not her real name) who was also fourteen, to join her in using the board.
(Doorways: ouija board, spirit guide, Bobby, spirit guides Black & Caa)

Caa was the most powerful of the demon spirit guides. He gave Jane a satanic name of "Enna." He did this when Jane signed a contract selling herself to Satan. In just three months from the time Jane first started using the board, these demons lead her into signing a contract in her own blood selling herself to Satan, body, soul, and spirit. Then, self-mutilation, drinking of her own blood and the blood of her friend Susan, blasphemy of God, desecration of Christian churches, animal sacrifice, astral-projection, all sorts of incantations and, finally, the attempted human sacrifice which Caa said was necessary so that Jane could

become a "bride of Satan." Please remember, this all happened in just three months! Jane never, at any time, had contact with other satanists or a satanic coven of any kind! All of this came about through her contact with the spirit world through the ouija board !
(Doorways: satanic name of Enna; blood contract with Satan; self mutilation; blood drinking; blasphemy of God; church desecration; animal sacrifice; astral-projection; human sacrifice; incantations)

Jane and her friend had become very unpopular at school because it became known amongst the other kids that Jane had the ability to inflict illness and all sorts of accidents on anyone who made her mad. Jane and Susan became close friends and withdrew from the other kids at school.

One week before the two girls tried to sacrifice Deborah's baby, Jane had an experience that greatly frightened her. She was sitting in class when Caa appeared to her and told her that she would gain much more power if she would allow Caa to come inside of her. Jane agreed, and followed Caa's instructions to call him into her. He came in with such force that Jane was knocked out of her chair onto the classroom floor. She was engulfed in searing heat and cried out in pain. Then she had a convulsion.

I asked her what happened then. She said that her teacher just thought she had overdosed on drugs and asked Susan to help her down to the nurse's office to lie down for awhile. The convulsion was of short duration, and though Jane was groggy afterwards, she could walk. Susan helped her down to the nurse's office. She lay down there for an hour or two and then returned to class. I was horrified! "But Jane," I exclaimed, "didn't the teacher want to send you to the hospital or report you to the authorities if she thought you were taking drugs?"

Chapter 13
Deliverance of Those Involved in Satanism

"Oh no," was Jane's reply. "There are so many kids on drugs at school that the teachers just look the other way. If they reported all the kids on drugs, there wouldn't be any kids left in class. Besides, many of the teachers are on drugs of some sort themselves." What a terrible state our country has fallen into!

Not only was Jane terribly frightened by Caa's painful entrance, Caa was very cruel to her. Jane began to remember all the warnings Bobby had given her. But she was trapped. She didn't know what to do. Caa was obviously much more powerful than she was. He told her that she could NEVER get rid of him. It was because Caa had threatened her with torment and death that she tried to sacrifice her aunt's baby to appease him.

She readily accepted Jesus Christ once she found out that He could set her free from the demonic torment and bondage she was experiencing. Her friend was not so willing, and has, the last I heard, returned to Satanism.

I had asked Jane to make up a list of the doorways in her life before I saw her. She did so, very accurately, I might add, along with very accurate drawings of what her three spirit guides looked like. She is a talented artist for one so young.

The three familiar demons Jane worked with were:
> Bobby
> Black
> Caa

Jane's doorways were:
> inheritance
> rock music & MTV

Chapter 13
Deliverance of Those Involved in Satanism

> multiple sexual contacts
> drugs
> occult demons through sex with Bobby (the satanist)
> ouija board
> blood contract with Satan
> self-mutilation
> drinking of human and animal blood
> animal sacrifice
> blasphemy of God
> desecration of Christian churches
> incantations of all sorts
> astral-projection
> attempted human sacrifice

I asked Jane if she knew what it meant to "blaspheme" God. She defined the word correctly. I then asked her how she knew the correct spelling of the word as this is not a common word in the vocabulary of a fourteen year old. Her answer was "Oh, Black spelled it out for me on the ouija board."

Because of her involvement with the ouija board, astral-projection, and because Jane had gained the ability to communicate with the demons directly without the aid of the ouija board, it was clear that the link between her soul and spirit had been formed.

As I talked with Jane, I found that she was a very intelligent girl. I told her that she now had more power in the name of Jesus than the demons had. "Oh good!" she exclaimed. "Does that mean that I can get rid of these demons?"

Chapter 13
Deliverance of Those Involved in Satanism

"Yes," I said.

"When?" was her immediate question. I was delighted to be able to answer "Right now!"

In her deliverance, Jane first made an announcement to Satan and the demons that she would no longer serve them, that she was now a servant of the Lord Jesus Christ.

Then she kicked out the three familiar spirit demons who had become her spirit guides. (Please see sample prayers and statements in Case #1.) Then she kicked out a demon of death who was afflicting her physically. She had a real struggle to kick out Caa. This demon tried to take over her voice to growl through her and tried to knock her out. This child was so determined to get rid of him that I did not have to coach or instruct her what to do. She would slap her hand over her mouth to stop the growl, swallow hard and say, "NO! In the name of Jesus, I command you to be bound, Caa. You will NEVER control me again!"

The struggle was intense, but Jane never gave up for a moment. Oh the faith of children! How beautiful and simple it is!

After getting rid of the four demons, Jane then went through and repented for her sins and confessed them and closed all the doorways. I had talked to her very seriously before starting the deliverance and told her that, if she chose to make Jesus Christ her Master, that meant she could never again have sex until she got married and never again do drugs or obtain power through demons. She said she understood that and was willing to agree to that. This girl was smart. She realized how much trouble these sins had brought into her life and was willing to make a complete change.

Chapter 13
Deliverance of Those Involved in Satanism

After closing the doorways, Jane then did a general cleansing of:

> Spirit

SEVER BETWEEN SOUL AND SPIRIT

> Mind

> Will

> Emotions

> Physical Body

(Please see sample prayers and statements given for Case #1.) Lastly, she prayed and asked the Lord to fill her up with His Holy Spirit, everywhere the demons had been.

I kept track of Jane through her Aunt and local pastor for about a year after her deliverance. Jane left her mother's home and moved in with her aunt. She had trouble with nightmares, and the demons attacked her day and night for several months with thoughts that she wasn't really saved, or wasn't really delivered. Jane persevered. Her aunt was a great help to her. The last I heard, Jane was still serving Jesus and growing in the Lord.

She had to sever her friendship with Susan, however, because Susan refused to give up her sexual and occultic activities. Both girls were offered the same gospel and the same opportunity for deliverance. The one chose eternal life, the other, eternal death.

Satan is after our children! Jane was just a child in physical age, but an old woman in sin. How many Janes are there, I wonder? How I pray that our Lord will reach down into the lives of these youngsters and bring them to committed Christians willing to pay the price to help them be set free! Not very many Christians would be willing to help Jane in

Chapter 13
Deliverance of Those Involved in Satanism

the way her aunt did after finding Jane in the very act of trying to kill her baby! Truly this is what Jesus meant when He commanded us to "love our enemies!"

Satanic Ritualistic Abuse

More and more psychiatrists, psychologists and Christian workers are being faced with the problem of helping people who were abused in Satanic rituals. Some are still young, but most are adults who have survived the abuse. This is an area that is extremely difficult to deal with. Many times the adults will have an almost complete loss of memory of their childhood. Once again, I must say that this is an area where I still have more questions than answers. Each person I see helps me to learn more. I am going to give a case history here of a young woman I worked with recently to illustrate some of the problems faced, and my approach to deliverance.

Lyn's (not her real name) story:

Lyn grew up a very troubled young woman, but it was not until she turned 25 that she began to find out why. During her high school years she took drugs continually and drank heavily as well. Finally, at the age of 19, some teens her age shared the gospel with her. She accepted Jesus Christ at the age of 19, but she continued to have terrible struggles. She quit taking everything except pot (marijuana). By the time she turned 21, the Lord convicted her that she had not made Jesus Christ the master in her life. It was at that time that she quit pot.

Just quitting drugs was not the answer for Lyn. She continued to have struggles with deep depression and great difficulties in her spiritual walk. She attempted to commit suicide twenty times before the age of 25. She had continual and very painful problems physically with her reproductive tract. When she finally married, sexual intercourse was extremely painful. She had extensive vaginal and uterine scarring for which she had no explanation.

In her 25th year, she began to see a Christian psychologist. During counseling, she abruptly realized that she had no memories at all of her childhood. Over the next seven painful years, she began to retrieve memories of her childhood until at last she had a pretty complete picture of what had happened to her. She went to several counselors, but just remembering wasn't enough. Somehow, she had to put an end to the torment and the difficulties in her walk with the Lord. Then, she came across my books. As she read them, she came to the realization that she must need deliverance. I met her when she was 34 years old. Lyn was ritualistically abused as a child, and also in her teens. Because Lyn's story is so long and complex, I am simply going to summarize it here, and then make a list of the doorways at the end.

Lyn was born into a family where her father was a satanist associated with one of the well known groups here in the U.S. Lyn still does not know how involved her mother was. Her mother spent much time in the hospital during Lyn's childhood.

Lyn was dedicated to Satan as a baby, more specifically, to "Prince Set" and "Eternal Father" (Satan) -- One of her earliest memories was of a "scary thing" put into her as a baby. This "scary thing" must have been a demon.

She was put through various "purification" ceremonies which were all sexual rituals. She was forced into sex with people, animals, and demons. She was also used in child pornography and snuff films. She was abused with every sort of sexual perversion possible. During one of the rituals, salt was poured into her vagina. This is a common ritual. Salt is always used in the occult for the placement of demons of

Chapter 13
Deliverance of Those Involved in Satanism

destruction. No doubt, all products of her womb were dedicated to be sacrifices to Satan. These salt rituals are sometimes called "salt protection rituals."

Lyn had many memories of human sacrifices, both children and adults. She was forced into cannibalism and drinking of blood. Parts of some of these sacrifices involved a ritual of washing her hands in the blood of the victims.

She was given a "secret name" which was actually a craft name. This was first given to her during what was called a "re-birthing ceremony." During the re-birthing ceremony, she was placed inside the abdominal cavity of both a dead human and an animal after their sacrifice. She was also placed in a coffin and buried in the ground for a period of time and supposedly re-birthed when she was brought out of the ground. The terror she experienced during these rituals is beyond description.

At the age of four, Lyn was so severely abused that she nearly died. Here is that experience as Lyn wrote it in her diary of memories.

> "I remember lying on a cold table with bright lights that hurt my eyes. I must have realized what was going on because I knew I could die and I really wanted to. I can remember letting the blackness take me. The blackness felt wonderful. No pain, no hurt, no tears, just nothing but warmth and a feeling of eternal patience. (I fully understood this.)
>
> "It was like, 'We have all the time in eternity, slow down, don't rush. Relax, breath me in.' Then I saw the Lord standing off to my left with his arms to His sides. Oh the bliss I felt when I looked at His face. Such love, such patience and sadness. It immediately felt like I was running, pushing, struggling to get closer to Him, to jump into His arms. But it was like a strong father holding

Chapter 13
Deliverance of Those Involved in Satanism

his three year old, holding her off the ground while her feet are still moving. I became frustrated and yelled, 'Lord, I want to come home!' It was then that I really focused in on the sadness I had briefly noticed earlier. I suddenly felt this terror and panic in my heart that I knew I couldn't stay. I would have to go back. Oh the little girl screamed in terror and pain, 'Please Jesus, please big brother, don't tell me to go back!

"I can't! It hurts too much. I want to stay." And on and on and on. I pleaded and then just broke down in sobs, knowing I would go back because that's what He wanted. He never moved, just looked into my heart and mind, shook His head and said, 'Not yet my little one. You will understand one day. I love you.' He talked to me more, but I can't remember. And I was suddenly feeling slapped in the face, saw the bright lights again as I opened my eyes. I was angry because I was back. From then on I've been in conflict with wanting to go back home and knowing there is something to be done here."

Lyn continues: "After my near death experience I knew deep inside that the cult had been lying to me and although I was angry for not being able to go home, I held onto that experience. I went through the motions and did what I was told, but I vowed that they would never have me completely. I KNEW "the Light" was stronger than Prince Set and the Eternal Father. Why else were they so openly disturbed about a three or four-year-old child talking to "the Light?" They had taught me to use telepathy and, that time, I turned it against them. I blocked that part of my mind and they never knew what happened during my near death experience. They had lost me -- I belonged to Jesus and they could not do anything about it."

Although Lyn never told anyone about her experience, those around her somehow knew that she had had an experience with Jesus Christ. They kept telling her that she

Chapter 13
Deliverance of Those Involved in Satanism

must have nothing to do with Jesus. They accused her of bringing "the light" into the meeting, and even killed a small boy about her age to punish her for "bringing the light into the meetings." Then they did a special ritual to "place a wall" in her mind so that she could not get" over the wall to Jesus." BUT, the victory had been won. No matter how Lyn was tormented after that day, the satanists never gained complete control of her mind. Part of her was owned by Jesus from that day on. However, later, when Lyn did accept Christ in her adult life, that wall in her brain still remained. She could not read the scriptures, was completely unable to memorize scripture, and had greatest difficulty praying. Once this wall was removed during her deliverance, she was set free to be able to read and memorize scripture and pray.

Lyn quickly learned to "fly," as she described it. This was, in reality, astral-projection. She also quickly learned to dissociate, blanking her mind and stepping out of her body to avoid the physical pain she experienced.

She was placed in cages along with other children. She was hypnotized and learned to perform hypnosis herself. She was forced to learn to use the demons to walk through fire and "breathe under water." Worst of all, she was put through a "black hole ceremony." This is a practice that is rapidly growing here in the U.S. I have known very few survivors of it." The hole is in the ground, no one I have talked to coming out of Satanism knows if these holes are dug by humans or opened up by demons. I suspect the later because no one I have talked to has ever known a human to be involved in the digging of these "Satan pits," as they are called. The children are impaled with metal hooks, usually placed in their legs or groin area. They are cut in the genital area so that they bleed freely. Then they are suspended down into these seemingly bottomless holes where the demons come up to molest them in any way they want. The freely flowing blood attracts the demons upwards much more quickly.

Chapter 13
Deliverance of Those Involved in Satanism

Usually the children die, but a very few do survive. Lyn was one of the few survivors. She received severe physical damage, the scars of which she still bears today.

During one of the ceremonies she remembers a "steel rod" being placed in her back which gave her much pain all of her life until the demons making up the rod were cast out during deliverance.

Lyn quickly learned various demonic skills such as the art of levitation, calling up spirits in seances, playing with the ouija board, starting fire without matches, fortune telling through rod and pendulum. She signed several blood covenants and was given several seals and yokes.

She learned to use visualization and ESP. She was given a "secret number" in addition to her secret name. She formed a very close relationship with a young man whom she called Michael. Michael exerted very powerful demonic mind control over her.

Various "cues" were placed into Lyn. These were such things as certain colors. Her father sent her a birthday card recently that was almost completely green. As soon as she saw that particular color of green, she immediately experienced a tremendous urge to return to her father so that he could take her back to the craft members. After deliverance, the cues no longer affected her.

She was given a powerful demon spirit guide named Tal at the age of six. Her school pictures show a remarkable difference in the five year old prior to receiving the demon spirit guide, and the seven year old with the spirit guide.

She was taken to ceremonies in Festus, Corpus Christi, California, and Egypt. As she grew older, she participated

Chapter 13
Deliverance of Those Involved in Satanism

heavily in rock music and drugs. She learned many of the demons by name and used them in various incantations.

As the memories came flooding back, the satanists contacted her again and she began to struggle with an overwhelming urge to go back to the cult. She was married to a Christian man in her late twenties who helped her to resist the urges to go back to Satanism. At the age of 34, we met and talked. I felt the Lord was leading me to help her clear out the many demons that had come into her through the years of abuse and participation in satanic rituals.

Lyn came and stayed with my husband and I for a week. The struggle was intense, but she was completely set free at last!

Below is a list of her doorways, followed by the approach we took to clearing out the demons.

> inheritance
> baby dedication to Set & Satan -- called "Eternal Father"
> "scary thing" placed into her as baby
> Roman Catholicism:
  baptism, communion, confirmation, praying to saints, false tongues, novena & rosary
> Sex: sexual molestation, group sex, ritual sex, lesbianism, pornography, snuff films, sex with demons, sex with animals, sex with other children
> salt protection ritual, re-birthing ceremonies
> human sacrifices, cannibalism
> blood drinking, blood covenants
> secret name & number
> fire walking
> levitation

Chapter 13
Deliverance of Those Involved in Satanism

> seances

> ouija board

> under-water breathing

> wall in brain against Jesus

> steel rod in back

> black hole ceremony (Satan's pit)

> black mass

> animal sacrifices

> cage torture

> astral-protection

> dissociation

> blanking mind, ESP & telepathy

> rod & pendulum

> ceremonies in Festus, Corpus Christi, California & Egypt

> seals, yokes, pacts, bondage to "Michael"

> various "power" ceremonies

> telekenesis

Each of these doorways was prayed about, confessed, and then closed, and the demons that came into her commanded to leave in the name of Jesus. It took us about three days just to work through the list of doorways. The struggle was intense because Lyn was so used to escaping torment by simply blanking her mind, or astral-projecting out of her body. Over and over again, Lyn could not remember what she was supposed to pray for, then she could not bring herself to rebuke the demons and command them to leave in the name of Jesus. The demons would blank our her mind or stimulate her to astral-project.

Chapter 13
Deliverance of Those Involved in Satanism

The demons created a tremendous drain on me also. Both of us battled with exhaustion and sleepiness. Much of Lyn's deliverance was done on our feet pacing the floor to help us stay awake and alert.

Early on in the deliverance, I told Lyn to kick out her demon spirit guide, Tal. At that point, she was still having some difficulty recognizing what was her and what was the demon. She was so used to having demon spirits dwell in her that she had difficulty recognizing the difference between them and herself.

As I talked to her about getting rid of Tal, she suddenly said, "Why should I tell him to go? He has never hurt me."

I knew at once that that thought was from the demon. With the guidance of the Holy Spirit I replied, "Can you honestly tell me you do not think Tal was ever jealous of your relationship with your husband or tried to keep you from entering into a close relationship with him?"

Lyn looked surprised, then sheepish. She admitted that she did realize that Tal was a major obstacle to her forming a close relationship with her husband.

I began talking about how Tal was a born loser and had chosen to serve a master who was a loser and how Tal was going to lose his home in Lyn forever. Lyn sat for a couple of minutes without saying anything. Then she spoke up saying, "I suppose it is only my free will that keeps me from letting Tal speak through me to cuss you out?" I laughed and answered that indeed it was.

As the demon got angry at me over the things I was saying, Lyn began to recognize for the first time with some clarity the difference between the demon and herself. Lyn herself was not angry because I said the demon was a loser, but she

Chapter 13
Deliverance of Those Involved in Satanism

began to feel intense anger at me. It was a real step in her deliverance. Once she recognized the difference between the demon and herself, she was better able to fight against the demon and kick him out.

Here is Lyn's description of the incident:

> "At different times in my life, I would think that I felt an alien presence in myself but immediately the thought would come into my mind that it was only me. I was just an evil person and these thoughts belonged to and were entirely mine. Two days into my deliverance with Rebecca, she and the Lord finally got it through my head that these were not my thoughts but the demons within me. That was a big breakthrough for me. I then began to see Satan's deceit and lies holding me in captivity. The purpose was to keep me defeatedly feeling such self-contempt and self-hatred that I would never feel worthy enough to believe Jesus Christ loved me and would forgive me."

Lyn's deliverance began to move forward more smoothly after she learned to recognize the difference between the demons and herself.

The next area we had to deal with was the problem with Lyn's passive mind. She used the technique of dissociation, blanking her mind and leaving her body to keep from feeling the tremendous physical torment during her abuse. There seemed to be no victory in this area. We struggled a whole day with the problem. Time and time again, when Lyn tried to address the demons that came into her through the blanking of her mind or astral-projection, she would blank out. I even had her write out the simple prayers and statements on a large sheet of paper. She was first unable to write the words, then unable to read or understand them once they were written.

Chapter 13
Deliverance of Those Involved in Satanism

Finally, after much prayer, I realized that she needed to confess, as sin, the fact that she had almost completely given up her free will. Then ask the Lord to restore to her her free will. The struggle to make that confession and then pray that prayer was one of the most intense ones of her deliverance. But at last, Lyn won through and the victory was won. Once this was done, she was then able to address the demons that had come into her through these things and kick them out in the name of Jesus.

Fortunately, Lyn retained enough control that she did not become a "multiple personality" as so many abused children do. I still have big questions in this whole area of multiple personalities. I firmly believe that a big percentage of the multiple personalities are simply demons that take over and control the person. But, I also wonder if an abdication of the free will does not allow the personality to fractionate. Will the confession of this as sin and a prayer asking the Lord to restore the free will be a key to "integrating" a person? I freely admit that I do not have the complete understanding of this whole complex problem, or the solutions. But I do believe that the Holy Spirit will give Christian workers the guidance they need.

Another difficult area was the control "Michael" exerted in her life. Once, a couple of years before, a therapist had tried to get Lyn to regress to about six years of age and then declare the tie between her and Michael to be severed. Lyn was not able to do so. As Lyn and I discussed the incident, I realized the folly of such an approach. A small child would not have the ability to stand against a strong adult, especially one that used physical abuse to punish them. Of course, Lyn couldn't break such a bond. She needed the strength of Jesus Christ to do so, and she did not have that strength at the age of six! But, as an adult, she had the strength in Jesus Christ to sever the bond. This is a big trap that many psychologist and psychiatrists fall into. They ask a person to remember an incident that occurred to them as a child, then, as that child to deal with the situation. How ridiculous. If the child had the strength to do so, they would have done so when the situation first happened. Be careful, much of the "regression therapy" being done is demonic! Never permit hypnosis! ALL hypnosis is demonic. The Holy Spirit is able to help a Christian remember what happened to them in childhood. AND, the Holy Spirit will bring back ONLY those memories necessary for the person's cleansing.

Step-by-step the doorways were closed. The blood contracts severed, the inserts renounced and the Lord asked to remove them. Lyn did not know what inserts she had received, but we had to assume that she had received several. Major changes occurred as we asked the Lord to remove them.

The last step was to go through and specifically kick out, by name, all the demons that Lyn knew personally. She had a list of about fifty names. As she worked through that list and commanded each one to leave, suddenly she began to cry.

"I can't go on. If I do, there won't be anything of Lyn left. I'm disappearing into nothingness."

We stopped and I assured her that this feeling of emptiness was normal. After the demons were out, we would pray and ask the Holy Spirit to fill her and remove the emptiness.

It took a step of faith and obedience for Lyn to finish commanding all the demons to leave in spite of the pain she felt. She had had demons indwelling her from birth. She had never experienced being without them. This feeling of emptiness is very common in such situations.

Chapter 13
Deliverance of Those Involved in Satanism

After she finished the list of familiar spirits, she then went through the general cleansing I have listed in previous case histories of body, soul and spirit.

After she was all done, we anointed her with oil and joined with her in prayer asking the Holy Spirit to completely fill her. We also prayed asking the Lord to erase her painful memories and heal all demonic damage done to her physical body and to her emotions and spirit. She said that the feeling of emptiness grew less and less as she spent most of her time reading the Bible and praying over the next week. She could feel herself literally becoming filled with God's word.

Changes Lyn experienced after her deliverance:

For a few weeks, she became very clumsy and felt as if she did not know how to control her own body. This is because since birth, she was used to having the demons operate in her body.

Lyn can now read and understand scripture for the first time in her life. She can also pray freely and can memorize scripture.

She felt a great lightness, as if a heavy burden had been lifted from her.

She can now laugh and experience all of the whole range of human emotions now. She was blocked from feeling emotions before.

Lyn can now write and play music. She knew she had a gift in this area, but was able to write only briefly after first accepting Christ in 1974. Now she can write freely.

Chapter 13
Deliverance of Those Involved in Satanism

Lyn had experienced a great improvement in her relationship with her husband, both emotionally and physically. She no longer has pain with sexual intercourse.

All five senses now function with much greater clarity, especially her vision. This is common. The demons keep a person from experiencing the physical realm in a normal fashion. This is particularly true in people who have been involved in the Eastern religions where the goal is complete withdrawal from experiencing the physical realm so that the person is aware only of the spirit realm.

It is now much easier to combat the demons because they are now on the outside of her rather than the inside.

Lyn no longer has the desire to go back to the craft. Also, she no longer has the urges to commit suicide.

The area of greatest struggle is to keep her mind from blanking out, especially around Satanic high days. She still has to fight occasionally as members of the craft come and try to force her to astral-project. She feels a tug on her spirit as they try to take her spirit out of her body. However, now she can rebuke them in the name of Jesus and completely stop them from being able to take her in the spirit to rituals.

She has lost her ability to see into the spirit world.

Lyn still has nightmares, but she can handle them now through the power of Christ.

She cannot levitate now and has lost her ability of mental telepathy.

She is no longer affected by the cues -- i.e., one cue was to drown herself, causing her to intensely fear water. That fear is now gone. Another cue was ringing bells, such as church

Chapter 13
Deliverance of Those Involved in Satanism

bells. When she heard bells ringing, she was supposed to astral-project. This cue no longer has any effect on her.

Lyn's struggle has been hard, but she is at last free from demonic torment, overwhelming urges to commit suicide, deep depression, etc. Lyn is at last free to grow in the Lord. The barrier in her mind to keep her from the Lord has been removed.

The road to freedom is long and difficult for those who have been ritualistically abused but victory CAN be won!

Chapter 13
Deliverance of Those Involved in Satanism

Chapter 14

TO SATANISTS ... WITH LOVE

To those still in Satan's service:

I have written this book because I love you. But, more importantly, the Lord Jesus Christ, who is God Almighty, loves you even more than I do.

You may not know your master's name. You may call him "The Master". Or, you may use other names. However, this master you serve is cruel. He demands pain, suffering and sacrifices for you to serve him and gain power from him. I want to tell you that there IS another God. He is a God who can be served with love and purity. This true God calls your master by the name of Satan. Satan is NOT the god he says he is. Satan is a liar. He is only a created creature, NOT the creator. Please stop and think a moment. How many times have you seen Satan and his demon spirits double-cross his servants? Why do the demons constantly demand that you shed blood -- particularly your own? Has Satan, or any of the demons, shed any of THEIR blood for you? You know they have not!

Tell me, WHY does your master Satan demand that you do those things that horrify human beings the most? WHY does he demand that you torture and kill one another? WHY does he demand the lives of your precious little children? WHY does he demand torture and abuse of helpless small children? WHY does Satan tell you this is the ONLY way to gain power? WHY? Have you ever stopped to wonder about these things?

Most of you have never experienced real love. You don't know what love is. How my heart longs to tell you that true love DOES EXIST!

What is true love? Here is the answer:

> "Greater love hath no man than this, that a man lay down his life for his friends." John 15:13

The Lord Jesus Christ did this for us! Jesus Christ IS GOD ALMIGHTY! How different Jesus is than Satan. Satan demands that you shed blood and perform sacrifices for him. Jesus, on the other hand, sacrificed HIMSELF for us! This Jesus, who is none other than the true creator God, chose to come down to earth and clothe Himself in human flesh. He was born of a virgin and walked this earth as a man without sin. He died on a cruel cross and took our just punishment upon Himself. But death could not hold Him because He IS very God. Jesus arose from the grave on the third day. He is NOT chained in Hell as you have been told. He is very much alive and currently sits in heaven at the right hand of God the Father.

> "God, who at sundry times and in divers manners spake in time past unto the fathers by the prophets, Hath in these last days spoken unto us by his Son, whom he hath appointed heir of all things, by whom also he made the worlds: Who being the brightness of his glory, and the express image of his person, and upholding all things by the word of his power, when he had by himself purged our sins, sat down on the right hand of the Majesty on high." Hebrews 1:1-3

Oh I beg of you, please read a little farther! You CAN get out of Satanism and live! Sister Courage, Sister Fortress, The Black Knight and many, many others are living witnesses to this. Jesus IS stronger than Satan. That is why these people have all come out of the craft and are still alive.

Chapter 14
To Satanists...With Love

What a harsh master you serve! How many times have you seen Satan's servants killed because they failed or made a mistake?

Ah, but I serve a Master that does not kill His servants if they fail. In fact, He died in my place, taking my punishment upon Himself! Satan would never do that! Do you know that the price and just punishment for EVERY evil you have done has been paid IN FULL? Jesus paid it on the cross nearly 2,000 years ago. Everything you have done can be wiped away! All your bitterness, hatred, jealousy, pride, FEAR and evil can be wiped away and be replaced with gentleness, love, peace, compassion and purity. All this is possible if only you will turn from serving Satan and make Jesus Christ your Lord and Savior and Master.

Please, please listen to me. Why continue in such bondage? Why walk every day in fear? You are in such terrible bondage -- to maintain your power, you must constantly perform sacrifices and endless rituals. You dare not miss a Satanic high day or you will be severely punished. If you do any little thing wrong, you will be punished. Sometimes you have done nothing at all wrong and you are still punished! Nearly every one of you suffers from some sort of demonic illness. Why?

PLEASE THINK! Why do the demons punish and torment you so many times if they care about you as they say they do? Oh how different it is to serve MY Master, Jesus Christ. This is what MY Master has to say:

"Come unto me, all ye that labour and are heavy laden, and I will give you rest. Take my yoke upon you, and learn of me; for I am meek and lowly in heart: and ye shall find rest unto your souls. For my yoke is easy, and my burden is light." Matthew 11:28-30

Chapter 14
To Satanists...With Love

The truth is that Satan and the demons hate all human beings. They know that Jesus IS alive and well. They know that Jesus offers forgiveness for sins and eternal life. It is their goal to keep as many people as possible from accepting Christ. They want as many people as possible to suffer for all eternity in Hell. SATAN HATES YOU! Satan is a liar. His promises to you are lies. Has he promised you power, money and fame? MY Master says:

> "For what shall it profit a man, if he shall gain the whole world, and lose his own soul? Or what shall a man give in exchange for his soul?" Mark 8:36-37

You may gain wealth, but you won't gain peace or eternal life. The ONLY way to have love, peace and eternal life is through Jesus.

> "Jesus saith unto him, I am the way, the truth, and the life: no man cometh unto the Father, but by me."
> John 14:6

I urge you to get down on your knees and ask Jesus to be your Lord, Savior and Master.

> "Behold, I stand at the door, and knock: if any man hear my voice, and open the door, I will come in to him, and will sup with him, and he with me." Revelation 3:20

Won't you open the door of your heart? How do you do this? Just get down on your knees right where you are and ask Jesus to forgive you and cleanse you from all your sins. Ask Him to become your Lord and Master. Then ask the Lord to place His precious Holy Spirit within you.

If you have made Jesus your Lord, then tell Satan and his demons that you will never serve them again. Command them to get out of your life forever in the name of Jesus.

Chapter 14
To Satanists...With Love

There are people who care, people who are true servants of Jesus Christ who will help you. Pray and ask the Lord to bring you to them. Will you accept Jesus today before it is too late? Remember, you are in my prayers and the prayers of many others.

Dear Heavenly Father:

I come before Your throne today in the precious name of Jesus Christ. I come before Your throne to petition You for each precious soul caught in Satan's cruel grasp. Father, I petition You to bind the demons so each person can have at least one chance to hear about Jesus and accept Him.

Father God, I petition You for each one that does accept Jesus. I petition You to send Your angels to surround and protect them. I petition You to guide them to true Christians who will help them.

Now, Father, in the name of Jesus, I come before Your throne to counter-petition Satan for every soul that comes out of the craft to You. I petition that You will not allow Satan to sacrifice these people or overwhelm them or lead them to false Christians. I petition You, Father God, that EVERY soul that comes out of Satanism will in turn be raised up to bring many more people out of Satanism into the wonderful kingdom of Jesus Christ.

I thank you and praise you Father for all of this in the wonderful name of Jesus!

Amen

Chapter 14
To Satanists...With Love

EPILOGUE

SURPRISED BY JOY

This book contains some of my adventures in the service of my Master over the past four years. So much has happened and I have learned so much in the past ten years since I first started in this ministry. This walk has been a very lonely one and the warfare has been intense. But. . .

After 41 years, 15 of them walking closely with the Lord, He has brought a most wonderful blessing into my life. He brought me a godly man to be my husband! What a surprise and joy this event has been! The blessing and increase in strength both physically and spiritually this union has wrought in my life is more than I can describe.

Now Daniel and I are joined together as one to continue this fight as servants of our beloved Master, Jesus Christ. We are close to the end. The return of our Lord is near. It is our prayer that each of you reading this book will be strengthened in the difficult days to come.

May all praise and glory and honor be unto our wonderful God for ever and ever!

APPENDIX A

BREAKING UP FALLOW GROUND

> "Sow to yourselves in righteousness, reap in mercy.
> Break up your fallow ground: for it is time to seek
> the Lord, till he come and rain righteousness upon
> you."
> Hosea 10:12

Do you feel a distance in your relationship with the Lord?
Do you feel you are not where you should be with Him?
Do you have difficulty praying? I would suggest you sit
down and take a careful, prayerful look at your life. If you
are in this condition, chances are you have sin in your life
that you need to confess.

> "If we say that we have no sin, we deceive
> ourselves, and the truth is not in us. If we confess
> our sins, he is faithful and just to forgive us our sins,
> and to cleanse us from all unrighteousness."
> I John 1:8-9

> "My little children, these things write I unto you,
> that ye sin not. And if any man sin, we have an
> advocate with the Father, Jesus Christ the righteous."
> I John 2:1

I cannot emphasize enough the importance of keeping short
accounts with God. Do not allow unconfessed sin to build
up in your life. Nothing destroys your relationship with the
Lord faster than unconfessed sin.

What does it mean to "break up fallow ground"? Fallow ground is hard ground that has not been plowed for several years. The hard ground must be plowed up and broken down into softer dirt so that plants can grow in it. As we allow unconfessed sin to build up in our lives, our hearts become hardened toward the Lord. In this section, I want to present some material that is not original with me. Many of the thoughts come from a book by Charles Finney called *Lectures On Revival*. I would strongly recommend that you obtain this book and read it. This is an outline of sins that are common to all mankind. I have combined some of Finney's thoughts with the things that the Lord has taught me in my own life.

> "Examine the state of your mind to see where you are right now. Many never think about this! They pay no attention to their own hearts, and never know whether or not they are doing well spiritually, whether they are gaining ground or going back, fruitful or lying waste. Shift your attention from everything else and look into this. Make a business of it. Don't be in a hurry. Examine thoroughly the state of your heart and see where you are.... Self-examination consists in looking at your life, considering your actions, remembering the past and learning its true character... General confessions of sin will never do. Your sins were committed one by one, and as best as you can they should be reviewed and repented of one at a time." (*Lectures On Revival*, by Charles Finney, Bethany House Publishers, 1988, pp. 30-31.)

Now, before you start reading the rest of this section, do YOU have a paper and pen in your hand so that you can write down the sins the Holy Spirit brings to your mind?

Appendix A
Breaking Up Fallow Ground

Dear Heavenly Father, in the name of Jesus I ask that you will, by your Holy Spirit, work in the lives of all people reading this. Bring to their memories the unconfessed sins in their lives. Shine your light of purity and holiness down into their lives. Help us all to be willing to bear the pain of looking at our sins so that we may be clean before you. Work in each of us so that we may become vessels of honor in Your service. I thank you for this in the precious name of Jesus Christ.

Sins of Commission

1. **Material Possessions.** What is your attitude towards your earthly possessions? Do you put them before God and others? Do you think you can do with them what you want? Are you willing to lose everything for the Lord? If you are not, then you need to confess this as sin. So many Christians are completely unable to hear the Lord telling them to make a move, for example, because they are too locked into the security of their current living situations and jobs. Many Christians have been warned by the Lord to prepare for the time of coming hardship and persecution, but they are unwilling to reduce their standard of living to do so. They want to continue living as well as they can until the last possible moment. Are you one of these?

2. **Pride.** How many times have you been vain about how your looks? How many times have you been hurt because others did not pay attention to you or compliment or thank you for something you did? How many times did you do something to become the center of attention? Do you look down on others as being less than yourself? This is sin.

Appendix A
Breaking Up Fallow Ground

3. **Envy.** How many times have you envied others, their looks, possessions, or even their positions and functions within the body of Christ? How many times have you talked about or dwelt on other people's shortcomings to make yourself look better? Write down these instances of sin.

4. **Criticalness.** Being critical of others allows a root of bitterness and then hatred to spring up within you. Bitterness and hatred will destroy you. Take a hard look at your daily conversations and thoughts. Are you critical of others? You don't think you have bitterness in your life? Remember, the heart is VERY deceitful. A good measure of bitterness is this: how easily do other people make you angry? How often do you have angry thoughts about someone? Anger is very often a symptom of bitterness.

5. **Slander.** Have you ever passed on gossip? The Lord hates slander and gossip! How many times have you spoken behind people's backs about their faults, real or imagined, unnecessarily or without good reason? How often have you assumed you knew what was in someone's heart? ONLY God knows our hearts! I have been amazed at the willingness of Christians to accept accusations against me without ever once contacting me to see if there is another side to the story. These Christians are also more than willing to pass on accusations against me without ever making an effort to validate them one way or another. What about the various ''Christian research'' organizations that give out information on people. Have you ever stopped to wonder if their information is accurate? I know for a fact that those passing out accusations against me have

Appendix A
Breaking Up Fallow Ground

never once contacted me. That makes me think they have probably not contacted others either. If you pass on such "information" and it is really slander, you are sinning. You are, in fact, guilty of shedding innocent blood — murder.

6. **Lack of appropriate seriousness.** How many times have you treated God lightly or spoken about God lightly? Scripture admonishes us that the "fear of the Lord is the beginning of wisdom." Do you lack proper respect for this God of ours? If so, that is sin!

7. **Lying.** Lying is ANY deliberate deception. Examine your daily life. How often do you lie, passing it off as "just a little white lie"? How often to you exaggerate? ALL lies are sin.

8. **Cheating.** Have you gone through the line at a grocery store and not said anything when the clerk mistakenly rang up less than the amount you owed? If so, you have cheated. Cheating is any time you have done to someone something you wouldn't want done to you. Write down the instances where you have done this.

9. **Hypocrisy.** How many times have you confessed sins you really didn't intend to quit? How many times have you pretended to be something you were not?

10. **Robbing God.** List all the times God wanted you to help someone or share the gospel with someone and you did not do it. Are you wasting time on "recreation" or other pursuits when God wants to send you out into the

Appendix A
Breaking Up Fallow Ground

harvest to bring souls to Jesus? Do you have time to watch TV but not for a daily quite time?

11. Bad temper. Scripture tells us to "be angry and sin not." We as Christians must discipline ourselves. If we are bad tempered, then we are sinning. We can choose not to take offense at what someone else does.

12. Keeping others from being useful. Have you weakened someone by criticizing him so that he is afraid to step out in faith and function as God wants? Are you a complainer? Do you waste other people's time by complaining about your own problems. Are you wasting your pastor's time by demanding endless counseling sessions with him? All this is sin.

13. Rebellion. How often have you refused to obey someone in authority over you? How often have you read God's word with NO intention of obeying what you found in it? How often have you known something that you should do but have not done it? How often has the Lord told you to do something and you have not done it? Remember, God regards rebellion very seriously.

> "Six things doth the Lord hate: yea, seven are an abomination unto him. A proud look, a lying tongue, and hands that shed innocent blood, an heart that deviseth wicked imaginations, feet that be swift in running to mischief, a false witness that speaketh lies, and he that soweth discord among brethren."
> Proverbs 6:16-19

> "He that overcometh shall inherit all things: and I will be his God, and he shall be my son. But the

Appendix A
Breaking Up Fallow Ground

fearful, and unbelieving, and the abominable, and murderers, and whoremongers, and sorcerers, and idolaters, and all liars, shall have their part in the lake which burneth with fire and brimstone: which is the second death.''

Revelation 21:7-8

Look at the list in these few verses alone:

lying
pride
shedding innocent blood — this is done most
        effectively through gossip
false witness
sowing discord among the brethren
murdering
involvement in the occult
sexual immorality
unbelief
fearfulness
idolatry
sorcery or witchcraft
rebellion

Sins of Omission

"Therefore to him that knoweth to do good,
and doeth it not, to him it is sin."

James 4:17

1. **Ingratitude.** How many times has God helped you and you have never thanked Him? The clothes on your back, the food on your table, your health, your family, your job,

Appendix A
Breaking Up Fallow Ground

everything is given to you by the Lord. How often do you thank Him for these blessings? Do you eat without first stopping to sincerely thank God for His provision for you? If so, you are sinning. Do you travel to work and back without an accident? You should thank God for His protection. Write down every instance you can think of when you have not thanked God for His provisions for you.

2. **Lack of love for God.** If you love someone, you talk to him and spend time with him. Have you neglected to love God? This is sin.

3. **Neglect of the Bible.** Put down the spans of time when, for days, or even weeks or months, you disdained God's Word. When you do read God's word, do you do it in a manner that is pleasing to Him? We MUST read the Bible with the attitude that we will immediately obey every commandment we find there!

4. **Unbelief.** How many times have you virtually charged God with lying? Do you believe His word? If not, this is sin.

5. **Neglecting prayer.** How many times have you skipped personal and/or family prayer? We greatly offend God by not praying.

6. **Neglecting the means of grace.** We are commanded to fellowship with others. If you are not doing this, you are sinning.

Appendix A
Breaking Up Fallow Ground

7. The way you perform duties. Do you do everything unto the Lord? Or are you lazy and slipshod in your work and everyday life? This is sin. Do you do ONLY those things at work your boss demands? You are required by Jesus to "go the extra mile." Are you lazy in doing the Lord's work? How many times have you known things you should do and have not done them.

How many times have you known you should do something like take out the trash or do the dishes and you have not done it? Write down these instances and confess them as sin.

8. Lack of love for your neighbors' souls. It is YOUR responsibility to share the good news of Jesus Christ to everyone around you. How many people do you know and associate with that you have NOT shared the gospel with? Write them down. It is sin. Every Christian is commanded by God to share the gospel with others. If you are not doing this, you are sinning.

As you make your list of sins, you should really make up three lists:

1. A list of all sins that have allowed demons to come into your life.

2. A list of all the rest of your sins.

Appendix A
Breaking Up Fallow Ground

3. A list of everyone that has hurt you or sinned against you in some way. You MUST forgive all of these people in order to receive forgiveness for your own sins.

After you have carefully gone through and confessed and repented for all your sins, kicked out all the demons that came into you through those sins and forgiven everyone who has hurt you, take your list and burn it! You now can start with a completely clean slate before God. You will have been totally set free from bondage to Satan.

Appendix A
Breaking Up Fallow Ground

APPENDIX B

SATANIC HIGH DAYS

I have had many questions from concerned Christians wanting to know the satanic high days. These are the days on which the Satanists perform special rituals and sacrifices. It is so very important that Christians everywhere begin to go before God's throne and counter-petition Satan for the sacrifices he does. I urge you to pray fervently asking our Lord to stop the human sacrifices and also to have mercy on the little animals being sacrificed and allow them to die before they can be so horribly tortured.

THE PRAYERS OF CHRISTIANS ARE EFFECTIVE. I have heard many, many stories from people coming out of satanism about episodes of interrupted human sacrifices. It is not uncommon for a coven to be gathered around an altar to do a human sacrifice when suddenly, a brilliant shaft of light comes down out of no where and lights up the whole altar and surrounding area. When this happens, the victim is not sacrificed and the satanists flee the scene. I know a number of people who were so shaken up by this shaft of light that they began to search for another god besides Satan and ended up accepting Jesus as their Lord and Savior.

Satanic holidays occur on different days around the world in order to set up a network of sacrifices 365 days a year. They vary from one group to another and from one location to another. To name them all would take a book in itself. I will give you the main high days here.

1. EVERY FULL MOON. Sacrifices are made every night of the full moon in many groups. The demons give people

maximum power during the time of the full moon. It is also the time when the incantations are fulfilled that were done earlier in the month.

2. HALLOWEEN. The highest time of the year is Halloween. Halloween is considered to be Satan's birthday. Frequently it is called "The Harvest Feast." The rituals and sacrifices to celebrate this time of the year are not just on Halloween night. They run from October 15 through November 15.

3. EASTER & CHRISTMAS. The satanists desecrate every Christian holiday. At Christmas, mostly infant boys are sacrificed to ridicule Jesus Christ. At Easter, and especially on Ash Wednesday, young men are sacrificed along with others as I described in *He Came To Set The Captives Free.*

4. SOLSTICES. Each solstice is celebrated. Spring, summer, winter and fall. You can find the dates for these on most calendars.

5. NEW YEAR. Sacrifices are done on New Year's eve, but the highest sacrifice is performed at midnight. This is to dedicate the New Year to Satan.

I have recently been in contact with a person who came out of a very high position in Satanism. He told me that, starting in the year 1990, Satan has decreed that all covens must perform human sacrifice on a daily basis. Satan's goal is to have a human sacrifice performed somewhere in the world every second! Satan is also pulling all his organizations together to unify them. He knows his time is short! Our Lord's return is near. We as Christians MUST stand against Satan and his activities in our prayers.

Appendix B
Satanic High Days

APPENDIX C

BOOKS WHICH HAVE GREATLY CONTRIBUTED TO MY OWN SPIRITUAL GROWTH

1 " Billheimer, Paul E., (Bethany House Publishers, Minneapolis, MN)

> *Destined For The Throne.*

> *Don't Waste Your Sorrows*

> *Adventure in Adversity*

2. Finney, Charles, G., (Bethany House Publishers, Minneapolis, MN)

> *Lectures on Revival*

3. Keller, Phillip, (Vine Books, Ann Arbor, MI)

> *In The Master's Hands*

> *A Shepherd Looks at Psalm 23*

> *Lessons From a Sheep Dog.*

> *A Shepherd Looks at the Good Shepherd and His Sheep*

> *A Layman Looks at the Love of God*

> *Predators in Our Pulpits*

4. Murray, Andrew, (Bethany House Publishers, Minneapolis, MN)

> *The Spirit of Christ*
> *The Believer's Secret of Obedience*

And many others.

5. Nee, Watchman, (Christian Fellowship Publishers, NY)

> *Spiritual Authority*
> *The Spiritual Man*
> *Characteristics of God's Workmen*
> *Assembling Together*
> *All To The Glory of God*
> *The Latent Power of the Soul*
> *A Balanced Christian Life*

and others.

6. Pember, G.H., (Kregel Publications, Grand Rapids, MI)

> *Earth's Earliest Days*

7. Penn-Lewis, Jessie, (Over Comer Publications, part of: Overcomer Literature Trust Ltd.) 10 Marlborough Road, Parkstone Poole, Dorset BH14 OHJ, England

> *Conquest of Canaan*
> *Communion With God*
> *War On The Saints*

Unabridged Edition of *"War On The Saints"* can be ordered through:
Thomas E. Lowe, Ltd.
P.O. Box 1049
Cathedral Station
New York, NY 10025

8. Tozer, A.W., (Christian Publications, Camp Hill, PA)

> *The Pursuit of God*

> *The Divine Conquest*

> *The Knowledge of the Holy*

> *The Root of the Righteous*

> *Man: The Dwelling Place of God*

> *Gems From Tozer*

9. Wesley, John, (Bethany House Publishers, Minneapolis, MN)

> *The Nature of Holiness*

There are, of course, many excellent books available today, but these have particularly helped me in my own spiritual growth. These books are not commonly available in most Christian bookstores. I have included the publishers so you can ask your local Christian bookstore to order them. I believe you will find them a real blessing.